Digital preservation

Other titles in the Digital Futures series
(Series Editors Marilyn Deegan and Simon Tanner)

Deegan, Marilyn and Tanner, Simon (2001) *Digital Futures: strategies for the information age*, ISBN 1-85604-580-3.

Hughes, Lorna M. (2004) *Digitizing Collections: issues for the information manager*, ISBN 1-85604-466-1.

Digital preservation

Marilyn Deegan and Simon Tanner

facet publishing

© This compilation: Marilyn Deegan and Simon Tanner 2006
   The chapters: the contributors 2006

Published by Facet Publishing
7 Ridgmount Street, London WC1E 7AE

Facet Publishing is wholly owned by CILIP: the Chartered Institute of Library and Information Professionals.

First published 2006

British Library Cataloguing in Publication Data
A catalogue record for this book is available from the British Library.

ISBN-13: 978-1-85604-485-1
ISBN-10: 1-85604-485-8

Typeset from editors' disks by Facet Publishing in 11/14 New Baskerville and Swiss 721.
Printed and made in Great Britain by MPG Books Ltd, Bodmin, Cornwall.

Contents

The contributors

Stephen Chapman is Preservation Librarian for Digital Initiatives in the Weissman Preservation Center, Harvard University Library. He advises the Harvard community about reformatting strategies to create sustainable digital collections and has been a member of the technical team managing Harvard's Digital Repository Service since its inception in 2001. He served on Digital Library Federation committees to develop guidelines and best practices for photograph and text digitization and, with Don Williams, co-authored the draft data dictionary for the NISO Z39.87 metadata standard for digital still images.

Marilyn Deegan has a PhD in medieval studies: her specialism is Anglo-Saxon medical texts and herbals and she has published and lectured widely in medieval studies, digital library research and humanities computing. She is currently Director of Research Development in the Centre for Computing in the Humanities at King's College London and was formerly Digital Resources Director of the Refugee Studies Centre at Oxford University. She has held a number of posts in digital library research and humanities computing over the past 15 years. She is Editor-in-Chief of *Literary and Linguistic Computing*, the journal of the Association for Literary and Linguistic Computing, and Director of Publications for the Office for Humanities Communication based at King's College London. Marilyn is co-author with Simon Tanner of *Digital Futures: strategies for the information age* (also in this series).

David Holdsworth studied physics at Oxford University and took first and second degrees there in 1964 and 1968. He has worked in computing at Leeds University since 1967, both as lecturer in the academic department and mainly in systems development in the computer centre under its several names. He was at one time its Acting Director. He was a prominent member of both the Cedars and CAMiLEON digital preservation projects and was the only person to have involvement with both projects throughout their lifetimes. He has been a long-time advocate of media-neutral data storage and has designed and built archive systems used at Leeds University and elsewhere since the 1980s. He is now retired, but retains an honorary staff post at Leeds University in support of his continuing activities in software preservation.

Jasmine Kelly is currently a research assistant at the Centre for Computing in the Humanities, King's College London. Armed with a BA in ancient and modern history from the University of Oxford, and latterly an MA in digital culture and technology, she has worked as an editor, writer, content manager, project manager, web communications specialist and researcher for, among others, the Cabinet Office and the BBC. Teaching English in China is her plan for the immediate future.

Brian F. Lavoie is a Consulting Research Scientist in the Office of Research at OCLC Online Computer Library Center, Inc. He has a PhD in agricultural economics. Since joining OCLC in 1996, he has worked on a variety of projects, such as revising and expanding the Cutter tables, developing metadata for digital preservation, and analysing the size and scope of the web. He is the author of many articles and papers on these and other topics. Brian's research interests include data-mining, digital preservation and the economics of information.

Julien Masanès is the co-founder and Director of the European Archive, a non-profit foundation for web preservation and digital cultural access. Before this he directed the Web Archiving Project at the Bibliothèque nationale de France. He also actively participated in the creation of the International Internet Preservation Consortium (IIPC), which he has co-ordinated during the first two years. Julien is a curator and received a degree in librarianship at enssib, the école nationale supérieure des sciences de l'information et des bibliothèques (Lyon) in 1999. He was a digital preservation adviser at BnF and has participated in various national and international initiatives in this domain, such as the European Project NEDLIB, the Global Digital Format Registry and the OCLC/RLG Open Archive Information System Certification Group. He has also launched and presently chairs the International Web Archiving Workshop (IWAW) series, the main international rendezvous in this domain. He has published several articles and contributions in this field and recently edited the first book on the topic (*Web Archiving*, Springer, 2006).

Elisa Mason is an independent information specialist. She has a Master's in library science from the University of Illinois at Urbana-Champaign. She has worked for the UN High Commissioner for Refugees, the Refugee Studies Centre at Oxford University and Tufts University on a variety of projects relating to the organization and management of electronic information resources and digital documents. Elisa has written a number of guides and journal articles on accessing forced migration information and currently maintains a blog on this topic.

Peter McKinney is Research Officer for the espida project which is developing a sustainable business-focused model for digital assets (www.gla.ac.uk/espida) and is based at the University of Glasgow's IT Services. Previously, he was Coordinator of the ERPANET project, which was a key international player in the area of digital preservation (www.erpanet.org). As a member of HATII at the University of Glasgow he taught on the successful digitization summer school at various international venues and, among other things, was part of the team that developed the NINCH (National Initiative for Networked Cultural Heritage) Guide to Good Practice in the Digital Representation and Management of Cultural Heritage Materials.

Simon Tanner has a library and information science degree and background. He is the founding Director of King's Digital Consultancy Services (KDCS) at King's College London. KDCS provides research and consulting services specializing in the information and digital domain for the cultural, heritage and information sectors. Before joining King's, he was Senior Consultant at HEDS, the Higher Education Digitization Service. He has also held IT, management and library roles for Loughborough University (Library Systems Manager), Rolls-Royce and Associates (Head of Library Services) and IBM (UK) Laboratories (Information Officer).

Simon is an independent member of the UK Legal Deposit Advisory Panel and chairs its Web Archiving sub-committee. He has been a consultant to many major organizations wordwide, and has also carried out research projects for the Andrew W. Mellon Foundation on charging models for digital cultural heritage in Europe and the USA. He co-authored the book *Digital Futures: strategies for the information age* (also in this series) with Marilyn Deegan.

Robin Wendler is Metadata Analyst in the Harvard University Library Office for Information Systems. She has been active in metadata standards development and deployment for many years, serving on the METS Editorial Board, the MARBI (Machine-Readable Bibliographic Information) Committee, PREMIS, the Digital Library Federation/OCLC Registry of Digital Masters Working Group, and the RLG Union Catalog Advisory Group, among other groups. She has published articles on automated authority control, preservation metadata, visual resource description, electronic resource description and other applications of metadata in libraries, museums and archives.

Series Editors' introduction

The Digital Futures series began its life in the book *Digital Futures: strategies for the information age* by Marilyn Deegan and Simon Tanner. What became obvious in writing the first book was that no single work can cover in great depth all the issues facing librarians and other information workers as they engage in digital activities. Thus the Digital Futures series idea was born to enable further volumes to explore in detail the major topics that concern our digital information age.

Written by leading international experts, each book in the Digital Futures series examines some of the key strategic and practical issues facing libraries and other cultural institutions in the rapidly expanding world of digital information.

Anyone interested in contributing to the Digital Futures series is invited to contact the Series Editors at marilyn.deegan@kcl.ac.uk and simon.tanner@kcl.ac.uk.

Marilyn Deegan
Simon Tanner

Introduction

This third volume in the Digital Futures series has been some time in gestation, and is intended as a contribution to the urgent debate about issues around the preservation of culture in digital form. It might seem ironic to some that we have chosen to edit and produce a book about digital preservation, rather than producing this work in some kind of digital form that could be updated regularly. However, we feel that the book still has validity as the appropriate format for sustained and reasoned argument, and we know that the book is a durable format for long-term preservation.

Digital preservation is a complex issue, with many different aspects and views, and we wish this volume to represent as many of these views as is possible within a single volume. We have therefore commissioned chapters from leading experts in the field, rather than producing a monograph, and we believe that the experts writing here are some of the best-qualified to share their vast experience on digital preservation. As with other volumes in the series, this book is aimed at the information professional who is interested in this area, but who is not an expert. Because this field gives rise to a great deal of new specialist terminology, we have provided a glossary of key terms, acronyms and abbreviations.

Chapter 1 offers a fairly detailed introduction to the field, and covers prevailing thinking on the different methods of preservation, as well as some of the practical and strategic issues not covered elsewhere. Some of the material covers the same ground as Chapter 8 ('Preservation') in *Digital Futures*, but this has been brought up to date and augmented considerably. In Chapter 2, David Holdsworth covers strategies and methods for digital preservation in more detail, and offers a very useful introduction to the OAIS Reference Model which is being widely adopted by digital preservation projects. Robin Wendler in Chapter 3 leads us gently through the minefield of metadata for digital preservation, pointing out the importance of excellent documentation for digital files and the methods used to preserve them.

Digital data are at risk if urgent positive action is not taken to ensure their long-term survival, and the most at-risk category of data is the vast amount of content on websites around the world. Chapter 4 by Julien Masanès looks in detail at a range of web-archiving methods and strategies, and Chapter 5 by Elisa Mason is a complementary piece presenting a number of case studies on web archiving activities.

One of the most difficult questions that has been asked over the last few years is 'What is long-term preservation going to cost?' We are all aware of the costs of not preserving digital information, but projecting cost models into the future is always fraught with difficulty. However, the two chapters here by Brian F. Lavoie (Chapter 6) and Stephen Chapman (Chapter 7) on the economics and costs of digital preservation are based on sound knowledge and a great deal of experience of working on both digital and non-digital preservation projects. This kind of approach is giving us a great deal more confidence that we *can* start to plan for the costs of preserving content into the future.

In Chapter 8 by Peter McKinney, we move away from technical and financial considerations in digital preservation, and look at more strategic national and international initiatives. We have chosen to commission a piece on European approaches because this offers a degree of diversity, given that different countries are taking slightly different approaches, but also a degree of cohesion as the European Commission, with its cross-border mandates for funding, is providing a framework within which countries can work together.

Chapter 9 by Jasmine Kelly and Elisa Mason brings together 60 short case studies of current digital preservation projects worldwide. These cover different media, different subject areas, and a wide range of technical and business models. They are intended to illustrate many of the points made throughout the book, and to give a wide-ranging reference guide, with enough detail for readers to know if they are worth investigating further.

Finally, we salute our friends and colleagues working to hold back the tide of digital obsolescence worldwide. We hope this book represents, through the thoughtful contributions of the authors, a fanfare for all the libraries, museums, archives, and other memory organizations. They play an essential role in preserving culture and in connecting people with their national and regional identities. Their work supports the very foundations of our civilization and enables one generation to pass information and knowledge, whether technical or cultural, to the next. This book is dedicated to you.

Acknowledgements

The worlds of digital library and digital preservation research are full of people who are making huge contributions to practical strategies and in-depth thinking about serious issues, but who rarely have time, because of their daily commitments, to reflect upon what they are doing and to share their insights with a wider audience. The authors of the individual chapters of this book are busy people who have been hounded and harried by us for the last two years, until they never wanted to see our names on an e-mail again. But they have cheerfully persevered and helped us to produce what we hope will be a major contribution to the literature on digital preservation. Our heartfelt thanks go to them.

We are particularly grateful to Jasmine Kelly and Elisa Mason, who as well as writing their authored contributions, have undertaken a great deal of extra research for the book. Elisa compiled the bibliography, and Jasmine the glossary of key terms, abbreviations and acronyms. They have also given us help and support throughout the process.

The Centre for Computing in the Humanities, at King's College London, provides much more than just our working home. We would like to thank all our colleagues for the inspiration they provide and their help in formulating this book. Special thanks to Professor Harold Short and Sheila Anderson are due for their friendship, sage advice, and support.

Our long-suffering partners, Jane Tanner and Louise Heinink, have endured our absences and our abstractedness with their usual fortitude, and the excellent team at Facet Publishing have, as ever, been a pleasure to work with. We'd like to thank Sophie Baird, Helen Carley, Rebecca Casey and Lin Franklin.

Glossary of key terms, acronyms and abbreviations

This glosses the main acronyms found throughout the book. The *Dictionary of the Internet* by Darrel Ince (Oxford University Press, 2003) is also recommended for terms not included in the glossary.

AAF	Advanced Authoring Format
ABA	North American Broadcasters' Association
AHDS	Arts and Humanities Data Service
API	Application Programming Interface
APSR	Australian Partnership for Sustainable Repositories
ARC	Augmentation Research Center
ARELDA	Archiving of Electronic Data and Records
ASBU	Arab States Broadcasting Union
ASCII	American Standard Code for Information Interchange
BAT	(Bibliothèque nationale de France) BnfArcTools
C	programming language
CAD	Computer-Aided Design
CAMiLEON	Creative Archiving at Michigan & Leeds: Emulating the Old on the New
CANDO	A consortium of four partner institutions: the University of Edinburgh; the University of Glasgow; UKOLN, at the University of Bath; and the Council for the Central Laboratory of the Research Councils, which together host the UK's Digital Curation Centre

CDX	a binary file format
Cedars	CURL Exemplars in Digital ARchiveS
CI	Content Information
CILIP	Chartered Institute of Library and Information Professionals
COM	Computer Output to Microfilm
CURL	The Consortium of Research Libraries in the British Isles
DACHS	Digital Archive for Chinese Studies
DAT	Digital Audio Tape
DELOS II	Network of Excellence on Digital Libraries
DIAMM	Digital Image Archive of Medieval Music
DIDL	Digital Item Declaration
DIP	Dissemination Information Package
DNS	Domain Name Server / Service
DOI	Digital Object Identifier
DPC	Digital Preservation Coalition
DRS	Digital Repository Service (Harvard University Library)
DSL	Digital Subscriber Line
DTD	Document Type Definition
EBCDIC	Extended Binary-Coded Decimal Interchange Code. An IBM code for representing characters as numbers
EMC	EMC Corporation is a company offering products, services and solutions for information management and storage
E-PROM	A rewritable memory chip that holds its content without power
ERPANET	Electronic Resource Preservation and Access Network
espida	Digital preservation project at Glasgow University
FCLA	Florida Center for Library Automation
FDA	Federal Drugs Agency
FIAT	International Federation of Television Archives
FORTRAN	programming language
GB	gigabyte

GDFR	Global Digital Format Registry
GIF	Graphics Interchange Format
GIS	Geographic Information System
GNU	A free operating system with features similar to Unix – its name is a recursive acronym for 'GNU's not Unix'
GPO	US Government Printing Office
HATII	Humanities Advanced Technology and Information Institute at the University of Glasgow
HTML	Hypertext Markup Language
HTTP	Hypertext Transmission Protocol
HTTrack	A free, offline browser utility that can download a website to a local directory
IA	Internet Archive
IBM SCRIPT	Programming language for IBM mainframe computers
ICOM	International Council of Museums
IEEE	Institute of Electrical and Electronics Engineers
IIPC	International Internet Preservation Consortium
IMS	Instructional Management System
InterPARES	International Research on Permanent Authentic Records in Electronic Systems
IP	Internet Protocol
IPR	Intellectual Property Rights
ISBN	International Standard Book Number
JISC	Joint Information Systems Committee
JHOVE	JSTOR Harvard Object Validation Environment
JPEG	Joint Photographic Experts Group, also a file format
JSTOR	The Scholarly Journal Archive
KB	Koninklijke Bibliotheek (National Library of Netherlands)
LEEDS	file archive at Leeds University
LIFE	Life Cycle Information for E-Literature
MARC	MAchine Readable Cataloguing record
METS	Metadata Encoding and Transmission Standard

MINERVA	MInisterial NEtwoRk for Valorising Activities in digitization. An EU co-ordination project
MPEG-2	Motion Picture Experts Group 2
MXF	Material eXchange Format
NARA	National Archives and Records Administration (US)
NDIIP	National Digital Information Infrastructure and Preservation Program
NEDLIB	Networked European Deposit Library
NESTOR	Network of Expertise in Long-Term Storage of Digital Resources. A German digital preservation project
NISO	National Information Standards Organization
NLA	National Library Association
NMDC	National Museum Directors' Conference
NPO	National Preservation Office
OAIS	Open Archival Information System
OCLC	Online Computer Library Center
OPAC	Online Public Access Catalogue
PADI	Preserving Access to Digital Information
PANDORA	Preserving and Accessing Networked Documentary Resources of Australia
PANDAS	PANDORA Digital Archiving System
PDF	Adobe Portable Document Format. A popular file format for digital documents
PDI	Preservation Description Information
PRONOM	an online registry of technical information about digital preservation maintained by the UK National Archives
PREMIS	PREservation Metadata: Implementation Strategies. A working group on preservation metadata
PRESTO	An EU project, headed by the BBC, to develop a cost-effective approach to the preservation of broadcast archives, audio and video
RFC	Requests for Comments. A set of technical and organizational notes about the internet beginning in 1969
RI	Representation Information

RLG	Research Libraries Group
SCORM	Sharable Content Object Reference Model
SGML	Standard Generalized Markup Language
SIP	Submission Information Package
TB	terabyte, equal to 1024 gigabytes
TCP / IP	Transmission Control Protocol / Internet Protocol
TIFF	Tagged Image File Format
TOM	Typed Object Model
UAF	Underlying Abstract Form
UCSD	University of California at San Diego
UKOLN	UK Office of Library and Information Networking
UNIX	operating system
URI	Uniform Resource Identifier
URL	Uniform Resource Location
URN	Uniform Resource Name
VM/CMS	Virtual Machine/Conversational Monitor System. An operating system on IBM mainframe computers
WARC	Internet archiving file format
WERA	Full-text web archive search, display and navigation tool
WIS	Web Information Systems
XFDU	XML Formatted Data Unit
XML	Extensible Markup Language

1

Key issues in digital preservation

Marilyn Deegan and Simon Tanner

Introducing the digital domain

The digital birth of cultural content and conversion of analogue originals into bits and bytes has opened new vistas and extended horizons in every direction, providing access and opportunities for new audiences, enlightenment, entertainment and education in ways unimaginable a mere 15 years ago. Digital libraries have a major function to enhance our appreciation of or engagement with culture and often lead the way in this new digital domain we find ourselves immersed within. The underlying information and communication technologies are still generally referred to as 'new' or 'high' technologies – they remain highly visible, and have not yet, despite their pervasiveness, become part of the natural infrastructure of society. 'Technology', as the computer scientist Bran Ferren memorably defined it, is 'stuff that doesn't work yet' (Adams, 1999).

The need to deliver cultural resources, especially from major cultural organizations such as museums or national libraries, has become an imperative closely associated with the core mission of these organizations to educate and elucidate, to promote and disseminate and to preserve culture. These attempts to reach out to new audiences and to refresh current audiences are major driving factors behind many digitization programmes and the shift towards digital repositories. The justifications for delivering cultural resources digitally can rarely be made on purely financial grounds as the fiscal returns on investment are relatively small, but the returns for culture, education and prestige are high (Tanner, 2004).

With the digital revolution, data and information can now be transmitted to all corners of the world. Some predict that we are reaching a period of cheap access for all, but the reality is that there are still political, cultural and financial issues which prevent low-cost access in certain strata of society and many parts of the world. The digital divide exists and could further disadvantage the poor, the under-educated and those in developing countries as the better-off, the better-educated and the economically developed forge ahead into the digital domain. Views on the democratizing nature of electronic networks vary wildly and we need to be cautious in our evaluation of these: for some we are on the verge of global utopia, an 'age of optimism' (Negroponte, 1995), for others the internet (our conduit to the digital library) 'continues to remain an expensive western toy' in a world where less than 2% of the population is connected to the internet and where 80% of the population has never even made a telephone call (Taylor, 2001).

We also have to be ready, both technically and psychologically, for major technological change to happen. Progress seems unlikely to follow a smooth linear rate of change, but more likely 'a series of stable states, punctuated at rare intervals by major events that occur with great rapidity and help to establish the next stable era' (Gould, 1980), a process characterized by Kuhn as 'paradigm shifts' (Kuhn, 1970). Gleick suggests that these changes are happening more regularly than before (Gleick, 2000), which is probably why change appears as a process of constant acceleration.

The subject of digital preservation is one that is often represented as being distinctly different from more traditional preservation issues due to the digital component. In many ways this is true but an exploration of the core concepts and principles driving preservation imperatives in both the digital and non-digital domains provides a useful introduction to the themes this book will explore in the coming chapters.

Preservation and the impact of nature, politics and war

Preservation is the continuous process of creating and maintaining the best environment possible for the storage and/or use of an artefact to prevent damage or degradation and to enable it to live as long a lifetime as possible. It has sub-activities, such as conservation and restoration, which involve specific treatments to an artefact to stabilize and preserve it for the future, or to restore it to a state of former glory. One of the key responsibilities held by libraries, museums and other memory organizations is that of preserving culture. This may be preserving the record of a way of life or the very roots of a culture, its language, literature, music and traditions. Digital libraries play an important role in preserving culture and in connecting people with their national and regional identities. This work is essential to support the very foundations of our civilization, which is based upon our ability to pass information and knowledge, whether technical or cultural, from one generation to the next.

Recorded information and knowledge resources are at constant risk from natural disaster and human mediated destruction. 'As Thomas Jefferson well knew with his family fire, there are few more irreparable property losses than vanished books. Nature, politics, and war have always been the mortal enemies of written works' (Coleman, 2006). The loss of archives includes examples such as the Catholic University of Louvain, Belgium, which burned down in both 1914 and 1940 due to wartime bombing, destroying 230,000 books, 800 of them incunabula printed before the year 1500, and 900 manuscripts. Most recently, the Asian tsunami, the New Orleans disaster accompanying Hurricane Katrina and the South Asia earthquake have all had an impact on a number of museums, libraries and archives as well as the people of many countries, affecting not just lives but cultural memories (Disaster Relief for Museums, n.d.). In the 1970s, the Khmer Rouge regime in Cambodia decimated cultural institutions throughout the country. They threw books from the National Library into the street and burnt them. Less than 20% of the library survived and the damage to Cambodia's rich cultural heritage remains an open and unhealed wound. In the last 150 years, a new danger has threatened: the ' "slow fires" of acidic paper' (Kenney, 1996), which has necessitated the large-scale microfilming of millions of pages of documents over many decades in order that the content is not lost. Many digital reformatting initiatives grew out of earlier microfilming projects, lighting the ' "fast fires" of digital obsolescence' (Kenney, 1996).

Culture is at constant risk and the digital domain, to a certain extent, may exacerbate this risk by maintaining resources in formats that have problems for long-term storage and retrieval. But the digital library itself is a powerful tool for holding back the tide of cultural diffusion and loss. Digital libraries are often the key tool by which citizens can engage with their own history, culture and language while also being of enormous value in restoring cultural artefacts to public view where the original is lost or too fragile for normal display.

The Gutenberg printing revolution led Europe out of the Dark Ages of loss of knowledge of the learning of the ancient Greeks and Romans; the digital revolution may land us in an age even darker if urgent action is not taken. In particular need of attention is the ever-changing information available on the internet, through e-mail and the world wide web. Details preserved in private communications, by accident or design, reveal much of the past, and offer many personal, literary and political insights unavailable in more public documents. The telegraph and telephone eroded epistolatory communications, and the rise of e-mail and text messaging has meant that communication through writing is popular again, but with the disadvantage that either the written products will be deleted or destroyed, or that we will be tempted to keep so much that the problems of data organization and the expense of handling them render them virtually useless (Gleick, 2000).

Materials published on the web may derive from professional sources such as publishers or libraries, with analogue versions available elsewhere which will continue to be available even after they disappear from digital view. But what of other kinds of digital documents? In the past, ephemera such as playbills, advertisements, menus, theatre tickets, broadsheets, etc. have survived, albeit sometimes rather haphazardly, and are now collected, stored, conserved and valued as vital witnesses to political, economic, social and private aspects of the past. Today, these artefacts appear on the web for a matter of days, to disappear from view as if they had never existed. There are, too, many government documents, records and other official papers which only ever have a digital form. What is to be done about these? We have a warning from recent history of the possible dangers here: tapes of many seminal radio and television programmes were destroyed after broadcasting, and many live broadcasts were never taped, resulting in serious gaps in the history of the performing arts of the twentieth century.

We must differentiate between digital preservation (which is about ensuring full access and continued usability of data and digital information), and preservation through digitization (which allows for greater physical security of physical analogue originals). Strategically it becomes self-evident that to reduce the stress upon the valued original, the data created must last as long as possible. Thus processes and intentions for preservation must be decided early in the digital lifecycle to ensure that repeating the digitization directly from the original is reduced or even eradicated.

The scale of the digital preservation problem

'Culture, any culture . . . depends on the quality of its record of knowledge' (Waters, 1997). As Waters points out, any society depends on the quality of its knowledge of its own past, and a falsification of that past, whether deliberate or accidental, damages the society. The Soviet Union is a prime example of a society which rewrote its history regularly to reflect the prevailing political mores, destroying valuable evidence along the way (Task Force on Archiving, 1996, 1). Lack of care in preserving our digital past and present will certainly ensure that we will have an impoverished digital future.

We now face a new threat in the form of digital obsolescence:

> Not brittle papyrus and crumbling mortar is the most severe threat to our cultural heritage today, but, as Mary Feeney expressed it, 'the death of the digit.' This 'death of the digit' is related primarily to two factors:
>
> •   First, technology develops ever more rapidly, reducing the time before a particular technology becomes obsolete.

- And secondly, unlike their analogue counterparts, digital resources are much more 'unstable' with the effect that the integrity and authenticity of digital cultural resources is corrupted.

(Geser and Mulrenin, 2002)

Digital data are now being produced on a massive scale by individuals, and by institutions of all types and sizes. Some data are created through digitization programmes but the vast majority of digital content is born, lives and dies in only digital form.

Digital preservation of cultural resources faces a number of challenges:

- preserving the data stream's integrity
- preserving the means to interpret the data stream
- preserving the means by which the resource is experienced.

Digital data are in danger, not because they are inherently fragile or flawed, but because there is a continually accelerating rate of replication, adaptation and redundancy of hardware, software and data formats and standards which may mean that the bitstream may not be readable, interpretable or usable long into the future. All data are stored as a code and therefore require an element of decoding before they are recognizable and usable in a computing environment, even if open data standards are used. For most people the bitstream for the word-processing document used to write this book would be totally unintelligible without the suitable computer applications, software and operating system environments to interpret and repackage the data into a readable form. We take this automatic decoding for granted until we try to read a word-processing file from 10 years ago and find that none of our current systems or software has any idea what the bitstream means without significant coaching or expert help.

The longer the data are left unattended, with the data coding unrecorded, the faster systems will become obsolete and the expertise to recognize and decode that specific type of bitstream will become unavailable. Data could be lost forever, unrecoverable without effort that will probably not be cost-effective. There is a direct analogy with the decipherment of ancient scripts where the knowledge of the language used and the system of coding of the written scripts is lost and must be recreated from scraps of knowledge, intuition, research and other language fragments that may be stems of the ancient script. The linguistic bridges to the past built upon the decipherment of hieroglyphics or Linear B are very highly valued for the historical information we now have about those societies and cultures of up to 3000 years ago. These decipherments were often life works for the people who succeeded and were preceded by centuries of hard worked failure. In the case of Linear A the battle continues (see Singh, 1999). As described by Maurice Pope,

> Decipherments are by far the most glamorous achievements of scholarship. There is a touch of magic about unknown writing, especially when it comes from the remote past, and a corresponding glory is bound to attach itself to the person who first solves its mystery.
>
> (Pope, 1975)

The challenge for our digital future is to not perpetuate a scenario of data loss and poor records that have dogged our progress over the last 25 years. Otherwise, in just 50 years from now the human record of the early 21st century may be unreadable, and its decipherment an expensive and intellectually challenging feat way beyond the achievements of the great codebreakers of the 20th.

Preservation through surrogacy?

Substitution of originals with other objects that simulate their content does, of course, pose its own problems. When is a facsimile a satisfactory surrogate for the object itself? This depends on both the needs of the reader and the quality of the reproduction, and is not an easy question to answer. The relationship between any original object and a reproduction of it is problematic, and is a question which has exercised theorists and practitioners of artefactual disciplines for many years.

The authenticity of surrogates and their acceptability to readers are of major concern, but so too is the preservation and conservation of these surrogates themselves. One great advantage of mechanically produced surrogates is the possibility of preservation through multiplication of the numbers of copies. In the analogue world this itself results in some degradation through recopying, in the digital world every copy is theoretically an exact copy of its precursor, even after many generations of copying.

There are two crucial questions to ask in the debate about the preservation of originals by the use of surrogates. What is it that we are preserving and for whom? Are we preserving the objects themselves or the information that they contain? With certain unique, intrinsically valuable and highly significant works – the Rosetta Stone, the Lindisfarne Bible – the object itself is as important as what it says. With more ephemeral materials such as newspapers or government documents, while there may be key issues or volumes where it is worth preserving the originals, in general it is probably the content, and the physical arrangement of that content, that needs to be preserved, rather than the objects themselves, though these are matters of much controversy.

Authenticity of digital data

Authenticity of digital documents must be distinguished from authentication as generally defined in the digital world. MacKenzie defines 'authenticity' of a documentary source as 'reliability over time' (2000, 59) while 'authentication' is a term usually used for the process of validating who is allowed access to digital data, and what they might be permitted to do with it. As Rothenberg has pointed out, 'whenever informational entities are used, and for whatever purpose, their suitability relies on their authenticity' and goes on to remark, 'the technological issues surrounding the preservation of digital information entities interact with authenticity in novel and profound ways' (Rothenberg, 2000a, 1). This is a key and crucial issue in the preservation of digital data, as validating authenticity is so much more problematic than in the analogue world. It is frighteningly easy to change a digital document, leaving no trace, no ghostly palimpsest to tell us what was there before. If we alter the words on a written document, generally we can decipher the original and the changes become part of the cultural accretion of meaning gained by the document. A digital document always appears pristine, despite changes made by accident or design, and this means that if two readers are discussing a document, they may not always know that they are using the same version, or if there has been some hidden change. One major consequence of this is that digital data may not be legally valid (see below), and an analogue version may need to be stored for legislative purposes.

As Cullen says, 'The problems of preserving digital objects have received more attention than questions of authentication . . . But why preserve what is not authentic?' (2000, 3). Users of libraries and archives have, in the past, relied on curators to validate the authenticity of the resources on offer; curators are trained to know what they have and what its status is, and they rely on a broad professional network in the production and care of the documentary heritage. They purchase materials from reputable sources, have access to experts who can be called upon for second opinions, and they have bodies of meta-information (catalogues, bibliographies, etc.) regarding the provenance and history of rarer works. Forgery or misidentification is not unknown, but the former is a painstaking and difficult process. There are, too, physical characteristics of originals which can reveal information about the age, provenance or history of an object. And falsification is much more difficult than actually creating the object in the first place. As Bearman and Trant point out of forgery in the digital world, 'the underlying technology makes purposeful fakery easier and more tempting' (1998, 3).

Digital authentication is difficult, and it is a problem which will increase over time as digital documents are preserved for the long term. Version control is also problematic, as very slightly different digital versions of the same exemplar could be circulating without being discovered, unless the changes are fully documented throughout the life of the resource. Digital dissemination is almost unthinkably rapid, as people who have circulated a private e-mail to a public discussion list have sometimes found to their embarrassment. Some accepted system of authenticity validation needs to exist in the digital world, but this is difficult to establish and to enforce for all potential uses and purposes. Responsible agencies producing digital documents are likely to use metadata structures, collection records or unique document identifiers which can be checked, but again these could be subject to abuse.

Librarians and archivists are going to have to face questions of digital authenticity more often than they faced the same issues in the analogue world, and the solutions are likely to be more diverse. In order that digital data can be considered legally valid, certain conditions need to be met. There are legal recommendations that must be followed if digital documents are to be considered authentic in the eyes of the law, and, for example, admissible as evidence in court. Legal implications will also need to be considered when planning long-term archiving. For many libraries, as trusted repositories and intermediaries, validating authenticity is nonetheless important and extends beyond legal validity,

Surrogate versus original

Can surrogates ever truly replace or faithfully represent the original? In his seminal essay 'The Work of Art in an Age of Mechanical Reproduction', Benjamin states that:

> Even the most perfect reproduction . . . is lacking in one element: its presence in time and space . . . This unique existence of the work . . . determined the history to which it was subject throughout its time of existence.
>   (Benjamin, 1992)

The notion of representation of an original by a surrogate is always problematic and in some sense it is always a falsification, for instance, photographs of buildings or sculptures, transcriptions or editions of texts are interpretations as much as they are representations. Creating surrogates can never replicate or preserve *everything* about an original object, but creating no surrogates could mean that *everything* is lost in the case of fragile or compromised originals: brittle books printed on acid-based paper, older newspapers, ancient and medieval books and manuscripts, crumbling sculptures, ruined buildings, photographs on glass plates, explosive nitrate film stock.

Disposal of originals and their replacement by surrogates

We discussed briefly above the advisability or otherwise of replacing originals with surrogates. The most controversial questions here arise when actual disposal of originals is proposed. Sometimes, there is no real choice to be made: for instance, the Department of Preservation and Collection Maintenance at Cornell University recommends that, for brittle books, a printed photocopy surrogate is created on archival paper, and the original then discarded (see www.library.cornell.edu/ preservation/operations/brittlebooks.html). This is done using a digital scanning process, and therefore digital images are also available. The Cornell Brittle Books project also experimented with computer output to microform technologies to create preservation microfilm copies of the books. The content is therefore safe for the long term. Cornell has become a world leader in digital reformatting and preservation, and runs many courses and workshops on the topic (see www.library.cornell.edu/preservation/training/index.html).

The decision to discard originals by libraries and archives is never taken lightly, but over time materials do have to be discarded for reasons of space and cost. This is not a new issue: repositories have always discarded materials to make way for new items. In the past, materials were sometimes reused. Vellum, for instance, was so costly that it was scraped down and reused which has paradoxically allowed the recovery of materials that were not actually supposed to survive. The Digital Image Archive of Medieval Music (DIAMM, see www.diamm.ac.uk/) has recovered music from 15th-century fragments of vellum that had been used for other purposes, for instance as binding reinforcements for non-musical sources. Vellum is so durable that it was possible to recover readings, despite damage by water, dirt, rats, glue or the effects of being stuck down to a wooden board for 600 years or more, and some hitherto unknown pieces of medieval music have been discovered in this way (Craig-McFeely and Deegan, 2005).

If some economical means of preserving access to the content can be found, this is often done. This process is part of the responsible stewardship of cultural materials by librarians and archivists, but there are times when these issues become matters of public concern. In the second half of 2000, for instance, there was mounting controversy in the UK and the USA about the jettisoning by major libraries of some of their historic newspaper collections. These collections were all preserved on microfilm, but the disposal of originals caused an outcry in the press. Major libraries such as the Library of Congress in the USA and the British Library in the UK have been microfilming newspapers for many decades in order to preserve the historical record rather then the objects, but the critics of the disposal policy advanced many arguments for the retention of the paper copies. As a society, we are wedded to objects rather than surrogates, even if this causes expensive problems, and some of the objections to the disposal were romantic rather than rational.

Digital surrogacy: is it a preservation alternative?

The example of the microfilming and possible destruction of newspapers (see above) begs a question. Can digital surrogacy replace tried and tested analogue methods? Is digital preservation well-enough understood and sufficiently robust for it to replace photographic techniques? Microfilm is predicted to last 500 years; other photographic materials, especially colour film, are perhaps less durable, but they have been in existence for long enough for there to be some knowledge of deterioration rates. The costs of storage are known and can be predicted into the future, and the surrogates generally do not require costly and time-consuming processes to be carried out on them every few years, as is the case with digital objects. Many librarians and archivists are still cautious about the digital medium as a preservation alternative, feeling that there has not been enough research into the long-term issues, and in particular costs, around the archiving of digital information for indefinite periods. Few librarians would de-accession originals and put all their trust in digital storage without perhaps having also a film surrogate as an insurance policy.

Why data needs preservation

The nature of data

Data are at risk because they are recorded on a transient medium, in a specified file format, and they need a transient coding scheme (a programming language) to interpret them. Another problem is that digital data can be highly complex, and meaning derived from data can depend as much on how individual data objects are linked as on what those objects are. Of course, written documents are also highly complex objects, but their structure does not need to be comprehended for their preservation, only for their interpretation. Over time, knowledge of how to interpret documents can be lost, but this can usually be recreated, as their textual and physical characteristics are explicit. Their decipherment generally needs only human faculties. Digital documents differ from analogue, too, in that they are not inextricably bound to their 'containers', and therefore preserving them is not necessarily a matter of preserving containers as it is in the analogue world. As Rothenberg points out, with physical documents 'saving the physical carriers saves all those attributes of the original that it is possible to save' (Rothenberg, 2000b).

With digital data, a machine needs to be interposed between the data and the human interpreter, which adds another layer of complication. Meanings recreated in modern contexts will necessarily differ from 'original' meanings, but this is generally the case in the interpretation of the past, even when the language and contexts have come down to us in an unbroken line: the past is always interpreted through our own historical moment.

The complexity of digital data

The complexity of digital data will not be apparent to the readers and users of the future if the creators of the present have not made them explicit. An innovative, multimedia DVD derives as much of its meaning from links between digital objects as from the informational content of those objects themselves. Complex digital objects, too, need complex programs to run them, and these programs are constantly in flux, with new versions appearing frequently. If the DVD has been produced by a publisher with today's market in mind rather than tomorrow's users, then documentation of the links and the methods used to create them might not be a priority: the objective is sales, not preservation. After all, some publishers may not even want the products preserved for too long, as they will want to produce new versions, updates, etc. which they can sell again and again. The library which purchases, delivers, then tries to preserve that DVD could have a very expensive task, especially because, in order to maintain market advantage, many publishers have very different interfaces, encoding schemes and media structures. Librarians can be faced with thousands of products in hundreds of formats: a difficult and expensive enough situation for providing access to them, a disastrous one for their preservation. Now that copyright libraries are facing the responsibility of accepting non-print materials, these questions are critical for them.

How is digital data to be preserved?

There are two key issues for data preservation, which surprisingly have little to do with preserving the original bitstream:

- preserving the physical media on which the bitstream is recorded
- preserving the means of interpreting, reading and utilizing the bitstream.

Given that the bitstream is merely a very long series of binary codes, the preservation of the physical media should maintain its integrity over time. However, being able to read, use or interpret that bitstream may become increasingly difficult as systems evolve, adapt and eventually become redundant, so presenting a fog through which the bitstream becomes unusable.

Why the urgency?

Digital data do not have a long enough natural lifetime for us to wait for better media to come along. The life of data written even to optical media, such as CD-ROM or DVD, may be measured in years rather than decades. Finding machinery to read the bitstream might become tricky within a few years, very hard after a decade and require some very serious computer archaeology after 15–20 years. As yet data storage has not found its stability equivalent of paper or microfilm, but the evolution of the technology may be around the next corner. The storage of data started with punched cards only some 50 years ago and has transitioned through paper tape, magnetic tape, to magnetic disc, optical disc and portable memory such as flash memory to the present day. It is now extremely difficult to find card or tape readers if old archives of the originals come to light.

Data are bad at self-preservation

Unlike many analogue originals such as paper or paintings, data are very bad at self-preservation. Active measures must be taken at birth to ensure that they survive longer into the future: this is known as the 'retention intention' and is essential to data preservation. Data preservation cannot and must not be left to chance. At particular risk is the category of data which are 'born digital' – that is, which have no analogue originals. A great deal of data are being produced in this category, much of which it is necessary to preserve: government documents, e-mails, electronic journals, dictionaries and encyclopedias, computer games and, probably the most ephemeral category, websites. While it is of course necessary to propose strategies for dealing with all categories of digital data, it is not feasible to propose that all digital data should be preserved for the long term.

Selection of data for preservation

In any format, analogue or digital, data are selected for long-term preservation because they are felt to have some long-term value. For why preserve something which has no value? But whose values are taken into account, and how can they be known? Historians of the future will rely on what is preserved from today, but their needs will be different from those of present historians, and their research paths will be partly chosen by the data which are available. Given that it is not possible to preserve everything, it is a complex matter to decide what should be preserved. Even the world's major copyright libraries which are offered copies of every published product of their nation do not accept everything, though most of what is offered is stored somewhere. It is a vital strategic decision to have selection and retention policies for digital data, just as it is for analogue, and the decisions should be made on the value of the content, not the ease of preservation. It will take complex teams of data originators, librarians, archivists, historians and others concerned with the documentary heritage to decide upon robust selection and retention policies, and these are strategic issues of national and international importance.

The Digital Preservation Coalition has produced an interactive decision tree on the selection of digital resources for long-term retention (see www.dpconline.org/graphics/handbook/dec-tree. html). The first question posed is 'Does the content of this resource fall within the institutional remit/collection development policy?' Several surveys have found that while many institutions feel that they *should* have such a policy, very few have produced and implemented one. See, for instance, *Mind the Gap: assessing digital preservation needs in the UK*, a report prepared for the Digital Preservation Coalition (DPC) (Waller and Sharpe, 2006) or the Arts and Humanities Data Service (AHDS) Digital Images Archiving Study and Moving Pictures and Sound Archiving Study (see http://ahds.ac.uk/about/projects/archiving-studies/index.htm).

Methods of preservation of digital materials

As is clear from the discussions above, the paradox of digital materials is that they are fundamentally simple, being made up of only two electrical states, but those states can be configured into patterns so complex when using programming techniques that a limitless number of different documents and other artefacts can be represented. Digital data derived from different sources differ greatly in the amount of storage needed. Electronic text, even with complex encoding, is compact; still images can be very space hungry, with digital cameras now available which can capture files of 400 Mb or more from visually rich objects; sound and video, especially if captured at high quality, take much more storage than images or text; satellite images or complex maps created with GIS systems can be even larger. While file sizes can be reduced to some degree by compression of the data, the compression techniques which offer the greatest economies have the disadvantage of the loss of information. There are some lossless compression algorithms, but these do not produce a significant reduction in file size.

There is also a great variety of media on which digital materials can be stored, from punch cards and tapes which represent the patterns as a series of holes, to the wide range of electronic recording materials: floppy disks, hard drives, tapes, CD-ROMs, DVDs, etc. The methods of digital preservation or digital archiving we introduce here and which are discussed in more depth in this book are:

- technology preservation
- refreshing
- migration and reformatting
- emulation
- data archaeology
- output to analogue media.

Technology preservation

Technology preservation is the maintenance of the hardware and software platforms which support a digital resource; if adopted as a preservation strategy it would need to be accompanied by a regular cycle of media refreshing. It is relatively impractical and financially unfeasible, given the large number of computers and programs which would need to be managed over a long period of time: 'any collection manager in charge of a large collection of digital resources who relied solely on this strategy would very soon end up with a museum of ageing and incompatible computer hardware' (Feeney, 1999, 42). One can imagine a library reading room littered with PCs with every version of Windows and Macintoshes running ten generations of operating system; that is to name just two current platforms. For certain rare and important resources, perhaps the technology could be preserved for a time, until a better long-term solution could be found, but this is an approach clearly fraught with difficulty.

Refreshing

Digital storage media have short lives, the length of which can be estimated but which is ultimately unknown. Data therefore have to be moved periodically to new media to ensure their survival. Sometimes this involves a change of media: CD-ROMs will be copied onto hard disks in a digital data store, floppy disks may be copied onto CD-ROMs, at other times refreshing may take place because a particular substrate has become unstable, and the files may be copied to a newer, more stable version of the same medium. Refreshing copies the bitstream exactly as it is – it makes no changes to the underlying data. It is a process that needs to be carried out whatever other preservation strategies are adopted. It is technically relatively straightforward, with low risk of loss if performed and documented properly.

Migration and reformatting

Migration involves change in the configuration of the underlying data, without change in their intellectual content. This is necessary when hardware and software changes mean that the data can no longer be accessed unless they are migrated to the newer machines and programs. Migration will generally involve some reformatting, which begs the question of whether the data still convey the same content information as they did before they were migrated. The simpler the data structures, the more likely it is that the content will be preserved. With complexly linked artefacts such as websites, it is difficult to see how they can be preserved without loss unless complex (and costly) documentation is produced which annotates the structures. Web archiving is discussed in some detail in Chapters 4 and 5. If libraries and archives have to cope with a plethora of digital formats, one approach to their sustainability over the long term is to convert the digital objects into standard formats when they are first accessioned. This involves assessment of the object and extracting its data formats and inner structure, and conversion of the structures into the institution's own models. This is expensive initially, but could prove cost-effective over the long term, making migration easier and faster. The costs here are front loaded; with other preservation strategies they come later in the life-cycle.

Strategic issues in refreshing and reformatting data

Migration, reformatting and refreshing of data are processes that may need to be carried out many times over the lifetime of digital objects identified as sufficiently significant for long-term preservation. Instability or obsolescence of media means that data will need to be moved regularly and changes in software and hardware platforms will dictate constant reformatting. Refreshing and migration cycles will not necessarily coincide, which means that documentation and management of the digital archives will be complex.

The main disadvantage of a reformatting approach to digital preservation is that *all* data must be converted in each reformatting cycle, whether there is any indication that particular resources will be accessed in the future or not. Missing a cycle could mean that the data are unreadable in subsequent cycles. Reformatting is costly and labour-intensive and is likely to stretch the resources of all libraries, large and small, which could compromise decisions about effort to be apportioned for other activities, digital and non-digital.

During refreshing and migration, too, time and care needs to be spent in validating data to ensure that there has been no corruption. The (relatively straightforward) process of copying the bitstream from one medium to another can sometimes be problematic, and even slight corruption can be cumulative, resulting soon in unrecoverable data. Reformatting *ipso facto* involves the loss of the original digital object, given that the premise upon which it is based is that the original is not preservable. Lorie says of migration:

> It is the most obvious, business-as-usual, method. When a new system is installed, it coexists with the old one for some time, and all files are copied from one system to the other. If some file formats are not supported by the new system, the files are converted to new formats and applications are changed accordingly. However, for long-term preservation of rarely accessed documents, conversion becomes an unnecessary burden. Another drawback of conversion is that the file is actually changed repeatedly – and the cumulative effect that such successive conversions may have on the document is hard to predict.
>
> (Lorie, 2001)

Migration is also time-critical and needs to be carried out as soon as new formats are defined and before the current format is obsolete. If a generation is missed, the data may already be difficult to recover; if more generations are missed, it could be completely lost. Migration cycles need to be relatively frequent – few digital originals will survive more than five to seven years without some attention.

Emulation

The more complex a digital object is, the more loss there will be in its migration to new formats and generations of hardware and software. This has led some researchers to suggest that for such resources emulation might be a better technique. 'Without emulation it is unclear how interactive digital objects could be preserved in a useful way' (Holdsworth and Wheatley, 2000; see also 2001). Emulation is the process of recreation of the hardware and software environment required to access a resource. It would be theoretically possible to emulate either the hardware or the software: software could be re-engineered in the future if sufficient metadata about it could be stored, or the software and operating systems which created the digital object could be stored with it, and the hardware platform to run them could be emulated in the future. Russell is of the opinion that 'although emulation as an approach for preservation has been viewed with some scepticism, it is gaining support because it offers potentially a solution for the very long term' (1999, 8). She argues that this is a long-term solution because the technical environment is emulated only when it is needed, rather than being preserved along with the data. This means that costs occur at a later stage than if data are constantly reformatted. Emulation is discussed in more detail in Chapter 2.

Data archaeology

Sometimes it may be necessary to rescue a digital resource which has not been migrated and which contains vital information, or to which some unforeseen disaster has occurred. Occasionally data are discovered on old disks or tapes that have been accidentally preserved and data archaeology has successfully rescued them. A wide range of techniques can be employed for this, with varying degrees of success. Data archaeology has also been proposed as a preservation strategy. In this model, data would be refreshed regularly, but no migration would be performed, and no programs would be preserved to be emulated at a later stage. Instead, data archaeologists of the future would be left to puzzle out the data structures and connections in order to reaccess the information. This is an extreme form of just-in-time rescue which has the virtue of being low-cost, but which is highly risky. One argument for it is that better techniques are likely to be available in the future to recover data and, if the resources are felt to be of sufficient value, methods would be developed. This is analogous to present recovery and interpretation methods of historians and archaeologists, and has the virtue that it would be for them to decide what has value to their society, rather than current content creators and managers making decisions about the future which could easily be misguided. See the excellent report by Ross and Gow (1999) for some approaches to data archaeology.

Output to analogue media

For many years an integral part of the conservation of fragile materials was the creation of a high-quality surrogate during repair, restoration or rebinding. This might be produced using photography, but more likely microfilming or even high quality photocopying would have been employed to provide a surrogate that would satisfy the access needs for the majority of users and would thus help to preserve the original. Now that valued originals are being captured in digital form, does there still also need to be an analogue surrogate of the item? Is the production of an analogue version of the data file an appropriate preservation strategy?

In any digitization project, consideration must be given to the question of whether to microfilm before the digital imaging is done. This provides a preservation copy in an analogue format and circumvents some of the concerns over the longevity of the digital files. However, there are often features in an original that microfilm cannot capture but digitization can, and so the digital file is a valuable primary surrogate in its own right. For access purposes high-quality prints and large-sized screens for viewing might satisfy most users' needs. The printing company Oce Limited even has technology that can print out full colour images straight on to vellum, thus recreating the experience of a manuscript as accurately as is feasible. However, these address only the preservation of the original analogue or the provision of analogue surrogates for access. To consider using analogue output as a preservation mechanism for digital files the options are fairly limited to 'computer output to microfilm' (COM).

The COM process involves printing the digital data file directly onto microfilm – so that each page of data becomes a separate frame in the film. The COM approach is thus most successful for large volumes of straightforward alphanumeric text or for bitonal images, as the Cornell project found:

> The Cornell project showed that computer output microfilm created from 600 dpi 1-bit images scanned from brittle books can meet or exceed national microfilm standards for image quality and permanence.
>
> (Chapman, Conway and Kenney, 1999)

It is not really suitable for greyscale or colour images, because too much information is lost in the process to consider it for preservation purposes.

The COM process is also limited in useful application to linear text-based resources such as books, journals, catalogues or collections of individual images, such as engineering drawings. Other digital products are likely to be rendered almost meaningless in analogue form, unless what is stored is the underlying code, plus supporting documentation, from which they can be recreated. This is probably an unrealistic expectation.

Preservation metadata

Whatever strategies or techniques are adopted to preserve digital data, they will be successful only if the data are fully documented throughout their lifecycle. This is a strategic issue for data creators and curators, and one which has long-term organizational, managerial, practical and economic consequences. As a resource moves through its cycle, responsibility for its documentation will pass to different agencies and individuals who will have different needs and sometimes divergent views. As Lagoze and Payette suggest, 'preservation metadata does not exist in isolation . . . it can be thought of as the union of all metadata that pertains to the continued discovery, use and integrity of an object' and 'all types of metadata have the potential to affect long-term preservation' (2000, 96). Metadata for digital preservation is discussed in detail in Chapter 3.

Rights management

Issues of intellectual property rights and copyright will need to be considered when preserving digital materials for long-term access, and it may be necessary to obtain permission from the rights holders for any reformatting. Given that laws, customs and practices differ from country to country, we offer no particular examples here, but merely warn that this will be an issue that librarians must consider when preserving, reformatting or even emulating data. As Day points out:

> Solving rights management issues will be vital in any digital preservation programme. Typically, custodial organizations do not have physical custody of digital objects created or made available by other stakeholders (e.g. authors or publishers). Instead they will negotiate rights to this information for a specific period of time. Permissions to preserve digital information objects will also need to be negotiated with rights holders and any such agreement may, or may not, permit end user access. A digital archive will have to collect and store any relevant rights management information which could be stored as part of the descriptive metadata. (Day, 1999)

The rights are similar in both the analogue and digital environments, with the obvious exception that in the digital environment almost every action taken on a digital object may be classed as making a copy, broadcasting or performance.

Copyright

Copyright applies to work that is recorded in some way. Rights exist for musical and dramatic work as well as films, sound recordings and literary, artistic or typographic arrangements. It gives the author/creator specific rights in relation to the work, prohibits unauthorized actions (mainly copying or broadcasting), and allows the author to take legal action against such infringements.

In the UK and much of the western world, a person's work is automatically copyrighted. As a result there is rarely such a thing as copyright-free material so, even where no action has been taken to register or claim copyright, there is a copyright issue to be addressed. However, some material may have had its rights waived (such as certain kinds of public documents) or the rights may have expired.

The issues for copyright in digital preservation are:

- Under what circumstances does the preserving organization have the right or permission to ingest the content into the preservation system or storage environment? This activity may be deemed illegal copying under copyright laws unless the permissions to store and make available have been clearly agreed, with associated written evidence.
- Especially for moving image and sound recordings there may be many creators and copyright holders. For instance, the background music for a documentary may have different restrictions on use from the visual content, and each of these will have to be addressed.
- There may be restrictions on the separation of elements of a work or their independent use, for example, removing a sound track from the visual track or GIS data from satellite imagery.
- Under what circumstances may the content being preserved be made accessible as this may be defined as publication, performance, or broadcasting? The digital domain creates this new problem because of the naturally one-to-many relationship of digital content and networked access. Dark archives may be able to address this issue of acceptable archiving but may then conflict with the initial purpose of preservation – to provide future access.

- Metadata to record and track copyright will be required to enable digital preservation and eventual use. Sufficient metadata fields and associated records must be available to record all the rights holders and their relationships with each other and the wider collection. Management of this data can be time-consuming and costly to achieve. Without it, however, the digital preservation strategy would remain open to litigation risk and continuing uncertainty in the long term.

Within the current UK law, the rules for making archival copies allow certain exclusions under which copyright may not apply to that activity. These circumstances include:

- for archival replacement
- unpublished documents
- material of historical and cultural importance
- out-of-print items
- abstracts (of scientific and technical papers).

However, such rules are not easily adapted to the digital preservation framework and the very properties of digital moving images and sound make them difficult both to preserve useful metadata and to deal with Intellectual Property Rights (IPR) issues arising.

Moral and ethical rights

Whatever the copyright circumstances, creators have moral rights under IPR that relate to paternity and integrity. The moral right of paternity is the right to be identified as the author of the work. Unlike copyright, which will eventually expire, this moral right will persist for as long as the digital item persists or the estate of the creator is prepared to pursue the issue.

Ayre and Muir (2004) identify the moral right of integrity as being problematic as publishers and creators 'interpret the right of integrity to mean that their digital publications should not be changed in any way as a result of preservation activities'. However, a legal expert cited in their report states that the integrity right is to object to derogatory treatment of the work. From a digital preservation perspective the consideration will need to be whether reformatting, migration or even different compression algorithms could be deemed as potentially derogatory. While unlikely to lead to litigation, preservation organizations take moral rights seriously, and this issue remains a somewhat vague but present concern, without yet any definitive answer for moving images and sound content.

A person's image is also their property. If a person is to be filmed then a release form should be signed allowing that filming. Click and Go have produced a release form template (see http://clickandgovideo.ac.uk/releaseform.htm). This may cause unexpected issues at the point of digitization and digital preservation. For example, a choreographer who, over many years, films rehearsals and performances of their work would not necessarily have written permission to film those performing. So, while they own copyright in their own filming, they may be restricted in what they can do with that film due to the lack of permissions to film the individuals involved.

Valuing digital preservation

It can be argued that concerns about the immediate value of digital preservation have created one of the most significant barriers to organizations developing their own digital preservation programmes. In the context of a rapidly changing and volatile environment, and the constant backdrop of the need for accountability and restraint in spending, it is understandable that managers have been likely to exercise caution before embarking on such a programme. Aschenbrenner and Kaiser (2005) suggest that 'costs of a digital repository are hard to calculate due to the lack of hands-on data from other initiatives . . . the lack of experience with digital preservation costs obstructs a complete picture'.

While there is a strong growth in the general application of digital preservation technologies and techniques, we have yet to see a maturing of the economic basis for this activity. Mainly this is due to the costing assumptions used by institutions differing significantly from each other. Differences include the means of estimating: the cost of labour and infrastructure, the cost of investment and expected returns, and how costs are allocated between distinct activities that share resources.

Most of the published material relates to cost models, rather than fully fledged business models. A cost model provides a framework in which all costs can be recorded and allocated or apportioned to specific activities. A business model shows how the service functions and outlines the method by which it can sustain itself. This involves both strategy and implementation. Costs, economic factors and business modelling are dealt with in depth in Chapters 6 and 7.

However, a number of factors have begun to emerge in a gradual shift away from an apparently stark choice of yes/no in the decision to develop a digital preservation programme. These factors can be broadly summarized into:

- growing awareness of loss/risk of loss of digital materials
- growing awareness of the brief timeframe during which action can be taken
- increasing dependence on digital materials
- increasing understanding of cost elements
- increasing number of case studies with practical models for identifying costs
- increased awareness and understanding of lifecycle management and a cyclical/iterative approach
- increased influence of the Open Archival Information System (OAIS) model.

The OAIS model is discussed in full by David Holdsworth in Chapter 2.

Risk of loss

As the volume of digital information being created continues to grow exponentially, personal experiences of losing digital materials also grow to the point where everyone will have had some experience of losing their own material and/or access to something they had cited or bookmarked. Depending on what the material was and how great the consequence of loss is, this experience can range from a minor irritation all the way through to a major catastrophe. No one can give blanket advice on what could/should be kept but every individual organization will have *some* digital material which is of such key strategic, business or legal importance to them that they cannot afford to risk losing it.

Brief timeframe

We also know that the life of digital material can be alarmingly short. The UK Web Archiving Consortium refers to the average lifespan of a website being around the same as a housefly (44 days). In such an environment, the option available in the non-digital environment of leaving preservation until later, or to someone else, is not viable. Moreover, there are an increasing number of case studies which illustrate the cost-effectiveness of taking action sooner rather than later.

This is not something which need only affect organizations with national responsibilities for permanent preservation, it will affect everyone at some stage.

Increasing dependence

The degree to which we have all become dependent on digital resources to satisfy a whole range of information requirements has been accelerated by the increased ubiquity of high-quality digital resources and also by government initiatives, such as the UK's Modernizing Government agenda. The move to open access is also fuelled by the obvious capacity of digital technology to provide rapid access to scholarly material to the benefit of those working in the same or related field of activity.

There is great potential to exploit the capability of digital technology to provide efficient, seamless access to a whole range of resources. The inevitable consequence of this is that *all* organizations, whatever their mission, whatever their size, will have made some investment in digital technology to assist them in meeting their mission. To make such an investment without giving thought to identifying which digital resources created by the organization need to be retained, whether for a defined period of time, or forever, is not economically sustainable. There will therefore be increasing economic and strategic imperatives to undertake digital preservation activity. The extent and nature of that activity, and the priorities for allocating resources for digital preservation, must be determined by the organization's mission.

Cost elements and practical models

When organizations such as libraries and archives began to embark on digital preservation programmes ten or so years ago, it was really both a leap in the dark and a leap of faith. Early pioneers of digital preservation programmes had no basis on which to estimate their costs so it was a question of 'learning by doing' and making the decision to allocate resources to this activity and then to develop from there. These were sometimes very difficult decisions as they often required reallocating resources from elsewhere, always a painful process.

It was therefore no surprise that the organizations making this commitment tended to be those that already had either a strong mandate to preserve national heritage and records (such as national libraries and archives) or were already in the business of preserving digital resources (such as digital archives). The situation is different now. Because cost has been such a frequently asked question, there have been a number of articles and studies that have defined cost elements to be considered and these provide some guidance.

Even more helpful are case studies which provide much more detail about the actual costs incurred in a practical context. While no one would suggest slavishly following these or that there can be a kind of magic formula which can always be applied to work out costs – there are too many variables for that – it is now possible to determine cost with much more confidence and precision, the costs relating to the specific requirements of an organization. This can be assessed at least for a 3–5 year period (a significant time period in the digital environment).

Lifecycle collection management

The concept of lifecycle management has been used in libraries and archives for many years, to help them allocate costs associated with processing non-digital materials. It also has the potential to be used as a tool for allocating costs of managing digital resources, particularly as the cost-effectiveness of managing digital resources rests heavily on decisions made early in the lifecycle of the resource.

Figure 1.1 shows the British Library's Collection Management model and illustrates all the activities which may be needed during the lifecycle of a non-digital resource, and their cyclical nature. It reminds us that this needs to work within a wider context of national/international agreements and collaborations. The British Library has done useful work on using lifecycle costing for both digital and non-digital materials, and this is now being explored further in the JISC-funded LIFE project (see www.ucl.ac.uk/ls/lifeproject/).

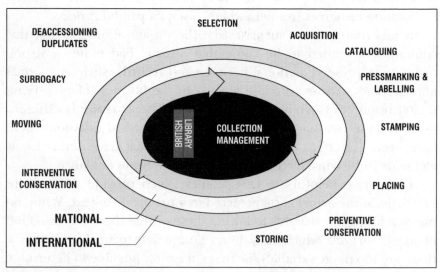

Figure 1.1 Lifecycle collection management (with thanks to the British Library)

Conclusion

The preservation of the written heritage in whatever format it is being produced is of crucial significance to civilized society. Given that it is so important, and that there are many strategic factors and costs which need to be established and predicted for the long term, it is an area where there are many uncertainties. Issues are hotly debated (sometimes in a wide public arena, as described above in the context of the disposal of newspapers) and different strategies have passionate adherents and opponents.

2

Strategies for digital preservation

David Holdsworth

In this chapter, the author is drawing on a number of projects at Leeds University which he has participated in over many years. His use of 'we' throughout indicates the multi-participant nature of such projects.

Introduction

Since computers were invented in the 1940s and 1950s, the impact of digital technology has grown to the point where it underpins the everyday lives of most people in the developed world. Increasingly, information stored and processed digitally is involved in preserving our cultural heritage. The technology itself is indeed a part of that cultural heritage. As digital information technology is barely 60 years old, and all the software from the earliest machines is already lost, we IT practitioners need to mend our ways. We should plan that our digital information will still be safe and accessible in 100 years. It is then likely that developments over that time will render the material safe for millennia. This involves a time-span over which all our existing hardware technology is likely to become obsolete, and also much of the software – a time-span often far from the minds of those of us who work in IT.

The purpose of preservation of anything, whether it be a painting by Canaletto or a database of climatic measurements, is to enable access at some unspecified date in the future, for purposes not necessarily anticipated by the creators. Furthermore, that future access has to provide meaningful access to the intellectual content of the original material. In the case of the painting, there is a certain self-evidence in the visual image, but more data about the image add markedly to the meaning of the image. Such data are, of course, metadata.

In the case of our database of climatic information there is a need for metadata about who collected it, and why. In order to make any sense of the data, future users will also need to know in what format the data are held, so that they can use appropriate software to access the information. Such metadata (sometimes called technical metadata) might seem to be a special requirement of digital information but, for the painting, information about the techniques used in its production can help in ensuring its material preservation.

In the case of digital information, material preservation is unimportant because the copies are perfect. In fact it is often impossible to identify something that can be called 'the original'. There is still justifiable concern about authenticity (see 'Authenticity' below).

There is always the question of which information will be accessed and which information will never be used again. As our current technologies do not encompass digital clairvoyance, the best that can be done today is to make the storage costs so cheap that there is little reluctance to keep things that have only a small probability of being accessed in the future.

Accountant: People tell me that 90% of this archive will never be looked at again. It seems that there is scope for a major cost saving here. Digital curator: You tell me which 90% we are talking about and I will delete it.

I have personal experience of having decided to discard material as useless, and now wish that I had kept it – and to keep it would not have been very difficult. I suspect that the contents of Canaletto's waste-bin would now be very valuable were they available today.

It is certain that the technological means for storage of digital information will change over time. The long-term preservation of printed material has focused on the preservation of the media of storage, namely ensuring the longevity of the paper and of the ink. For digital material, one must take an entirely different view. Even long-lived media such as optical discs (e.g. CDs) will become unreadable long before they decay because the devices to read them will become obsolete and unmaintainable.

However, if things are done properly, digital information can be preserved indefinitely, and at a cost that is reducing for the foreseeable future – in marked contrast to the preservation of paintings or printing on paper. The key to doing things properly is to take a view of digital data as an abstract quantity, divorced from the medium upon which they are stored, but associated with information (technical metadata – often including software) that permits ready access to its intellectual content. In this chapter we shall be concerned with this technical metadata. The metadata to do with provenance and other issues rightly of concern to preservation are covered in Chapter 3.

Leeds University was a major participant in three projects looking at digital preservation: Cedars (2002) (jointly with the universities of Oxford and Cambridge), CAMiLEON (2003a) (jointly with the University of Michigan) and the Representation and Rendering project (Wheatley et al., 2003). The author was heavily involved with the first two of these projects, and closely associated with the third. The strategies proposed in this chapter are very much the product of this work at Leeds University. It is based on a paper presented at the NASA Goddard/IEEE Storage Conference in April 2004 (NASA/IEEE, 2004).

Abstraction is vital

Over the few decades since computers were invented, there have been many changes in the representation of data. The binary digit has survived as an abstraction, and in today's world the byte is a world-wide standard, although in some circles it is called an *octet*.

All that is certain for the long-term future is that there will be further change. However, even though the technology used for representing such bits and bytes has changed enormously over time, the abstract concept of data in digital form lives on. Nonetheless, the uses to which those bits and bytes can be put have grown massively over the years. Society can be confident that the concept of information will survive the passage of time, and even the concept of digital information. There is a need to bridge the longevity of the information concept to the certain mortality of the media on which the digital data live.

The fundamental approach is to ensure that everything is represented as a sequence of bytes. I believe that it is reasonable to have confidence that the ability to store a sequence of bytes will survive for many decades, and probably several centuries. Current technology usually does this by calling this sequence a file, and storing it in a file system. There are many files in today's computer systems that had their origins in previous systems.

A new data storage paradigm may emerge in due course (and probably will), but it is unlikely to replace the digital paradigm, unless it can totally subsume it. In short, humankind will retain the ability to store bytes of data for a century or two. Conversely, it is certain that the medium upon which any digital information is recorded will be out of date in a decade or two. Recent developments of content-addressed storage (EMC, 2004) are completely consistent with this view. The 'blobs' stored within the system are still byte-streams and perfectly fit this model of viewing storage as abstract.

The challenge that remains is to maintain the ability to extract the information content of such stored byte-streams. The knowledge of the formats of such preserved data is itself information, and is amenable to being represented digitally, and is thus amenable to preservation by the same means used for the actual data.

By taking this focus on the storage of a stream of bytes, the problem is divided into two.

1 providing media for storage, and copying byte-streams from older technology to newer technology
2 maintaining knowledge of the data formats, and retaining the ability to process these data formats in a cost-effective manner.

Our work in the Cedars project concluded that in most types of collection of digital information, one should copy the digital information from obsolete media onto current media from time to time, and also update knowledge of data formats to reflect changes in current IT practices. There is also the possibility of repeatedly converting the data formats along the way to eliminate obsolete formats. The section on 'Format conversion – when?' below treats this subject in some detail.

The rest of this chapter is concerned with illustrating the viability of this strategy of abstraction and media-independence, by looking at some techniques for achieving preservation in practice. The IT industry is constantly bringing new products to market, and has a certain interest in rendering its previous products obsolete. The producers of digital material do not always take seriously the fact that the copyright laws which give protection to their intellectual property also stipulate that copyright expiry will eventually put their products in the public domain. Digital preservation technology is poised to protect future generations from the ephemeral nature of the products of the IT industry.

Above all, the strategic planning must be truly strategic and always keep in mind the long term. This means that there will always be change ahead that cannot be foreseen – but must not be forgotten.

Standards

Standards are a good thing. We are fortunate to have so many of them. However, not only do we need to take care in choosing which standards to use, but we have to avoid being overly prescriptive in their application. Systems for digital preservation have to be designed to adapt to changing ideas and practices.

A standard of prime importance in the field of digital storage is the Open Archival Information System, known to its friends as OAIS, and to officialdom as ISO 14721 (Consultative Committee for Space Data Systems, 2002).

Standards for metadata have evolved over the years and have sometimes been widely adopted. The use of MARC records (Furrie, 2003) has been standard practice for many years. This success bears testament to the widely felt need for digital metadata. However, we must not underestimate the difficulty of agreeing the format and content, as perhaps illustrated by the exercise to develop Dublin Core (2006), which managed to agree only 15 fields. Metadata is covered in depth in Chapter 3.

Open Archival Information System (OAIS)

This is a generic standard: it lays down the principles and style of operation of digital preservation, without specifying the detail of data formats or hardware technology. It was briefly introduced in the initial volume in this series (Deegan and Tanner, 2002). Section 2 of the standard gives a very good résumé of the subject area.

The overall picture is shown in Figure 2.1, which is taken from the Consultative Committee for Space Data Systems (2002) and also occurs in Deegan and Tanner (2002). Digital material is accepted by the process of *ingest*, and is then cared for indefinitely in the *archival storage*, thus allowing access by people in the future. There is also a *data management* function that 'contains the services and functions for populating, maintaining, and accessing a wide variety of information'.

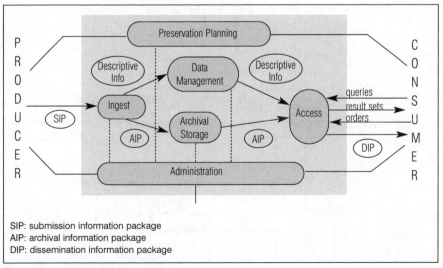

SIP: submission information package
AIP: archival information package
DIP: dissemination information package

Figure 2.1 The OAIS functional model

The OAIS standard talks of the *designated community*, 'an identified group of potential Consumers who should be able to understand a particular set of information. The Designated Community may be composed of multiple user communities.' For some types of archive, such as that held by a public library, the designated community is very large indeed.

In the OAIS model, the metadata is divided between *preservation description information* (PDI) and *representation information* (RI). The PDI is the type of information collected about most types of preserved information, and very little of it is specific to digital data. For proper coverage, see Chapter 3. On the other hand, representation information describes the digital format of the data – how to get the intellectual content from the stream of bytes.

Figure 2.2 combines two diagrams from the OAIS standard to show how the representation information and the preservation description information are related to the bare digital data. A preserved digital object is held as an information package, which has

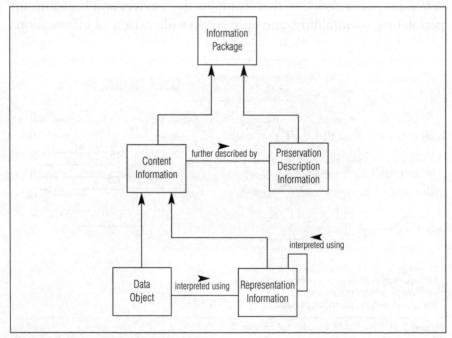

Figure 2.2 OAIS information model

two components: the *content information* (CI) and the *preservation description information*. There is no requirement that these are held together as a single blob of binary data, In many cases it might well be best to hold a large CI object in a low-cost near-line store, and keep the PDI online where it can be used for searching, or even updated as knowledge about the object is gained over time. This approach was learnt as a lesson the hard way by the Museum of Modern Art in New York, where the digitization project stored metadata on the same tapes as the digital images. The staff soon found that as people looked at the images, more metadata came to light, but that the data were already packed in such a way as effectively to render them read-only (Magraeth, 2001).

Representation information

In Figure 2.2 we see that the representation information is held alongside the data object itself. The representation information is that information without which the data object is just a sequence of meaningless binary information. Of course, representation information is just more digital data, and there is a need for some description of how to understand it. In other words, representation information can itself have representation information to describe its data formats. This is shown by the link looping round the right-hand side of the box labelled Representation Information.

As a simple example, we might wish to preserve a digital object which is an image file in GIF format. The representation information needs to tell the potential users of today how to access its intellectual content. Ideally we would like it to perform this function for the indefinite future also, but our limited digital clairvoyance circumscribes our ambitions in this area. As GIF is a format in wide use today and understood by many different software packages, the representation information needed for today's user is just the fact of it being a GIF file. The version number might be nice, but that is actually embedded inside the file anyway. Better still would be the URL of the file describing the GIF format (CompuServe, 1990), which is held by the World Wide Web Consortium (W3C, 2006). This file is itself a digital object, and as such should be associated with some representation information to describe how to access its intellectual content. Traditionally documents defining internet formats are written as plain text in a fixed-pitch font. Such documents (known as RFCs) are held in this form (in which they originated) by the Internet Engineering Task Force (www.ietf.org). For documents in this simple format the representation information can take the form of a digital object that is not very large.

In principle, the chain can go on for ever. In fact it is impossible for the system to describe itself completely, so we have to stop at some point where every likely user will already know what the format of the document is. In the Cedars project (2002) we called such stopping points Gödel ends, after the famous but difficult theorem known as Gödel's Incompleteness Theorem. The representation information for our GIF file thus naturally becomes a chain of linked nodes, as shown in Figure 2.3. In general, the structure can usefully be more complex than a mere chain, and become a directed acyclic graph. In the OAIS model it is called a *representation net*.

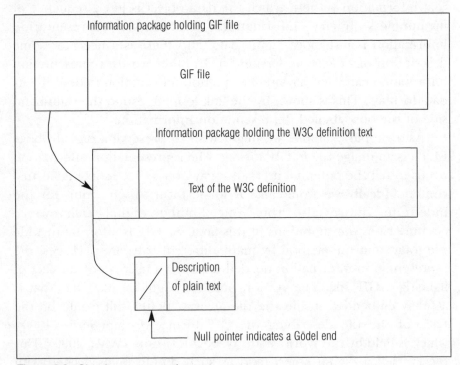

Figure 2.3 Simple representation net

Actually the vast majority of people who look at GIF images do so in an environment where the slight mouse click, or even hover, will cause the system to show the image the file represents. On the other hand, very few of them have ever read the above-mentioned definition, and many are even unaware of its existence. We actually need our representation information to tell us which software will render the image, and perhaps also to record that it is a format in common use today, and is understood by common desktop operating systems.

The OAIS representation net is the means by which the knowledge is retained. By treating all data as an abstract byte-stream at the lowest level, we have a common frame of reference in which we can record representation information, independent of any particular data storage technology, and any particular data storing institution. We have a framework in which representation information will be globally relevant.

Keep the original data

The Cedars work led to the conclusion that it is folly to have faith in long-lived media (Holdsworth, 1996). The Cedars approach is always to keep the original data as an abstract byte-stream and to regard it as the master.

Why? Because it is the only way to be sure that nothing is lost. Format conversion can lose data through moving to a representation incapable of handling all the properties of the original. It can also lose data through simple software error in the conversion process that goes undetected until it is too late to read the previous data. (I have personal experience of both situations. One in which the data were damaged, and one in which potential damage was avoided by keeping the original and producing a format conversion tool.)

How? It is certainly impossible to preserve the ability to read the medium upon which the data are stored. In the Cedars project we developed the concept of an *underlying abstract form* which enabled us to convert any digital object into a byte-stream from which we could regenerate the *significant properties* of the original. The approach is to preserve this byte-stream indefinitely, copying it unchanged as storage technology evolves.

The question then remains as to how to achieve continued *access to the intellectual content* (another Cedars phrase) of the data, and not merely a stream of bytes. Our answer to this is that the digital curation exercise should evolve the representation information over time, so that it provides the means to transform the original into a form that can be processed with the tools current at the time of access. We believe that our work in the CAMiLEON project has shown this to be feasible in the case of a very difficult original digital object of great historical importance. Using emulation we successfully preserved the accessibility of the BBC's 'Domesday' project, see below and CAMiLEON (2003b).

The very essence involves identifying appropriate abstractions, and using them as the focus of the rendering software. We achieve longevity by arranging for the rendering software to be implemented so as to remain operational over the decades. The application of our approach to emulation is covered in *Emulation, Preservation and Abstraction* (Holdsworth and Wheatley, 2001). We have also investigated the same technique of retention of the original binary data coupled with evolving software tools in the context of format migration (Mellor, Wheatley and Sergeant, 2002).

Ingest

In the OAIS model, the word 'ingest' is used to describe the process whereby digital information comes into the archive. This probably involves an appropriate form of agreement between the data producer and the archive. Alternatively there may be a requirement for digital legal deposit, or even a curator's decision that the material should be preserved for posterity. Whatever the politics, there is a need to take in digital information held on some medium, and to preserve it so that it can be accessed after technology has moved on to the use of different media, and probably also different software systems.

We propose a process of ingest which contains two steps:

1 Separate the data from the medium
2 Map to a byte-stream (i.e. make the *data-object* in Figure 2.2), and produce representation information that allows access to the intellectual content of the original.

This byte-stream is then preserved indefinitely within the archive store in such a way that it contains a reference to the appropriate representation information, of which, more later.

The form of the data between steps 1 and 2 is the *underlying abstract form* (UAF – see below). These two steps are the parts of the *ingest* process that involve the actual data. Of course, there are other steps involving the metadata, dealt with in Chapter 3, and which the OAIS model sees as construction of the PDI. We find that the UAF concept enables us to identify the *significant properties* of the original that must be preserved if subsequent meaningful access to the preserved digital object is to be achieved. This includes such processes as recreating the experience of viewing (or even interacting with) the original, or analysing it for a concordance. For particularly complex objects, emulation might be necessary.

We are concerned here with generating the *representation information* (RI) that goes alongside the data object within the content information of Figure 2.2. For various good reasons explained below, the representation information is best included by reference, rather than as a copy. At its most basic, the RI enables a reversal of the ingest process to deliver a copy of the original. This observation provides a useful minimum criterion for testing the acceptability of any scheme for RI and also for the RI of any particular information object. 'The representation information must allow the recreation of the significant properties of the original digital object, if one assumes that appropriate hardware technology is available' (Holdsworth and Sergeant, 2000). This chapter does not address the other metadata aspects that must also comprise part of the ingest process.

Underlying abstract form (UAF)

In the Cedars project we used the term *underlying abstract form* (UAF) to encapsulate the recognition that the data have an existence and a content separate from the medium upon which they are written. It is not a term used in the OAIS model. The concept will apply to any attempt to preserve digital data in a medium-independent form. Any given digital object is likely to have a number of possible UAFs. Choice of the UAF for preservation is part of the ingest process (either in the *receive submission* box or the *quality assurance* box).

Some examples of UAFs are:

- Many a CD actually contains a file system, and successful operation relies on that file system. Copying such a file system onto a partition on a hard disk delivers an equivalent working representation. File placement is unimportant. Thus the file system is a viable underlying abstract form.
- In some cases it is important only to have a file tree, and the CD contents can be copied into a directory within an existing file system.
- In the case of a complex game CD or DVD, the underlying track structure of the disc may be important for some of the special effects. This track structure then becomes a significant property, and the picture of the disc as a file system would not be a valid UAF, because it would not encompass all the significant properties.
- Data held in a relational database can equally well reside in a variety of database engines, and still deliver their original content. The comma-separated files holding the content can be used as a system-independent representation of that content.
- A plain text document consisting of lines of characters drawn from the ASCII character set is meaningful in a variety of environments. Internet RFCs are typical of such documents.

Access involves realizing the UAF on the technology appropriate to the time of access in such a way that the desired form of access (which may not necessarily be viewing) can be achieved. If we take the simple example of the internet RFC, the same UAF is stored slightly differently on a UNIX system from a PC file system, because of the different conventions for line termination. However, the UAF of lines of text is the same in each case, and the UNIX cat command clearly displays the same information as the PC's NOTEPAD. The same lines of text represented in an EBCDIC (Extended Binary Coded Decimal Interchange Code) system would be represented very differently in terms of binary digits. The same data would be displayed in the same form. The underlying abstraction of lines of text is the same, but the different platforms represent the information differently internally.

The actual process of future access will involve the use of some kind of computing platform, at whose characteristics we can only guess. It seems likely that the idea of software will continue to exist. Certainly in the early 21st century it shows not the slightest sign of going away in the near future. As well as assisting the identification of significant properties, the UAF can be used to partition the process of access:

1 Recreate the data in underlying abstract form on technology commonly available at the time of access
2 Access intellectual content (e.g. view it – a process sometimes called rendering) using software.

The software for each of these steps will be identified from information in the representation net. It is important to choose a UAF that is likely to last for a long time, such as a file tree. In some cases the UAF may itself be just the preserved byte-stream, and all the work of viewing is done by the rendering software, after a trivial copying process in step 1.

It is very likely that the rendering will be done by some widely available software, after some conversion of the data format from that in which it was submitted to the archive (i.e. 'ingested'). In the next section we discuss the future-proofing of this process.

A digital object may be configured for a variety of platforms (for example, many CDs work with both Mac and PC), and the chosen UAF may well encapsulate this. It is up to collection managers to decide whether it is a significant property of the original digital object. The technology should give them that option.

Format conversion – when?

It is obvious that when data are to be accessed some time after their initial collection, the technology involved in this access will differ markedly from that in use when data collection took place. There is also the real possibility that other technologies have been and gone in the interim. Thus, format conversion is inevitable. If a policy of copying the unchanged original digital information from obsolete media onto current media from time to time is adopted, format conversion must be performed when access is required. To do this, it is necessary to update knowledge of data formats to reflect changes in current IT practices. The question as to who might undertake this open-ended commitment is dealt with in the section on 'Share and cross-reference representation nets'.

There is also the possibility of repeatedly converting the data formats along the way to eliminate data held in obsolete formats. This is superficially attractive, in that access is always easy, but the convenient division of the problem is undermined. The only time at which format conversion of the whole data is likely to be cost-effective is when copying from one medium to another, thus changing a basically straightforward job into a much more complex one. It is vital that the copying process does not lose any information, because the data input to the copying process are about to be destroyed. Any mistakes in this complex process will lead to erosion of the intellectual content over time. On the other hand, errors in the representation net relating to past data formats will usually be amenable to correction.

Repeated format conversion may be suitable for an archive addressing a particular restricted field (for example, the CAD data for nuclear power stations), where the number of formats is small, and the whole regime includes specification of allowed formats at the outset. Archives such as libraries do not have this luxury, and must be able to absorb all appropriate material, in whatever format it is held.

For data held in currently common formats, the amount of representation information needed is trivial. Meaningful access to the data normally happens at the click of a mouse. A current computer platform will render a PDF file merely by being told that the format is PDF. Conversely, faced with an EBCDIC file of IBM SCRIPT mark-up, the same current platform might well render something with little resemblance to the original, whereas in 1975 the file could be rendered as formatted text with minimal formality. (Actually, the user had to type the word SCRIPT followed by the name of the file.)

However, if the representation information for IBM SCRIPT files is updated over time so that it points at appropriate software for rendering the file contents on current platforms, the historic data become accessible to today's users. Alternatively, all the world's IBM SCRIPT files could have been converted into Word-for-Windows, or LaTeX, and so on. The argument about the choice could continue until all the current formats become obsolete, and it could well be that the chosen format quickly becomes obsolete. Of course, there would be the temptation to convert from EBCDIC to ASCII, but that could lose information because EBCDIC contains a few more characters than ASCII.

My colleagues and I at Leeds University debated in 1990 whether to convert the EBCDIC text files in our VM/CMS archive to ASCII characters as we shifted to a basically UNIX and PC platform. Instead we kept the EBCDIC data in their original format and wrote a program to convert the files to ASCII on demand. A small enhancement to this program produces a program that converts to UNICODE instead, preserving all the characters that exist in EBCDIC and not in ASCII. Back in 1990, UNICODE had a very low profile.

This chapter argues for a policy in which the format of preserved data is converted only when access is required to the data, i.e. on creation of what the OAIS model calls the *dissemination information package* (DIP). For a popular item, it would obviously make sense to cache the data in a format that is in current use, but not to allow the reformatted data to replace the original as master. This means that the tracking of developments in storage technology involves only the copying of byte-streams. Moreover, when the format conversion has to be done, there will be improved computational technology with which to do it (Wheatley, 2001a).

Authenticity

A further concern regarding format conversion concerns authenticity. The current technique for ensuring the authenticity of any digital document is to use a digital signature. This involves computing a *digest* of the document, and then encrypting that digest with the private key of the authenticating authority (e.g. author). The corresponding public key can then be used to confirm the authenticity of the document. A converted document would not pass this test, and re-signing would involve access to a private key that may well not be available.

Indirection is vital

There isn't a problem in computer science that cannot be solved by an extra level of indirection. *Anon*

The essence of the Cedars approach involves keeping the preserved data unchanged, and ensuring that we always have representation information that tells us how to access it, rather than repeatedly converting to a format in current use. Without doubt, it is very difficult (impossible?) to provide representation information that will be adequate for ever. This is likely to be true even if the format of the master is periodically changed. The work at Leeds and elsewhere has led us to propose that representation information evolves over time to reflect changes in IT practice, but that the preserved digital objects are kept in their original abstract form. This implies a structure in which each stored object contains a pointer to its representation information. This is easily said, but begs the question as to the nature of the pointer. This must be a pointer that will remain valid over the long term (i.e. 100 years). The world needs to be wary of depending on institutions whose continued existence cannot be guaranteed. What we need is not so much a pointer as a reference ID for each preserved object. This needs to be distinct from the location of the object, but there needs to be a service that translates a reference ID into a current location. The reference ID has thus become a pointer to a pointer. This is the essence of the Cedars architecture (Holdsworth, 2002). Reference IDs could be managed locally within an archive store. Such IDs could then be made global, by naming each archive store, and prefixing each local name with that of the archive store.

There are various global naming schemes – ISBN, DNS, Java

packages, URL, URI, URN, DOI, etc. It may even be necessary to introduce another one, just because there is no clear candidate for long-term survival. What is certain is that there have to be authorities that give out reference IDs and take responsibility for providing resolver facilities to translate these IDs into facilities for access to the referenced stored objects. Currently the DOI handle system (DOI, 2005) has a resolver service at http://dx.doi.org/.

There is the prospect that if the digital storage community grasps the nettle of a global name space for reference IDs of stored objects and keeps the representation information in the same name space, the evolving representation information can be shared on a world-wide basis. Some discipline will be needed if dangling pointers are to be avoided.

Enhance representation nets over time

In the Cedars project we produced a prototype schema for a representation net following the OAIS model, and populated it with some examples. After this experience, we had some new ideas on the schema of the representation net. We believe that it is inevitable that this area is allowed to develop further, and that operational archives are built so that evolution in this area is encouraged. It is important to accept that there is likely to be revision in the OAIS model itself over the 100 year time-frame.

Also, we could see that to require a fully specified representation net before ingest is allowed could act as a disincentive to preservation of digital objects whose value is not in doubt. In many cases, representation information exists as textual documentation. An operational archive needs to be capable of holding representation information in this purely textual form, although with an ambition to refine it later. Such information would not actually violate the OAIS model, but there is a danger of being over-prescriptive in implementing the model. For instance, the NISO technical metadata standard for still images (NISO, 2004) has over 100 elements, at least half of which are compulsory.

For some formats the most useful representation information is in the form of viewing software. It is desirable for representation nets to enable the discovery of such software (see below). Many current objects need only be introduced to a typical desktop computer in order for them to be rendered. On the other hand, at Leeds we experimented with obsolete digital objects (from the 1970s and 1980s) in order to understand some of the issues likely to arise when our grandchildren wish to gain access to today's material. We even tried to imagine how we would have gone about preserving for the long-term future using the technology of the 1970s. It was abundantly clear that ideas are very different now from those of 30 or 40 years ago. Designers of systems must expect that today's ideas will be superseded over the long term.

In order to accommodate this, systems must allow the content of objects in the representation net to be changed over time, in sharp contrast to the original preserved objects where the recommendation is for retention of original byte-streams. It is vital that the reference ID originally used for representation information be reused for newer representation information produced as a result of development of new tools and ideas. That way, old data benefit from new techniques available for processing them. The representation information that is being replaced should of course be retained, but with a new ID, which should then be referenced by the replacement.

Representation nets should link to software

The representation nets of the Cedars project very deliberately contained software, or in some cases references to it. Ideally software should be included in source form, in a programming language for which implementations are widely available.

A format conversion program that is known to work correctly on many different data objects is clearly a valuable resource for access to the stored data, and should be available via the representation network. As regards the issue of longevity of such software, programming languages are abstract concepts (like bits, bytes and byte-streams), and they too can live for a very long time. Current implementations of C or FORTRAN run programs from long ago. Other languages which have been less widely used also have current implementations that function correctly.

The source text of a format conversion program which is written in a language for which no implementation is available is still a valuable specification of the format, and has the benefit of previously proven accuracy. The issue of evolving emulator programs is addressed in *C-ing Ahead for Digital Longevity* (Holdsworth, 2001), which proposes using a subset of C as the programming language for writing portable emulators.

The way in which representation information is likely to evolve over time is illustrated by three examples drawn from rather different computational environments.

Example 2.1   Acrobat files

In today's IT world it is very common to use Adobe Acrobat® portable document format (PDF) for holding and transmitting electronic forms of what are thought of as printed documents. The only representation information needed by today's computer user is the URL for downloading the Acrobat® Reader™. The representation net for PDF files is basically this single node, detailing how to gain access to the software for rendering the data. In reality, it should be an array of nodes with elements for different platforms. All preserved PDF files would reference this one piece of representation information. The recent appearance of the GNU open-source Xpdf (Foo Labs, 2004) would be reflected by adding it to this array.

Example 2.2   IBM SCRIPT files

Once upon a time, the representation information for a preserved IBM SCRIPT file would point to the IBM SCRIPT program for the IBM/360 platform. Unfortunately, there was no OAIS model in the 1970s but, if there had been an OAIS archive for storage of our VM/CMS data, this is the only representation information that would have been needed. (Actually the CMS file-type of SCRIPT performed the role of representation information, much as file extensions do today on a PC.)

As the 30 or more years elapsed, our putative OAIS archive would have expanded the representation information for SCRIPT by information suitable for more current platforms – including the human-readable documentation for a live-ware platform. There would probably also be reference to the Hercules project (2001) which allows emulation of IBM/360/370 systems of yesteryear. This need to keep up to date was highlighted in the InterPARES project (2001).

Example 2.3   The BBC Domesday project

In 1986, to commemorate the 900th anniversary of the Domesday Book, the BBC ran a project to collect a picture of Britain in 1986, to do so using modern technology, and to preserve the information so as to withstand the ravages of time. This was done using a microcomputer coupled to a Philips LaserVision player, with the data stored on two 12 inch video discs. Software was included with the package, some on ROM and some held on the discs, which then gave an interactive interface to this data. The discs themselves are robust enough to last a long time, but the device to read them is much more fragile, and has long since been superseded as a commercial product.

Here is a clear example where the preservation decisions placed (mis-placed) faith in the media technology of the day, and more crucially in the survival of the information technology practices of the time. The CAMiLEON project used this as a test case to show the effectiveness of emulation as a preservation technique. A detailed treatment is to be found on the CAMiLEON website (2003b).

We can look at this example with particular reference to its long-term viability, both with regard to the original efforts in 1986, and to the emulation work of 2002. It illustrates ideas about the appropriateness of emulation software as part of the representation information.

In the CAMiLEON project, data were preserved from the original discs as abstract byte-streams. We can represent this step as the process marked A in Figure 2.4 (taken from Holdsworth and Wheatley, 2001):

The technique was to show that we could use emulation to bridge from the Original platform to a different host platform, labelled Host platform 1 in Figure 2.4. The ingest step (marked A) involves identifying the *significant properties* of the original. The data consisted

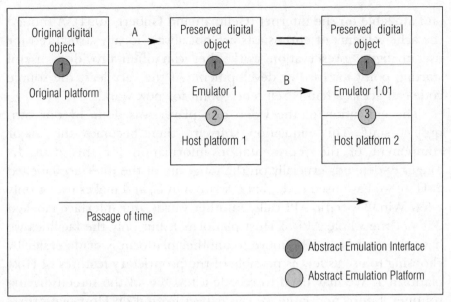

Figure 2.4 Emulation evolving over time

of the four disc surfaces, each with 3330 tracks, and some software in ROM held inside the BBC microcomputer. Some tracks were video images and some held digital data which were often textual. We preserved the ROM contents as binary files, and made each track of the disc into a binary file of pixels for the video images, and a straightforward binary file for each of the digital data tracks. This we claim preserves the significant properties of the software and data necessary to run on the BBC computer with its attached video disc player. An example representation network describing the capture process was constructed as part of the Representation and Rendering project (Wheatley, 2001b)

To demonstrate the validity of this claim, we produced the emulator shown as Emulator 1 in Figure 2.4. The original software relied on an order code and an applications program interface (API) labelled 1. In order to achieve successful preservation of this digital object, we need to reproduce this API with software that operates with a more modern API, labelled 2.

The emulation of the BBC microcomputer was obtained from an open-source emulation written by an enthusiast (Richard Gellman)

53

and available on the internet (Gellman and Gilbert, 1994). Although the achievements of enthusiasts are not always ideally structured for use in digital preservation work, they can often provide a useful starting point for further development. At the very least the source code can act as a handy reference point for new work.

The emulation of the video disc player was done by our own project staff. This emulation software then becomes the major component of the representation information for this data. Its longevity depends crucially on the longevity of the interface labelled 2. Here we have used code that is written in C, and makes use of only a few Win32-specific API calls. In other words, our interface labelled 2 is not the whole API of Host platform 1, but only the facilities we have chosen to use. The move to another platform is made easier by choosing to use as few as possible of the proprietary features of Host platform 1. We may need to recode a few bits of the screen driving routines, but by and large we can expect to find on Host platform 2 an API (shown as 3) that has most of the features needed on the new platform. We expect that a slightly revised emulator called Emulator 1.01 will readily be generated (step B) to run on Host platform 2. Meanwhile, the preserved digital object will be completely unchanged, as indicated by the large equals sign.

Evolution of representation information

At the outset, the storage media consisted of two 12 inch video discs. The representation information (a booklet supplied with the discs) advised the purchase of the appropriate hardware including the two E-PROM chips holding software that is used in accessing the video disc player. In addition, the BBC microcomputer had a well documented API for applications programs. This API (or preferably the subset of this that happened to be used) provides the interface labelled 1 in the diagram.

Our preservation of the data from its original preservation medium created byte-streams that closely mirrored the actual physical data addressing. This maximized the validity of the existing representation information, namely the documentation of the API mentioned above.

The emulator then implements this API, opening up the question of the API upon which it itself runs. Thus we add to the representation information the emulator, and the information concerning the API needed to run it. This is not yet stored in a real OAIS archive, but we do have the materials necessary to achieve this, and the data from the discs are stored in the Leeds archive (Holdsworth, 1992).

Our care in producing an emulation system that is not tied too closely to the platform upon which it runs illustrates our desire to produce representation information that will indeed stand the test of time by being easily revised to accommodate newly emerging technologies. This revised emulator becomes an addition to the representation information, extending the easy availability of the original data to a new platform. InterPARES (2001) identified clearly the desire of users to access the material in the technology of their own time.

So why emulate in this case? The interactive nature of the digital object is really a part of it. There is no readily available current product that reproduces that interaction, so we treat the interaction software as part of the data to be preserved. On powerful implementations of current desktop hardware, it runs faster than the original.

Since the CAMiLEON work, the National Archives in London have outsourced a modern web implementation of the access to the original information (Pearce, n.d.). This information should now be added to our representation information for the original data.

Share and cross-reference representation nets

As argued above, it is impossible to produce an adequate standard for representation information which would retain its relevance over the decades. To attempt to do so would stifle research and development. It is therefore to be expected that different data storage organizations may develop different forms of representation information. Initiatives such as the PRONOM (National Archives, 2004) file format database and the proposed Global File Format Registry (Harvard University Library, 2005) will also produce valuable resources that should be linked from representation information. It would seem that collaboration should be the watchword here. The emerging solutions for IBM SCRIPT files in Example 2.2 are likely to be applicable to any institution holding such data. With our proposed global namespace, they can all reference the same representation net, and benefit from advancing knowledge on the rendering of such files.

Global considerations

The NASA Goddard/IEEE Storage Conference in 2004 (NASA/IEEE, 2004) had as its theme Long-term Stewardship of Globally Distributed Storage, and this chapter draws heavily from the author's paper at that conference (Holdsworth and Wheatley, 2004).

The implementation of preservation on a global basis means there will be no overall command, and co-operation will have to be by agreement rather than by diktat. This situation has some aspects that resemble the problems of achieving true long-term preservation. We cannot predict the future accurately, nor can we control it to any great extent, so the ambition to operate on a global scale despite being unable to control activities everywhere in the world sits well with the need for future-proofing. The future is another country whose customs and practices we cannot know.

Referential integrity

On the world wide web, links that lead to pages that no longer exist (known as dangling pointers by computer scientists) are perhaps inevitable (though annoying) in such a dynamic and anarchic network. Before criticizing the anarchy, it is important to acknowledge that it is the source of much of the dynamism.

Digital storage archives referencing representation information on a global scale also have potential for the generation of dangling pointers. Furthermore, the whole *raison d'être* of the archive makes it inevitable (and desirable) that there will be lots of pointers into the archive using the archive's own reference IDs for its stored digital objects.

I would contend that once a reference ID has been allocated, it should exist for ever in the resolver services. Ideally, the object to which it points should have the same longevity but, if it is lost or deleted, that fact should be revealed by the resolver. In the case of representation information, it may be modified, but never deleted. Thus, anyone may use a reference to an object in the OAIS digital storage world confident that it will never become a dangling pointer.

A vital part of the management of such an archive will involve keeping an inventory of the external references in the representation nets (so called Gödel ends), and maintaining a process of review of the inventory in the search for things that are no longer generally understood or refer to information that is no longer available. The remedy in such cases is to update the referring nodes to reflect the new realities. Clearly it is in the interests of good management to try to keep such nodes to a minimum.

For example, a store would have a single node that describes the current version of Microsoft Word to which the representation information for any ingested Word file would refer. When this version becomes obsolete, this one node is updated with information on how to access data in the old format, or to convert to a newer format.

The two-level naming proposed earlier helps greatly in implementation of such a policy.

Cost-effectiveness

It is necessary to keep down the cost per item stored so that there is less pressure to discard things that might be useful in the future. Many things that survive to be exhibits in museums were initially seen as current fashion, then went downhill in the scale of importance, often descending to the level of rubbish, before scarcity and antiquity made them interesting. Much of what survives had a period when its survival was purely by accident. Archaeologists spend much of their time sifting through the rubbish bins (and worse) of ancient settlements. Things which survive tend to do so because there is little to be saved by destroying them. If it costs very little to keep digital data, we might resist the temptation to discard those items of little interest to us, but which later researchers might find valuable.

Digital data have a very special and convenient property: the cost of keeping it falls over time. Regan Moore's (2004) group at UCSD has a policy of copying data when the medium upon which they are stored costs twice as much as current technology. Thus each copying involves half the expenditure of the previous copying. So the total media cost of keeping the information for ever is only twice the cost of original storage media, including that original expenditure:

$$1 + \frac{1}{2} + \frac{1}{4} + \frac{1}{8} + \frac{1}{16} + \frac{1}{32} + \frac{1}{64} + \vdots = 2$$

The policy of keeping the original byte-stream, unmodified after ingest, means that the incremental cost of keeping something which shares its representation information with other items is little more than that of the media cost.

Summary

I argue strongly for retention of the original in the form of a byte-stream derived as simply as possible from the original data, and for the use of representation information to enable continued access to the intellectual content. For much material it is impossible to have perfect representation information at the time of ingest, but we must preserve the data and develop their representation information over time. Ideas on the nature of representation information will evolve over time. We must have systems capable of taking on board changing schemas of representation information.

A two-level naming system, separating reference ID from location (and translating between them) should be the practice for implementing pointers in an OAIS archive, as a prerequisite for the proposed policy of evolving representation information over time, and sharing it on a global scale.

A footnote on bits versus bytes

This chapter talks of preserving byte-streams rather than bitstreams, even though the OAIS model uses the bit as the lowest level. However, the byte is the ubiquitous unit of data storage. In today's systems one cannot see how the bits are packed into bytes. When a file is copied from one medium to another we know that whether we read the original or the copy, we shall see the same sequence of bytes, but we know nothing of the ordering of bits within the byte, and these may be different on the two media types. On some media (e.g. 9-track tape) the bits are stored side-by-side.

Pragmatically, we regard the byte as the indivisible unit of storage. If the OAIS model requires us to use bits, then we shall have a single definition of the assembly of bits into a byte. This would enable us unambiguously to refer to the millionth bit in a file, but not constrain us to hold it immediately before the million-and-oneth bit.

3

The status of preservation metadata in the digital library community

Robin Wendler

Introduction

It is a truism that preserving digital objects is quite different from preserving physical ones. While a 400-year-old book may be held and read today, digital content can be made manifest only through the use of specific hardware and software. This dependency on a technological intermediary means that not only must the object itself be kept secure and intact, as is true for all preservation, but that the means to reveal its content must also be maintained. In order to do this, a preservation agency must know a great deal about the object and the environment in which it can be used. Collectively, the information that an archive will need to ensure the survival of digital objects over long periods is called preservation metadata.

In recent years, the digital library community has dedicated focused effort to three main areas related to preservation metadata:

- determining what metadata will be needed to maintain objects over time and identifying or creating appropriate metadata standards
- designing tools to facilitate the creation, extraction and verification of certain types of metadata
- planning and in some cases test-bedding registries that will enable common metadata about digital formats and hardware and software configurations to be shared throughout the community.

Digital repositories routinely contain many kinds of information about the objects they manage. Some of this information supports the administration of the archive, such as information about the depositor, the rights holders and the contractual agreement outlining the respective rights and obligations of the depositor and the repository. Additional information may support functions such as discovery, storage management and access management. All such information may also be useful or even necessary for preservation. However, there are additional categories of information that primarily or exclusively exist to enable long-term preservation.

Techniques for preserving digital material are still in their infancy, with many fundamental questions of methodology and best practice still under debate. Most discussions about digital preservation have been theoretical: as of 2005, few digital archives have active preservation programmes. As experience in preserving digital information grows, understanding of the information that will be required in the preservation process will continue to evolve. We are trying to anticipate what our needs for information will be at some point in the future, and as our understanding grows about what those future processes might be, so does our sophistication in thinking about the information that will be needed to perform them. Although the details are still under discussion, there is agreement that successful long-term preservation of digital objects will depend on the quality of the information known about them.

Goals of preservation

Preservation metadata encompasses a range of documentation that supports five key functions: *viability, renderability, understandability, authenticity* and *identification* (www.oclc.org/research/projects/pmwg). This chapter discusses each of these functions, outlines the creation and use of metadata in each of these areas, and discusses efforts in the community to improve the prospects for gathering such metadata in an economically sustainable way.

Viability

At the simplest level, preservation requires that a digital object be kept safe and intact. Maintaining the integrity of a digital object as a sequence of bits over time is a well understood process that can be carried out with little metadata: an identifier, a checksum or some other means of verifying the integrity of the object, dates of creation and maintenance, and an indication of who may access or act upon the object. The process of ensuring continued viability requires a rigorous system of backups, checks and cross-checks, but once in place it is a mechanical operation based on a slim set of objective criteria. Maintaining reliable content that carries the key properties of an object forward over decades or centuries in a usable form, however, is expected to require more than bit-level preservation.

Renderability

Renderability, or the ability to open, play, display, execute or otherwise access digital content, is a far more difficult undertaking. Maintaining such usability requires compatibility between the form of the resource and an available hardware and software environment. This may be achieved by changing the resource into a form that can be used in a contemporary environment or by maintaining or emulating the environment in which the resource can be used in the form in which it was archived. Knowing the detailed specifications of the object's format can enable the archive to identify or, if necessary, write software to use it even if the programs with which it was originally used are long gone. Knowing the detailed specifications of the environments where the object can be used helps the archive preserve or recreate such an environment in the future.

In addition to the content files, information may be necessary to bind multiple files into a usable object. A simple example is a book with images of pages and accompanying OCR text. *Structural metadata* can be used to express the relationship between components of a complex object and supports the user behaviours of viewing pages in sequence, jumping to earlier or later chapters, and so on. Structural metadata underlies audio, video and multimedia presentations as well. Like all metadata, structural metadata is also data that must be preserved if the object is to persist.

Understandability

In order for a digital object to be useful in the future, it must not only be intact and 'playable'. The content must also be meaningful. Where renderability addresses the physical or syntactical form of the object, understandability deals with the semantic integrity, or the meaning of the content. The Open Archival Information System (OAIS) model recognizes that this need can be met through both explicit representation information and implicit 'community knowledge' (Consultative Committee for Space Data Systems, 2002). An archive can decide to rely on community knowledge of German, for example, rather than decide to keep a German dictionary and grammar in addition to a German text. On the other hand, an archive must retain a codebook for a social science data set, or else perfectly preserved and rendered columns and rows of numbers will be meaningless.

Authenticity

One of the great fears about relying on digital information is its susceptibility to change. Archives need to document any action taken on an object so that future users can judge whether an object has been altered and, if so, in what way, by what process, when and by whom. This documentation is variously known as digital provenance metadata, event metadata and process history metadata. Capturing information about events in the history of an object provides an audit trail, and makes it more likely that an archive can not only account for the current state of an object but possibly even reverse actions that were taken in error or flawed in execution.

Digital signatures and similar technologies provide a means of certifying that a given object has not been altered, by joining an identifiable and verifiable signature to a computed fixity value. By recording details of a digital signature and the chain of certificates that authenticate the signature, an archive can document that a signed object has not been changed.

However, it may be necessary to subject an object to controlled and authorized change in order to ensure that the content survives in any form. In that case, any certificate of authenticity that relies on bit calculations breaks down. While canonicalization, a method for 'guarantee[ing] that for a given object the reformatted version is equivalent to the original version with regard to some specific set of object characteristics' has been theorized (Lynch, 1999), for many digital formats it has not yet been realized. For now, archives may need to have the body now responsible for the object re-authenticate and re-sign an object after an authorized transformation. The long-term preservation of signed objects remains a topic of investigation.

Identification

The actions that preserve the integrity and usability of a digital object can happen without knowing what the object is, for example, its title, creator and so on. However, most practitioners agree that a preserved object must also be discoverable and identifiable, even if only within the confines of the archive, for preservation to make any sense. Therefore, any discussion of preservation metadata is likely to include the descriptive metadata and persistent identifiers such as URNs or handles that support identification and discovery.

Evolution of preservation metadata

The process of understanding and defining the metadata needed for preservation of digital content is ongoing. Groundbreaking archiving efforts such as Cedars, NEDLIB and PANDORA developed preservation metadata element sets that continue to influence new archiving projects. The Open Archival Information System reference model, released in January 2002, defined high-level metadata categories needed to support archival functions including preserv-ation planning, and those categories continue to be elaborated on and refined by international working groups such as PREMIS (Consultative Committee for Space Data Systems, 2002). The OAIS model states that an information object consists of not only data content, but also the information necessary to interpret that content. This is a critical point: content alone is not an archival object. OAIS defines four primary levels of information, the majority of which are not content but metadata:

- content information
  - content data
  - representation information
- preservation description information
  - reference information
  - provenance information
  - context information
  - fixity information
- packaging information
- descriptive information.

The OCLC/RLG Working Group on Preservation Metadata took the OAIS framework a step further in 2002, refining the representation information of OAIS into a description of the data object, including its technical characteristics and description of the environment, including hardware and software (OCLG/RLG, 2002).

The second preservation metadata group jointly sponsored by OCLC and RLG, PREMIS, moved beyond the OAIS reference model. Based on a simple data model with five entities, PREMIS created a data dictionary of specific elements deemed essential for preservation of digital content (www.oclc.org/research/projects/pmwg/). The PREMIS data model describes intellectual entities, objects, rights, agents and events. Objects can be bitstreams, files or representations (digital objects 'instantiating or embodying an intellectual entity').

In order to achieve the PREMIS-defined preservation goals of viability, renderability, understandability, authenticity and identity, an archive needs to know the following kinds of information:

- storage management and fixity characteristics
- technical characteristics, including for barriers such as encryption and compression
  - characteristics that apply to a class of objects
  - characteristics that are specific to an individual object
- process history or provenance
- digital signature trail, where applicable
- structural metadata that enables a complex object to be assembled from its constituent parts

- descriptive metadata and identifiers.

The metadata categories above are roughly congruent with those identified for an OAIS-compliant archive and with divisions within the PREMIS data dictionary.

In addition to the characteristics that directly support preservation, the archive must also track further information, such as administration and rights metadata, that supports other management functions within the archive. It may also need to accept and interpret so-called submission information packages (SIPs) and to produce dissemination information packages (DIPs). The SIP/DIP terminology, defined in OAIS, refers to standardized packages of content and metadata used for communication purposes. Standardizing the communication format of digital objects permits flexibility in local systems while facilitating interaction among such systems.

How is preservation metadata created?

Where does all this metadata come from? Metadata for preservation – its creation or capture, its management and its use – is complex and expensive, and archives are always looking for ways to improve the quality of metadata while reducing the cost and effort involved. Documentation of digital objects can be created by people or programs that create and process objects, or a combination of both.

Technical settings are most accurately and efficiently captured automatically, although even automatic capture is not absolutely reliable. In some situations people supply the values that an automated process uses to populate metadata. In that case, a machine may perpetuate human error. For values a device sets automatically, settings may be left with default values that are inaccurate if the device cannot determine the correct value.

Certain kinds of documentation, however, cannot be supplied by machine. For example, the rationale and methodology for the creation of the object and for preservation processes do not lend themselves to automation. Information that cannot be extracted from the object must be supplied by the creator, depositor or other agent, or the archive must do without it. Most archives do not have the luxury of receiving at ingest all the metadata that might be useful in preserving an object. The depositor may not know all the relevant technical or provenance information, or the content may be harvested and ingested with no information beyond what it carries itself.

For some formats, important characteristics can be derived from the object itself, stored internal to the object as metadata in a header or other defined structure. Libraries and archives continue to encourage device manufacturers to incorporate automatic capture of standardized technical metadata in their products. Initiatives such as Automatic Exposure at the Research Libraries Group (RLG) advocate for manufacturers of cameras, scanners and other devices to bring the technical metadata captured automatically during image creation in line with preservation standards (www.rlg.org/en/page.php? Page_ID=2681).

Even when the characteristics used in preservation planning can be found within the object, however, most repositories find it easier, safer and more efficient to monitor and manipulate them as external metadata. An increasing number of tools exist to extract such metadata, which can then populate database tables or other structures where they will be readily available for reporting. Checking for validity and consistency across received metadata, internal metadata and inherent characteristics is becoming an increasingly important way for archives to ensure that they accurately assess the materials for which they take responsibility.

Sharing tools and expertise

Most technical metadata is by its nature specific to a class of formats, such as images or audio. Some of the metadata is common to all objects in a given format, while other characteristics vary from object to object within that format. In the OAIS model, representation information, of which technical metadata forms a part, is required down to the most detailed level. Not only must an archive know that something is a TIFF, it must know enough about the TIFF format to be able to write software such as viewers. For TIFF and other publicly documented standards, this is a realistic if significant task for any single repository. When you consider the number of formats – some public, some proprietary – that an archive can expect to manage, having such expertise in-house for every format would be wildly expensive. The sheer quantity of information needed about any given format has driven archives to try to share the burden. Two major efforts are (1) format characterization and validation tools, and (2) format registries.

Format characterization and validation tools

In recent years, several major digital libraries, including the Library of Congress and the National Library of New Zealand, worked along similar lines to develop tools to identify the format of a supplied object, to determine whether the object is valid – that is, whether it conforms to the specification for its purported format – and to capture any included metadata. The JSTOR/Harvard Object Validation Environment (JHOVE) is perhaps the most widely adopted of such tools. JHOVE is a framework that can invoke a sequence of modules to analyse a file or a directory of files (http://hul.harvard.edu/jhove/). Developed at Harvard under a Mellon-funded contract from JSTOR, JHOVE is being used at various points in the archiving process by many digital archives. By combining JHOVE with other tools and scripts, a basic submission information package can be generated for a digital object with a minimum of effort. The modular nature of JHOVE ensures that any institution can write and contribute parsers for formats of interest to them, enriching the tool for the entire community.

Format registries

Format registries are still largely in the planning and prototype stages, but there is widespread interest in the concept among digital archives. The idea behind a format registry is to establish a repository of information about digital formats: technical specifications common to all compliant instances of the format, software that can render or process the format, and so on, where both information about the format and responsibility for monitoring continued viability of the format is shared among institutions. Format registries also address the problem of proprietary formats, where a company unwilling to release the format specifications to individual archives might be open to escrowing those specifications for future use given adequate guarantees.

Several initiatives are working on format registries. The first phase of PRONOM at the National Archives in the UK is a database that stores information about 'software products used to create or view electronic records (www.nationalarchives.gov.uk/pronom).' The Global Digital Format Registry (GDFR) is an effort to capture 'knowledge of how typed content is represent[ed]' in a way that is 'inclusive in coverage, detailed in representation, rigorous in validity, public in discovery and delivery, and sustainable over archival time-spans' (Harvard University Library, 2005). The GDFR is modelled as a distributed system for sharing format information, and PRONOM has expressed interest in participating in that system. Dr John Ockerbloom has developed the Typed Object Model (TOM) and a prototype database (FRED) for 'managing diverse data formats' (http://tom.library.upenn.edu/). The hope is that these efforts can converge into a robust, sustainable co-operative that both lessens the costs to archives of monitoring digital formats and improves the chances that digital information in registered formats will be preservable.

Although format registries allow archives to share an enormous quantity of metadata common to a set of objects, there remain those technical characteristics specific to the object in hand. Where possible, definition of standards for technical metadata has been left to industry committees or other interest groups based on the type of file. Groups such as the DIG35 Initiative Group, National Information Standards Organization (USA), and the Audio Engineering Society have all developed valuable technical metadata standards for classes of files. While some widely deployed formats are covered by these efforts, many digital formats have never been documented in this way. In addition to the gaps in format-by-format coverage, there remains a need for archives to develop a deeper understanding of the specifications of many digital formats in order to develop accurate data models and to ensure they are tracking the information in the right way.

Modelling

As archives have gained experience, they have become more knowledgeable about the technical characteristics of their digital content. Many digital formats are complex and, in order to characterize them accurately, archives need to model and record metadata at the correct unit of description. Although many archives manage metadata about files and logical objects, it has become clear that other layers of description may be needed.

File formats may include one or more bitstreams with distinctive technical characteristics that should be independently tracked. For example, values for x resolution, y resolution, and bits per sample for a TIFF file more appropriately describe the bits that comprise one image, of which there may be several, within the TIFF. When each TIFF has only one image, an archive can get away with conflating file and bitstream metadata, but for multi-image files, the need to be precise about what unit is being described becomes clear. In this case, technical metadata needs to be recorded for each included image bitstream. The reasons for this are as follows:

- Content files may be encapsulated, singly or in groups, through compression or encryption. In that case, all the 'layers of the onion' need to be described, because each of them poses a barrier to usability and a preservation risk.
- The phrase 'logical object' is sometimes used in digital archives for two distinct concepts that are better modelled separately: an intellectual entity and the particular technical instantiation of complex content, for example, a PDF and a series of page images. The intellectual entity is abstract, and corresponds to a work or expression as defined by the Functional Requirements for Bibliographic Records (FRBR), while the instantiation is an FRBR 'manifestation' and may exist in multiple copies, i.e. items. PREMIS models these concepts as intellectual entities and *representations* which, like FRBR manifestations, may exist in many copies. A representation may be comprised of many content and application files, each with metadata of its own. Because some kinds of metadata, such as ownership, rights, process history and preservation policies, may apply to either the intellectual entity or

the representation, many archives find they need to be able to identify, describe and manage both kinds of logical object in addition to the management of the component files and bitstreams.
- Groupings or collections of digital objects may also require preservation actions and corresponding metadata.

Clearly, there is an enormous amount of information that can be known about a digital object, daunting both in the detailed technical understanding required and the effort involved in its creation.

Being controlling is good

Most technical metadata can be expressed in unambiguous quantitative terms. Bits per sample and number of channels are examples of objective characteristics that can be rigorously controlled. Structural metadata, too, must be rigorously expressed in order for rendering applications to work correctly. However, other kinds of metadata are more difficult to pin down. Tension exists between the desire to leave a copious record of decision processes and digitization methodologies on the one hand and the cost and efficiency – both of creation and use of metadata – on the other. Narrative or discursive metadata that requires human review and interpretation may be appropriate to support digital archaeology or for exceptionally precious and complex resources. However, as archives grow in size, most find that in order to monitor the risk of obsolescence and design the most effective preservation strategies, they must be able to identify groups of objects within a single format that share characteristics which impact preservation decisions. In order for preservation to be affordable, preservation processes for most materials must be automatable based on controlled metadata.

The challenge of significant properties

Archives continue to struggle with an idea called *significant properties*: functions or characteristics of an object that are essential to its meaning. Preservation of digital objects will in some cases necessitate changes in look, feel, functionality or content if the object is to remain usable at all. Identifying significant properties lets an archive know what features must not be lost during preservation actions. It is easy to grasp the concept of significant properties but difficult to define what they are to express them so that they can be used effectively in preservation processes.

Although significant properties may be seen as individual and specific to a given object, most digital archives try to explicitly or implicitly create classes of objects based on common properties. In the Cedars project, 'significant properties' were associated with the Underlying Abstract Form (UAF) of an object. Therefore objects with the same UAF shared the same significant properties (Cedars, 2000). Conversely, if significant properties varied, than objects that were otherwise similar could have different UAFs. The National Library of Australia's (NLA) *Digital Preservation Policy* describes significant properties by example: 'such as formatting, "look and feel", function-ality, and information content' (National Library of Australia, 2002).

The PREMIS working group, following on the work of OAIS, Cedars and NLA, defined significant properties as those 'character-istics of a particular object subjectively determined to be important to maintain through preservation actions', noting 'Significant properties may be objective technical characteristics subjectively considered to be particularly important, or subjectively determined characteristics' (PREMIS, 2005).

One example of a significant property often cited by Dale Flecker of Harvard University is the case of two JPEG images of paintings – one by Monet, one by Mondrian. They might share technical characteristics such as bits per sample, *x*-resolution and *y*-resolution, etc. However, in a conversion from JPEG to JPEG2000, they would benefit from different processing parameters in order to optimize for colour or sharpness, respectively. The tricky part is knowing at the time an object is archived that colour versus sharpness is a trade-off the archive may have to make in the future. Capturing subjective significant properties in an actionable, that is to say controlled, form requires that archives and curators determine *in advance* the qualities that might be at risk during a future preservation action and record them as metadata. The foresight to 'know what you will need to know' is one of the most problematic aspects of preserving digital content.

Standards

Information needed to preserve digital objects is in fact a patchwork of related documentation, governed by standards from different domains. Virtually everything that can be known about an object has a place in the preservation process. Some kinds of metadata, such as descriptive metadata, are thoroughly represented by established standards. Most archives will adopt, in whole or in part, existing standards in these areas. New efforts to develop standards for preservation metadata have focused on filling in the gaps.

The 2005 PREMIS report provides guidance about what information a responsible archive must know about its content and must be able to supply to partners as required. The PREMIS data dictionary, the largest portion of the report, provides a baseline set that spans preservation metadata needs. The data dictionary is independent of any particular architecture and is agnostic about whether the metadata values are explicit or implicit in any local implementation. It omits detailed metadata about description, rights and agents (which are already well defined and well served by existing standards) as well as format-specific technical metadata. The XML schemas that accompany the data dictionary can facilitate implementation and exchange of preservation information, but their use is optional.

The PREMIS metadata set includes an event entity to tie information about digital objects with information about the events and actions in which the objects play a part. The PREMIS event entity defines events at a general level. Other standards, such as the Audio Engineering Society's Process History Metadata (2002), can be linked in to provide precise details (such as equipment makes and models, processing parameters and channel patching) about technical transformations.

One of the most active sectors of metadata development has centred on the related areas of digital object modelling, structural metadata and content packaging. While standards in these areas are remarkably similar and can in fact serve similar purposes, they arose from different information sectors and were intended to serve distinct needs. The phrase 'structural metadata' often implies representation of one resource (for example, a monograph or serial publication), while content packaging may refer the aggregation of such resources into a course of instruction. Structural metadata represents the relationships among component files of a complex digital object, along with the descriptive, technical, administrative and rights metadata associated with the object as a whole or with any of its parts.

Because a user's experience of digital content is determined in part by the way the object is structured for presentation, structural metadata must be captured, archived and maintained along with the actual content files in order for the object to be usable in the future. METS is the structural metadata standard that arose within the digital library community itself (www.loc.gov/standards/mets/). Developed under the auspices of the Digital Library Federation, METS is a generalized and flexible XML schema based on an earlier format developed in the Making of America II Project (http://sunsite.berkeley.edu/MOAZ/). METS has evolved from a format primarily designed to drive display applications for multipart objects such as imaged books into a full-featured archiving package.

The heart of METS is an inventory of components and one or more 'structure maps' – views of the content that support navigation among components. In its simplest form, METS supports functions such as 'next' and 'previous', but it may also support jumping to a given file in a sequence or a given page or track number, to a particular segment of content within an image, audio file or text file, and so on. With the wide range of metadata it supports and the ability to encapsulate content and metadata or to point to external content files and metadata, METS truly is a kind of map to a digital object. METS can be adapted to many technical environments and serve a variety of needs.

SCORM (Sharable Content Object Reference Model), administered by the Advanced Distributed Learning Initiative of the United States Department of Defense (www.adlnet.org/scorm/index.cfm), and IMS Content Packaging (IMS, 2004), come out of the learning object community and are designed to represent sequences of objects intended for use in a courseware or training environment As such, they often include metadata that characterizes the intended audience, learning methods supported and other pedagogical context. Digital libraries in an academic setting increasingly need to generate learning objects from library content and to take in learning objects created by external agencies and format them for long-term preservation.

MPEG21 Part 2: Digital Item Declaration (DIDL) is yet another structural metadata and packaging format, arising primarily from the commercial sector (MPEG 21, 2003). DIDL has been adopted by some digital libraries, most notably Los Alamos National Laboratory Digital Library in the USA (Bekaert, Hochstenbach and Van de Sompel, 2003). While it is unclear how widely DIDL will be adopted as a packaging format for long-term preservation, its origins in the commercial sector make it likely that archives will be given responsibility for DIDL objects that the archive must either transform or manage. Similarly, the Advanced Authoring Format (AAF) and its derivative Material eXchange Format (MXF), developed by the motion picture and broadcast media industry, serve as wrappers encompassing content and metadata, and complex objects in these formats can serve an archival purpose (http://aafassociation.org/index.html).

Another name worth knowing in this arena is XFDU (XML Formatted Data Unit), a document modelling format developed by the Consultative Committee for Space Data Systems, the group responsible for OAIS. XFDU draws on METS, but has streamlined that schema to deal specifically with space data. The goal is to support 'the packaging of data and metadata, including software, into a single package (e.g. file or message) to facilitate information transfer and archiving' (Consultative Committee for Space Data Systems, 2004).

The proliferation of formats in this area testifies to the importance of keeping a handle on all the parts of a digital object and their accompanying metadata, and to the complexity of doing so. While a single standard has its appeal, each of these formats fulfils a particular need within its community and is seen as responsive to that community. Any effort to impose a 'super-standard', at this time, would not only be *perceived* as being less responsive to each community, it would *be* less responsive. It would also be overly complex for every community, by virtue of incorporating special concerns from each. For now, the METS, IMS, MPEG, XFDU and other structural metadata communities work at keeping lines of communication open, trying to insure that objects created by one community can be transformed to another with minimal loss. Several projects are actively working on transformations between IMS and METS (and the reverse) to enable traffic between libraries and courseware.

Future steps

Thanks to the dedicated efforts of many groups, the role of metadata in preservation is now fairly well understood, and a solid foundation has been laid in the development of standard element sets and exchange mechanisms. With those in place, digital libraries and archives can work more productively on practical areas of common concern:

- Implementing metadata sets such as PREMIS and testing their effectiveness is an immediate goal. Refining and iterating those standards and developing community-wide best practices will enable the development of additional common tools to make the creation, capture and use of preservation easier, more consistent, more reliable and less costly.
- Developing a sustainable infrastructure for documenting and monitoring digital formats is essential. Format registries offer the promise of harnessing distributed effort and expertise, ultimately reducing the burden on individual archives and improving the chances that objects in obsolete formats will be recoverable. Such a utility seems fundamental in a modern world increasingly dependent on digital formats as the medium for commerce and culture.
- Improving the ability to readily convert between the many flavours of structural and content packaging metadata is crucial. Consolidation on a single format is not in the offing, and yet producers and consumers in many industries as well as digital libraries and archives need to be able to import and work with digital content and metadata from other domains. Being able to

do so easily will increase both productivity and creativity and lower the barriers to and cost of bringing digital objects into a preservation environment.

Developing understanding of the information that will be needed to preserve digital content has been an impressive co-operative effort on an international scale. It is an ongoing task, and technology is not standing still while we figure it out. However, great gains have come and will continue to come from sharing expertise throughout the digital archiving community. Co-operative efforts including metadata standards, metadata extraction and conversion tools, and format registries offer the hope of a longer life for digital content worldwide.

4

Web archiving

Julien Masanès

Introduction

In order to be able to conserve artefacts in the long term, it is necessary to understand not only their content, but also their organization, including their physical structure. Librarians have been able to play their historic role as the preservers of books because they have an in-depth understanding not only of the content of books but also of their tabular organization and their physical shaping. Based on this knowledge, they have built the methods, from collection development to preservation policy including shelving, cataloguing, etc. that enable them to fulfil their mission.

There is a wealth of information on the web. The size of the web is difficult to estimate but certainly ranges in the hundreds of terabytes (1 terabyte = 1024 gigabytes),[1] if not in the petabytes (1 petabyte = 1024 terabytes). The largest libraries in the world hold tens of millions of volumes, which represent, if we consider the text only, tens of terabytes of information (1 megabyte per volume on average). If we take into account images, the total can be estimated at 50 times more. If we consider moving images, information held by libraries is even larger. The Bibliothèque National de France (BnF) for instance is running a digitization project for its videotapes collection that will yield an estimated 400 Tb of data. Nevertheless, it is reasonable to assume that the volume of information that the web contains already equals if not exceeds those of the largest libraries in the world.

Content on the web has not been, for the most part, selected and edited. We can estimate that around 40 million active webmasters co-ordinate the production of hundreds of millions of contributors. A very conservative estimate of the number of web logs indicates that 10 million people use this new publication tool and therefore enrich content available on the web.

This impressive growth in size and number of producers would have resulted in a catastrophe from the preservation standpoint in the analogue world. But, as this has happened in a digital realm, the consequence is more a displacement of problems and practices than a disaster. The main reason for this is that the preservation of born-digital material can benefit from the possibility of automatic processing and falling storage costs that have enabled such growth. Manually selecting, cataloguing and shelving such a tremendous mass of information would have been impossible. But automatic processing of information makes it possible.

Web archiving is, in this regard, the test bed of a larger transformation of preservationist activity. For the first time, size of data, variety of content, number of producers scale up to the point where entirely new methods and approaches have to be introduced. As a consequence of this, the web should not be considered only as a content repository, but also as an information space with its specific structure, rules and organization.

Making an isomorphic copy of a website is in most cases almost impossible for practical reasons. The reconstruction of content that web archivists have to make requires a deep understanding of web structure to guarantee faithfulness to the original together with accessibility and long-term preservation.

This chapter outlines the main transformations that the preservation of web material introduces. Other chapters of this book deal with general digital preservation issues and approaches.

The web: an information space

The internet is built on several basic protocols (e.g. TCP/IP) and systems (e.g. the DNS) that together make it possible to connect computers in a very loose and open way. An important architectural decision has been to leave the 'intelligence' of the communication to the ends (that is computers connected to the network with their software). The network performs only neutral, basic data transportation tasks. The end-to-end architectural design (Saltzer, Reed and Clark, 1984) adopted for the internet has had important consequences. One of the main ones is to allow anyone to build extra protocols enabling new usages on top of this basic infrastructure and have them easily adopted by others, as long as they provide the code implementing them. This means that new and unexpected usages can flourish on the internet (only) if someone has conceived them, translated them into protocols and coded an application that can implement these protocols. There is no need for prior agreement from the infrastructure providers, no need for heavy development and deployment (the coding of a new application protocol can be made in only a few days depending on its complexity).

This has led to the tremendous creativity of the internet as a platform (Lessig, 1999), giving birth to, among hundreds of other functions, mail, ftp, instant messaging, internet telephony and of course the world wide web itself.

As an application protocol, the web is oriented to document publishing. It implements a hypertext information space through three protocols/languages (Berners-Lee et al., 1994):

1 URI (Universal Resource Identification) is a standard for addressing resources. It is composed of a prefix that uses the domain name server (DNS)[2] system for host naming, and it allows great flexibility to webmasters regarding the right part of the URI. These two characteristics have made the URI a powerful integrating standard. It is indeed possible to address with a URI not only web documents, but also other entities (ftp, wais, gopher). This was crucial in the early and rapid adoption of the web (Gillies and Cailliau, 2000).

2 http (Hyper Text Transport Protocol) is a protocol for the request and delivery of documents. It allows the client to send a request for documents (based on the URI), get a status of the request, and get the document from the server if it is possible.

3   html (Hypertext Mark-up Language) is the best known of the
    three standards of the web because it is used by millions of people
    to create web pages. It is a mark-up language (actually a DTD of
    SGML) that enables the layout of pages.

These three essential bricks of the web are implemented at the client-
side by a browser that interacts with the server and displays pages,
and at the server-side by an http server or web server that responds
to http requests on a network port (80 by default), processes them
and provides an interface to the file system or the database that
accommodates the actual content. These form the underlying
infrastructure of the web information space characterized by its
segmentation in documents connected together by hypertext links.

To give an overview of its underlying mechanisms, we can say that
navigation consists for the user in clicking on objects (words, phrases,
images) that the browser then transforms into requests to the server
for the files, the URI of which is embedded in these links.

The physical organization of files that the web gives access to is a
virtual file system integrating all the web servers' files via the network.
For instance, the site www.example.net is stored in a specific directory
(often called www) of the web server as a hierarchical structure of files
and directories. The filenames and structure will form the basis of the
linkage structure. Requesting the document www.example.net/index.
html is equivalent to sending the request for the document named
index.html in the directory /www/ of the server. The web server
receives the request on port 80 of the network, recognizes the request
(http://) and finds in the directory called /www/ of its local file system
the appropriate file. If it has it, it sends it with some extra information,
notably status code ('200' for instance means 'OK'). In other words,
when navigating on the web, you actually navigate in a virtual or
abstract file system made of all the file systems of all the web servers.

The abstraction provided by the web as a system can be even
greater when pages requested are dynamically generated from
content stored in databases. In this case, the file system you navigate
in is virtual not only because it integrates several local file systems,
but also because it mimics a file organization that does not even exist.
Dynamic pages have 'names' (URI) that consist of parameters for

programs that will be interpreted and used for generating the final content displayed to the user. Even if these names don't correspond to actual files stored somewhere on the web server, these pages are labelled with these 'names' (URI) and you can use them in links. This feature has given an extremely powerful and flexible addressing capacity to the web, allowing almost any sort of content to be included, with programs calling and parameter passing through URIs.

This brief description of the web as an information space system suggests some consequences from an archiving point of view. As a first approximation, we can say that web archiving consists of constructing a 'local' and preserved version of certain parts or segments of this virtual information space. What is new compared to traditional preservation is, first, that the web information space exists only as a result of the interaction of several complex and active web information systems (WIS). And, second, as navigation paths in the web are embedded and actionable in the documents themselves, the archive has to be built in a way that will enable this mechanism to work.

This means that an archived segment has (1) to be collected through interactions with web servers, with all the constraints and limits that this entails, and (2) to be organized in a way that enables navigation. The two stages will be considered in the next sections and we will see that they raise specific problems for digital preservation.

Content acquisition

Archiving a website is a non-trivial task. First, all files of the website have to be found. The web protocol does not provide a full list of the documents of a site, in contrast to FTP, for instance. The same has to be done for every page, ensuring that no linked document is omitted (Roche, 2006). This is done with automatic tools for content gathering such as crawlers (also called spiders) that allow massive content acquisition at relatively low cost. For a recent review of crawler literature, see Chakrabarti (2002) and Pant, Srinivasan and Menczer (2003). With standard desktop computers and a digital subscriber line (DSL) connection, it is possible to retrieve millions of documents per week, even per day. Crawlers are also very efficient at exploring the web and discovering new sites through links, even when starting from a very small set of seed sites.

However, a crawler faces severe limitations when it comes to finding a path to certain types of documents (Boyko, 2004). First, access to sites or parts of sites can be restricted (with password or internet protocol (IP) authentication). In this case, getting due authorization from the producer is required. Second, the coding technique used to implement links can be difficult for crawlers to interpret. This can be the case when scripts use contextual elements or when the code is opaque (executable, server-side code, etc.). Although crawlers are getting better at link extraction (Mohr et al., 2004) they still face some limits in this area.

Third, a non-trivial interaction from the user can be required (more than a click). This is usually the case when entering a query is required to access a portion of the site. This part of the web inaccessible to crawlers is usually called the hidden or deep web (Bergman, 2001; Cope, Craswell and Hawking, 2003; Lin and Chen, 2002; Giles et al., 1998; Lawrence and Giles, 1999). Even if active research is done in this area (Lin and Chen, 2002; Lage et al., 2002; Raghavan and Garcia-Molina, 2001) gathering hidden website content necessitates a case-by-case assessment and some adapted actions. This can be limited to entering new parameters for the crawler, or downloading directly page by page a part of the site. In many cases, nothing can be done remotely, and obtaining the content through the hypertext transfer protocol (http) interface remains impossible. In these cases, direct contact with the producer is unavoidable, which is incomparably more time-consuming than online capture.

Last but not least, time is an important parameter to take into account while managing a crawl: given that the request load that can be put on a single server is limited, it is necessary to wait for a period of time between two requests sent to this server. This delay can be defined in absolute time (3 seconds for instance) or in relative time (3 times the average response time of the server). In any case, this means that downloading a complete website will take time – days or even weeks for very large websites, whatever the crawler's capacity. As a consequence of this, a certain temporal incoherence can arise: some pages linked from the homepage, for instance, may be different, when they finally get crawled, from how they were when the homepage was crawled. To avoid under-using crawling machines while waiting for responses, it is often practical to crawl several sites at the same time to keep crawling resources busy.

Shaping of the archive

Gathering content is not all that is needed for web archiving. In traditional preservation practice, for analogue as well as for digital objects, there is a clear delineation of document bounds and shaping. A book, digitized or not, is a defined and finite set of pages, in a particular order. A technical mediation is certainly needed for accessing digitized material (see other chapters of this book). But for web material, in addition to this, stability and finiteness of the object itself no longer exist: websites represent a mingled set of documents related in various ways (mostly by linking but not only) that makes a whole of itself. This implies that archivists have to recreate an information space not only out of flat linked files but also out of active information systems. As Antoniol et al. put it: 'A web site may be as simple as a single file or one of the most complex collection of cooperating software artifacts ever conceived' (1999).

Of course, ideally the archive could be isomorphic to the original (same hierarchical structure, naming of files, linking mechanism and format) but, for practical reasons, it is almost never the case. Creating an exact copy of a server's files in an archive is the least of the problems. More challenging is the re-creation of the web information system. Web information systems (WIS) represent complex architectures dependent on specific operating systems, server configurations and application environments that would, in most cases, even be difficult to re-create from scratch for their designers and managers. This is the reason why web archivists have skirted the problem and resigned themselves to adopting transformation strategies for obtaining versions of sites that can be preserved. These transformations can impact the addressing and linking mechanism, the format, as well as the rendering itself of archived objects.

Three strategies have been adopted so far for generating web archives. The first strategy is to make a local copy of the site's files and navigate through this copy in a pseudo-web manner (Roche,

2006). The second one is to run a web server and serve content in this environment to the user's clients. The Internet Archive with its now famous Way Back Machine has implemented this strategy. The third option is to reorganize documents in a different (non-web) logic of naming, addressing and rendering. The pros and cons of these different strategies as well as their preferred application domain are presented in the following sections.

Local file system archive

Description

In this case, web archivists take advantage of the possibility that the URI specifications (Berners-Lee, 1994) offer to use the local file system prefix 'file' in a URI scheme, as in this example: file:///User/example.html.

This enables the use of the local file system for navigating through web documents. It also requires using a partial (relative) form of the URI excluding not only the prefix but also the server's name and the path of the object to point to a relative address.

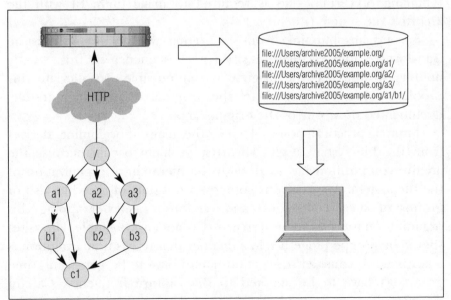

Figure 4.1 Local file system archiving

85

Standard browsers can open local files directly from the archive and, as long as all links in the document are or have been converted into relative ones, the navigation of the archive will be the same as on the original site, noticeable only if looking at the URI prefix in the address bar of the browser (here 'file' instead of 'http'). Navigation occurs in the context given by the starting URI, with the file system as its environment instead of the web.

Discussion

The main benefit of this strategy is to simplify access to the archive by smoothly migrating the original website linking structure onto the archive file system. Using a standard browser and file system avoids the extra overhead associated with running complex access systems. This makes it very convenient for small- and medium-scale web archives.

But there are several limitations in this approach. From a conservation point of view, the shortcomings are twofold. First, as file system naming conventions (case-sensitiveness, escape characters, forbidden characters) are different from those allowed by the web, renaming of certain files is required to make them fit with the archive's file system (Roche, 2006).

Second, absolute links from the original web documents must be transformed into relative links. As a consequence of this, strictly holding steadfast to the original is not possible. To alleviate this problem, changes applied to the original should be carefully documented or a copy of the original kept.

From a practical point of view, the main shortcoming derives from the file system itself. The first problem occurs because the archive composition has to fit with the hierarchical organization of the file system. An archive is composed not only of sites but also of groups of sites (collections) and versions of sites. Mapping this organization to a hierarchical structure is not always simple. How sites should be grouped together in a manner that resists time evolution is a key issue to consider. Collection names have to be persistent, time groupings have to be adapted to the capture frequency. Careful decisions have to be made beforehand that will impact on how the chosen structure will persist as the collection develops. Organizing time transversal navigation (from one version of a site to an older one for instance) is a key issue for which a middleware layer has to be added on top of the simple file system. This layer has to be able at least to bind together different versions of a site of various dates (versioning) and present this in an appropriate user interface that will allow navigation through time to proceed logically. This has often been implemented by an intermediary page with a list of dates where the site is available, generated by an external database of information on sites and their capture dates.

A second shortcoming of this approach is the huge number of files web archives have to handle. It is common to see archives with billions of files. This figure reaches the capacity limits of current file systems. Even when it can handle this number of files, the burden put on the file system threatens its performance. This is the reason why large-scale archives have used container files to store their files in order to alleviate the load put on the file system. But this of course breaks the direct correspondence in names and linking that the local file system archive's approach offers and makes it necessary to adopt the second approach, the web-served archive (see below) to deliver content from the container files.

Web-served archive

Though more difficult to implement, this option enables a better compliance to the original naming of documents. It also means that file system size limitations can be overcome, which is crucial for large-scale web archives.

Description

Files of the original website are stored in warc container files. This format has long been used by the Internet Archive and is now standardized in a new version by the International Internet Preservation Consortium (IIPC). A warc file records a sequence of harvested web files, each page preceded by a header that briefly describes the harvested content and its length. Besides the primary content recorded, the warc accommodates related secondary content, such as assigned metadata and transformations of original files. The size of a warc file can vary up to hundreds of megabytes. Each record has an offset, which permits direct access to individual records (web files) without loading and parsing all of the warc files. Offsets of individual records are stored in an index ordered by URI. It is hence possible to extract individual records rapidly based on their URI out of a collection of warc files. The records are then passed to a web server that sends them to the client. The conservation of the original naming scheme (including parameters in dynamic pages) allows navigation in the site as it has been crawled. All the paths followed by the crawler can be traversed again.

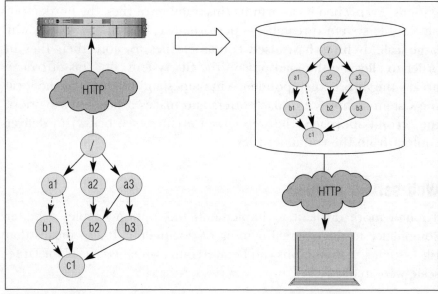

Figure 4.2 Web-served archive

Discussion

The main advantage of using warc containers is the possibility of overcoming the storage file system limitation in terms of size (fewer individual files are effectively stored in the archive) and namespace (the naming of individual web files can be preserved). The Internet Archive achievement through the Way Back Machine (that gives access to 400 Tb of web collections) shows that this approach scales up like no other.

The downside of this approach is that direct access to the stored files is not possible. Two layers of software have to be added: a warc file index system and a web server. These two layers are not outstandingly complex but it means that the access has to be done in a specific environment, which can be difficult to set up and maintain in small organizations.

Non-web archive

Description

In this approach, documents that were on the web are extracted from the hypertext context and reorganized in a different style in terms of access logic and/or format.

This can be the case when a set of documents taken from the web is reorganized from a link-based access logic to a catalogue-based one. This is also the case when a page or even an entire website is transformed into PDF format. Adobe's Acrobat has this functionality

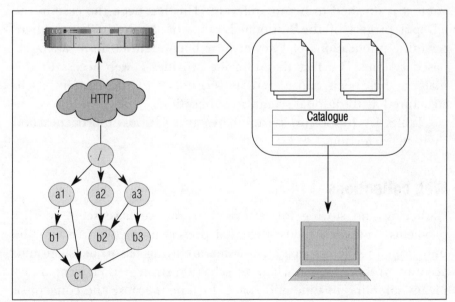

Figure 4.3 Non-web archive

(since version 6) and can transform an entire website into a PDF document, at the expense of a larger size and a paper-style reorganization of the web pages. In this case, the document appears as though printed, with a static rendering and a paper page-like organization, even if linking can be safely preserved through the use of a different and non-global naming scheme.

Discussion

This approach is a limited case of what can be called web archiving. It mostly makes sense for objects that have been created and organized independently from the web. This is the case, for instance, with large collections of digitized books, papers, music and videos made available on the web but whose original organization was not hypertext but catalogue-based. It can be preferable in this case to archive these collections and their catalogues and give access to them through the local archive catalogue itself. In these examples, the web has been used only as an accommodation for a pre-existing information system with its own structure. Archiving the original form (documents and catalogue) can make sense if the hypertext context is deemed to be non-relevant. This has been the case in the e-Depot project of the National Library of the Netherlands where scientific publications of Elsevier have been archived in a catalogue-based system. The fact that Elsevier provides a web access to this material has been considered as secondary to the content itself, structured as traditional scientific publications.

Table 4.1 (opposite) recapitulates the various approaches and their characteristics.

Web collections

Gathering and storing for access poses, as we have seen, specific problems compared to usual digital preservation. But it is not the only domain where specificity of web archiving has to be taken into account. Web archiving, whatever selection strategy is chosen, always means sampling in time and space. In time, because the concept of definite or final version does not apply on the web: web documents

Table 4.1 Summary of web-archiving strategies

Archive type	Local file system	Web-served	Non-web
Description	All links are converted into relative ones. Hypertext navigation is done directly on the local file system.	A web server is set up for access through which documents are served. Hypertext navigation is close to the original one.	Documents are extracted from the original hypertext content and reorganized along a different logic.
Preferred use	Single-site archiving and small- and middle-scale archiving.	Middle- and large-scale archiving.	Specific (non-web) collections archiving.
Tools	Website copier (e.g. HTTrack).	Archiving crawler (e.g. heritrix) and index system for warc files.	Depends on the final structuring of content.
Advantages	Simple to implement.	Authenticity, scalability.	Enables integration in traditional OPAC or other local collections organizations.
Disadvantages	Does not scale up. Requires renaming and limited reorganization of content for hypertext navigation. Needs a file system level management of archived collection and versions of items.	Difficult to implement in absence of integrated software (this might change in the future).	Loss of hypertext structure. Can be applied only to isolated, non-web documents.

are always prone to updates or removal. In space, because choices have to be made regarding the limits of the web sphere to archive (Schneider and Foot, 2005), together with the target site. Since a virtually unlimited set of pages link to, and are linked from, the target pages, what will be chosen as the appropriate sphere will always be a sample. Web archiving always means preserving a limited and frozen version of a larger and moving information space. In consideration of this, Niels Brügger introduced the interesting notion of 'document of' the internet:

the actual archiving of the Internet ('document of') is still a document, and therefore has, as mentioned, the characteristics of the document, inasmuch as there is a certain degree of representation and subjective involvement. An important consequence of this is that archiving of the Internet should be accompanied by a number of deliberations as to method. (Brügger, 2005)

This is why it is so important to preserve as much contextual information as possible – dates, crawling policy, etc. – so that future users can at least understand what portion of the original information space the archive represents and how it has been sampled (see section below on metadata).

Scope

Usually, sampling is organized accordingly to specific scope definitions. Most common web archiving scopes are site, topic and domain.

Site

Site-centric archiving is mostly done by corporations, institutions or even individuals for archiving purposes. The growing use of websites and intranets, for instance, and the increased accountability that comes with it (what has been published and when can be very important for liability cases) fosters this type of archiving. To do this, archivists use either a simple website copier (e.g. HTTRack) or the archiving functionality of their site manager software when it exists. They usually store their archive in proprietary site manager's tools or adopt a 'local file system archive' strategy (see above). The frequency can vary depending on expected results and accountability rules.

Topic

Topic web archiving is becoming more and more popular, often driven by direct research needs. While working with web material, many researchers are facing the consequences of its ephemeral nature. The lifespan of web material is inappropriate for scientific verification (falsification requires access to the same data) as well as for long lasting reference. This is the reason why several projects have been undertaken to preserve primary material for research, for example the Digital Archive for Chinese Studies (DACHS) at Heidelberg University in Germany (Lecher, 2006), or Archipol for analysis of Dutch political sites at Groningen University in the Netherlands (Voerman et al., 2002). These projects share not only a topic orientation but also the use of a network of informants (the researchers) who provide accurate and updated feeds for the archive. As they are often implemented with limited resources, they tend to adopt a 'local file archive' strategy for its simplicity. Other topic-centric projects have been carried out in libraries to archive electoral websites (Christensen-Dalsgaard, 2004; Masanès, 2005b, Schneider et al., 2003).

Domain

Domain-centric web archiving is not driven by content but by location. 'Domain' is to be understood here in the network sense of the word or, by extension, in the national sense. Projects implementing this approach focus on a generic domain, such as the .gov or the .edu. It can also extend to a national domain, such as Kulturarw started in 1997 by the Swedish Royal Library (Arvidson, Persson and Mannerheim, 2000; Arvidson, 2002), which covers the .se domain and also Swedish pages linked from it and located in generic domains such as .com.

Priority

As the process of archiving a site takes time (i.e. the time needed to download all the documents), it is necessary to manage the priority of this process. (This does not apply, of course, when making a simple copy from the server file-system.)

It has been proposed that the quality of a web archive can be defined by (1) the completeness of material (linked files) archived within a designated perimeter, and (2) the capacity to render the original form of the site, particularly regarding navigation and interaction with the user:

> Graphically, completeness can be measured horizontally by the number of relevant entry points found within the designated perimeter and vertically, by the number of relevant linked nodes found from this entry point. Usually, entry points are site home pages and links can direct either to a new entry point (another site) or to elements of the same site.
>
> (Masanès, 2005b)

Ideally, web archives should achieve completeness vertically as well as horizontally. But, in practice, this is difficult to achieve and priorities have to be set and managed to achieve the best result possible. Archiving can be called 'extensive' when horizontal completeness is preferred to vertical completeness (see Figure 4.4). This is the case for instance for the Internet Archive and its collection which is donated by Alexa. Alexa's crawler uses a breadth-first approach and adapts depth of crawl for a site on traffic measured for this site (Burner, 1997).

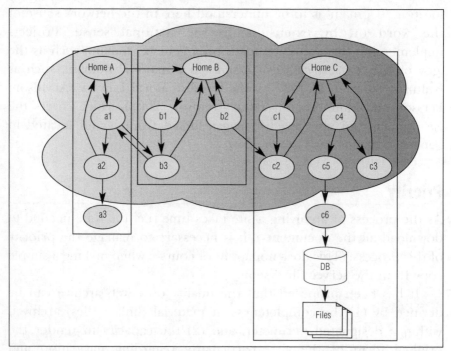

Figure 4.4 Extensive archiving (cloudy area). Some pages are missed (a3, c6) as well as the 'hidden' part of sites

Conversely, archiving is called 'intensive' when vertical completeness is preferred to horizontal completeness (see Figure 4.5). This is the case when a manual verification with supplementary archiving is made where needed (Phillips, 2003). Intensive archiving is even more demanding for hidden websites (also called deep websites) where access to the full content is not possible with crawlers. See some experiments in this area in Abiteboul et al. (2002); Masanès (2002b); Masanès (2002a) and Masanès (2006).

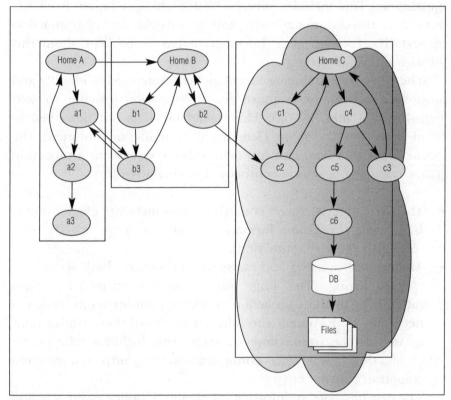

Figure 4.5 Intensive archiving (cloudy area). Collects fewer sites but collects deeper content, including potentially the 'hidden' web.

Metadata

Web archiving involves, as seen in the previous sections, choices with regard to what and how things will be archived. This has to be documented at least to enable future users to assess what the archived content represents compared to the original content. As we have seen, the scope and priority of the crawling process can result in huge differences in the results. Each interaction with a web server can also potentially generate a unique response customized according to who the client is supposed to be, which page might have been visited before, the time, etc. Database-driven websites enable almost every possibility in this domain and the least a web archive can do in this regard is to document the context of this interaction, or pseudo-transaction. This includes server–client exchanges (apart from the transfer of the document itself), and various element of transaction context (ID, cookies, etc.). Information has to be kept about this through metadata generation.

The IIPC Web Archiving Metadata Set is intended to identify and propose a scheme to capture this information specific to web archiving (Masanès, 2005a). This metadata set is not described in detail here, but the main elements it contains are outlined. The metadata set is broken into five main subsets: document, transaction actors, transaction, selection process and change history:

- The first subset *document* comprises usual metadata elements (e.g. URI, size, checksum, format) and also a more specific one (change frequency estimation).
- The *transaction actors* and *transaction* subsets are both specific to web archiving. The huge variety of responses that slight differences in the transaction conditions can generate makes it necessary to document carefully the actors of these transactions as well as the transactions as such. This includes information about the crawler, its configuration, the http request and response, cookies, etc.
- The *selection process* information includes policy, seed list and evaluation made for each page.
- The *change history* subset describes changes made mainly on files by documenting changes made on the original metadata of these files (date, old value, new values, tools used for the transformation, etc.).

It is worth noting that for each file archive, there are several date stamps (request, response, ingest) and it is also possible to determine when and from which page the link to this file was detected. This means that the archivist can know precisely the temporal gap between the identification of a page or an image (and from there its original hypertext context) and the actual archiving.

Conclusion

As we have seen in this brief overview, web archiving entails a tremendous adaptation of traditional preservation methods and approaches. With the end of finite and discrete objects to preserve, with the necessity to reconstruct a navigable version of the content, several of the traditional groundings of preservation disappear. Not only have archivists or librarians to define the scope of what they want to archive, but also the methods and choices they make to do it, with unprecedented implications for the result. This result can only be considered as a construction that relates in some ways to the original. Documenting precisely the processes and choices made can provide the cues for understanding, measuring and even modelling the gap between the preserved version and the original and thus bring some value to the resulting archive.

Notes

1   The Internet Archive currently receives donations from Alexa's 70 Tb snapshots of the web. These snapshots represent only a sample of the content available on the surface web, estimated at 1/6. This does not include the 'deep web' content. I have, for instance, encountered, while working on deep-web archiving at BnF, a major music site that contained more than 600 Tb in 2002. Based on this, it is reasonable to assume that the web already gives access today to petabytes of information (1 petabyte = 1024 terabytes).

2   The Domain Name Server (DNS) system is a hierarchical organization of names of servers that allows mapping from readable names (e.g. example.net) to the more obscure real numbering of machines used on the network (e.g. IP address 192.1.1.34).

5

Web archiving activities: case studies

Elisa Mason

Introduction

With the rapid expansion of the internet, particularly the world wide web, the increased dependence of users on the information to which it provides access, and the ephemeral nature of websites, greater emphasis is being placed on ensuring the preservation of and long-term access to online content. This review surveys some of the different strategies currently being employed to achieve these goals and introduces some of the principal institutions that have taken up the challenge. For a thorough treatment of the more technical aspects of web archiving, please refer to the preceding chapter by Masanès.

Approaches to web archiving

Many national libraries around the world have been taking an active role in archiving large segments of the web in the interest of preserving cultural heritage. Often, these initiatives are linked with legal deposit requirements that have been updated to include networked digital materials. The first challenge of a web archiving project is defining what to collect. Since the late 1990s, web archiving programmes have tended to adopt one of the following approaches: domain-specific, selective, topic-specific or a combination of the aforementioned. A domain approach involves automatically harvesting websites that make up a particular web space; for example, all sites within the so-called Swedish internet or that fall within the .se domain (more below). The advantage of this approach is that it is comprehensive. The Swedish Royal Library argues that one cannot predict what will be deemed of value to researchers in the future; therefore, resources should be spent on developing the technology to undertake large sweeps of the web and on storage to house what is collected, rather than on the human capital required to make selection decisions (Royal Library, 2005).

The disadvantage of the domain approach is that it does not allow for much control over what is collected. To address this issue, the selective approach prioritizes the online information that is collected; it archives 'defined portions of Web space or particular kinds of resources according to specified criteria. Selection may be based on the significance or quality of resources, their theme or topic, or by targeting a related set of Web sites' (PADI, n.d.). The model for this strategy is the National Library of Australia, which started development of its PANDORA archive in 1996 (more below).

As noted above, the topic approach is one type of selective web archiving. The objective here is to collect and preserve online content that focuses on a particular theme, subject area, discipline or even an event. Because the resulting data subset tends to be much smaller than one produced using a domain approach, more value can be added in the form of richer metadata and detailed search parameters. The Library of Congress in the USA has initiated a number of projects using this approach. Several projects based in academic institutions are also described below.

One caveat. Most of the initiatives described here are limited to archiving what is referred to as the 'surface web', that is, publicly accessible and static pages that can be harvested by search engines. While this represents a significant portion of the internet, it overlooks the 'deep web', which includes password-protected sites as well as database-driven, dynamically generated web pages. Masanès notes the deep web may be 500 times larger than the surface web. An archiving tool designed to tap into these online resources is referenced in the International Internet Preservation Consortium profile below.

Archiving national web spaces

The Royal Library of Sweden was the first national library to adopt a harvesting strategy to create an archive of the Swedish web space. Since 1996, the Kulturarw³ project (www.kb.se/kw3/ENG) has been collecting all websites within the .se domain, as well as seeking out Swedish content within the .com, .org, .net and other domains. The search engine robot utilized at the start of the project was first developed by the Nordic WebIndex; by early 2005, 13 sweeps of the internet had been performed in search of relevant websites. The archive is publicly available, but only within the Royal Library itself. In 2002, after a challenge to the Royal Library's activities, the government decreed that harvesting and collecting of websites could continue, but it set limits on public access. Currently, sites can be retrieved by URL only, with free text search to be offered in the future.

Other national web archiving projects that have adopted the harvesting approach have taken place in Finland, Iceland and Norway. In China, Beijing University uses a parallel and distributed crawling process to locate and retrieve pages within the .cn domain. Snapshots of the Chinese web space have been available since 2001 by URL from the Web InfoMall at www.infomall.cn/index-eng.htm.

The UK is pursuing a selective approach towards archiving the UK web space. The UK Web Archiving Consortium (www.webarchive.org.uk) is made up of the British Library, the National Archives, the National Library of Wales, the National Library of Scotland, the JISC and the Wellcome Trust. By working collaboratively, the partner institutions aim to sufficiently spread the costs, expertise, facilities and risk of their web archiving endeavour in order to limit the overall burden imposed on any single organization. Each Consortium member is responsible for selecting content from its specific areas of interest. As such, the British Library selects sites of national historical and cultural relevance, while the national libraries of Scotland and Wales focus on the history and culture of their respective countries. The National Archives collects material from governmental departments. And the Wellcome Trust and JISC select content in the areas of medicine and higher education, respectively. Pending the enactment of legal deposit legislation that will extend to networked digital material,

Consortium members are including only content that has been expressly cleared by website owners. The project uses the PANDORA Digital Archiving System (PANDAS) developed and tested by the National Library of Australia. The UK web archive thus has the same look and feel as its Australian counterpart, PANDORA (http://pandora.nla.gov.au/ index.html), the forerunner for the selective web archiving approach. Sites are organized by subject, with information provided about the institution that selected the site, dates when the site was archived, and a copyright statement, if available. The archive is also keyword-searchable. Work on the UK web archive will continue through 2006. By project-end, the Consortium anticipates harvesting some 6000 websites, along with greater expertise on the selection of web content and a better understanding of the technical challenges involved.

The web archiving community has recognized that taking *either* a strict domain *or* selective approach has its disadvantages. The more practical approach may be a combination of the two. And, in fact, both Sweden and Australia have decided to supplement their primary approaches with selective archiving and whole domain harvests, respectively (Phillips, 2005a). Australia, for instance, undertook its first harvest of the whole Australian web domain in July 2005 (Koerbin, 2005).

Other national libraries likewise have determined that using a combination of approaches will yield richer results. For example, Denmark has been engaged in selecting online documents since 1998. However, now that a new legal deposit law has came into effect (as of July 2005), the netarchive.dk project has begun actively harvesting the Danish portion of the internet. It will supplement these comprehensive sweeps with more focused selective and thematic approaches. Currently, the archive is accessible for research purposes only. New Zealand will proceed with its web archiving initiative using a similar strategy.

Topic-specific approaches

Through its MINERVA web preservation project, the US Library of Congress has been involved in the development of thematic archives.

Currently available are web archives that focus on September 11th, the 2000 and 2002 US elections and the 107th Congress. Future collections will cover the 2002 Winter Olympics and the Iraq War. Each collection is selective rather than comprehensive within the chosen theme, with suggestions for websites put forward by recommending officers or staff members with expertise in a given area. Collections are catalogued, and therefore have the added value of being browsed or searched in much more meaningful ways than simply by URL. The Library of Congress has also funded several university-based projects with a thematic web archiving component through the National Digital Information Infrastructure and Preservation Program (NDIIP). One example is the California Digital Library's 'Web at Risk' project, which aims to develop web archiving tools to help libraries preserve government and political information on the web.

Discipline-specific web archives are natural projects for universities to undertake. The University of Heidelberg's Digital Archive for Chinese Studies (DACHS) is an often-cited example of an archive designed to provide access to internet resources 'reflecting the Chinese social and political discourse'. The University of North Texas Libraries have teamed with the US Government Printing Office (GPO) to provide long-term access to defunct government websites; appropriately, the project is dubbed 'CyberCemetery'.

Archiving the internet

The domain approach takes on a new meaning when it is considered in the context of the internet as a whole. The Internet Archive (IA) was established in 1996 with a mission to ensure continued long-term access to the internet. It collects and archives not only publicly accessible web pages, but also moving images, texts, audio and software. Crawls are conducted by Alexa Internet, which provides the resulting snapshots to the IA after a six- to 12-month delay. Unlike the national library endeavours described above, permission to archive websites is not sought from website owners. Instead, the IA respects the robot.txt exclusions that websites incorporate to prevent crawling of their online content, and the IA will remove any web pages upon a content owner's request. Archived web pages are retrieved through the Wayback Machine by URL and date range, but not by keyword. (A beta search tool, Recall, was introduced in late 2003 that allowed keyword searching of a limited portion of the archive; it was withdrawn a year later because of instability.) However, the various special collections are searchable by a variety of fields, including title, creator, description, media type and date, among others. The Internet Archive collaborates with a number of international partners, including the International Internet Preservation Consortium (IIPC) and national libraries, offering technical expertise or assisting with the creation of specialized web collections. It is also involved in the development of new services to facilitate web archiving; for example, Archive-it, www.archive-it.org/learn-more.html, is a subscription-based service that allows users 'to create, manage and search their own web archive'. The various archive sets produced are publicly accessible and keyword-searchable.

International Internet Preservation Consortium (IIPC)

Established in 2003, the International Internet Preservation Consortium seeks collaborative solutions for 'selecting, collecting, preserving and providing access to internet content' (Masanès, 2004). Its members include the Internet Archive and the national libraries of Australia, Canada, Denmark, Finland, France, Iceland, Italy, Norway, Sweden, the UK and the USA. The IIPC is coordinated by the Bibliothèque nationale de France (BnF) and governed by a steering committee. Each member must participate in at least one of the consortium's six working groups, which include the following:

- Access Tools Working Group. Its objective is to better understand the various types of access required for a web archive (e.g. access for selection, access for content management, end-user access, etc.) and how each type of access can best be supported.
- Content Management Working Group. Its aim is to define a web archiving metadata set and to promote the development of core tools to support the different approaches that can be used when creating a web archive collection.

- Deep Web Working Group. Its objective is to identify strategies and produce tools for accessing and archiving content located in the 'deep' portion of the web that cannot be harvested by web crawlers.
- Framework Working Group. Its aim is to ensure interoperability among member institutions by defining a broad technical framework for web archiving activities, based on international standards.
- Metrics and Test Bed Working Group. Its principal activity has been defining and evaluating the challenges that might be encountered by a web crawler that is attempting to harvest content for archiving purposes.
- Researchers Requirements Working Group. Its mission has been to learn how best to support the needs of researchers by getting input from internet researchers about the scope and content of a web archive and how it should be accessed and maintained over time.

In the two years since its inception, the IIPC, through its working groups, has developed a series of open-source tools to facilitate web archiving tasks. These tools can be accessed from the IIPC website in the 'downloads' section, and include:

- BAT (BnfArcTools), an application programming interface that can be used to process Internet Archive ARC, DAT and CDX file formats
- DeepArc, a tool that allows users to map from a relational database to an XML schema and then export the database content into an XML document for archival purposes
- Heritrix, a flexible and extensible web crawler that is designed specifically to archive websites and allows for either very broad or very focused crawling; produces files in the ARC format, with associated DAT and CDX files
- NutchWAX, a tool designed to index and search the full text of small web archive collections
- WERA, a full-text web archive search, display and navigation tool, currently designed to work with NutchWAX

- Xinq, a tool developed to search and browse structured data archives stored as XML.

Many of these tools are actively being used. For example, the US National Archives and Records Administration (NARA) recently contracted the Internet Archive to conduct a harvest of 'Federal Agency public web sites as they existed prior to January 20, 2005'. The Internet Archive used Heritrix to capture the sites and NutchWAX to create the index.

The IIPC's original charter is set to expire in July 2006. The consortium's mandate will no doubt be extended, its scope broadened, and its membership expanded. The long-term challenge will be to help ensure that web archiving can be integrated easily as a standardized function into a national library's regular collection-building routine.

Conclusion

While these projects represent only a fraction of the work that is being done to archive the web, they illustrate the range of approaches that have been taken to meet the challenge. They also underscore the importance of the internet as a historical record which future generations will be exploring in order to remember, learn from and better understand their past and their cultural heritage.

6
The costs of digital preservation

Brian F. Lavoie

Introduction

Stewards of the scholarly and cultural record recognize that their curatorial responsibilities now extend beyond familiar forms of materials, such as print books, paper manuscripts, motion pictures, paintings, etc., to include the ever-increasing body of information manifested in digital form. These digital materials may represent old wine in new bottles, e.g. e-books or electronic government documents, but they also include digital creations with no obvious antecedent in the analogue world, e.g. software, websites and databases. If we are not to tolerate gaps in society's memory in the future, we must intervene in the present to secure the long-term availability of culturally significant digital materials. The 1996 report of the US Task Force on Archiving of Digital Information contains the call to arms that has been echoed in dozens of publications since: 'Failure to look for trusted means and methods of digital preservation will exact a stiff, long-term cultural penalty' (Task Force, 1996, 4).

But the best of intentions are almost always reined in by practical constraints. In the case of digital preservation, it is economic realities that intrude. A significant commitment in effort and resources is required to preserve digital materials, and for institutions operating within the limits imposed by static or even shrinking budgets, the costs of sustaining a programmatic digital archiving activity may simply be prohibitive. Scarcity of funds is hardly a new problem in preservation, of course: Kenney and Stam (2002) recently found that preservation generally commands less than 3% of the total budget in American academic libraries. But there is every indication that the economic requirements of *digital* preservation, fuelled by the immediacy and scale of the problem, will exacerbate this familiar problem to a degree heretofore unseen.

As institutions look to implement sustainable digital preservation programmes, the question 'Is digital preservation technically feasible?' becomes overshadowed by the question 'Is digital preservation *economically* feasible?'. And the corollary to this, of course, is that even the most elegant technical solution is no solution at all if it is not economically sustainable.

In this chapter, past work on articulating the costs of digital preservation is reviewed and synthesized. The costs of digital preservation are influenced by numerous factors, but one of the most significant is the preservation strategy chosen by the repository. This chapter traces some of the key ways in which choice of preservation strategy impacts the costs of digital preservation, with an emphasis on the preservation strategies described elsewhere in this book.

There has been much discussion of the costs of preserving digital materials, but relatively little attention paid to the reverse side of the problem, i.e. the costs of *not* preserving digital materials. This chapter discusses valuation of digital preservation activities, and the prospects for developing reliable techniques for doing so. Estimating the benefits from preserving a particular set of digital materials – or alternatively, the benefits foregone if the materials are not preserved – would aid institutions in planning digital archiving programmes that maximize the impact of scarce preservation resources.

Preserving the past is a fundamental mission of cultural heritage institutions, a public good that is conferred upon both current and future generations. The challenge in fulfilling this mission grows in parallel with the ever more diverse, complex forms in which digital resources are manifested. Extending long-term stewardship of the scholarly and cultural record into the digital world involves recognizing and overcoming challenges touching on the technical, policy and, not least, economic environments overarching digital preservation activities.

The costs of digital preservation[1]

Recognition that preserving digital materials requires active intervention throughout the information lifecycle leads naturally to questions about the costs of such intervention. The 1996 Task Force report, mentioned above and often cited as the definitive account of digital preservation's potential impact on cultural heritage institutions, takes pains to remind readers that '[i]n addition to managing their operating environment and the migration of information through hardware and software platforms, a third function by which digital archives fulfill their commitment to preserve electronic information is in managing the costs of these activities' (Task Force, 1996, 30). In short, a commitment to preserve digital resources into an indefinite future presupposes a parallel commitment to marshal, on an ongoing basis, the resources – funds, infrastructure, expertise, etc. – necessary to do so.

This point seems obvious but, somewhat surprisingly, it is often neglected. There is far more time and effort devoted to the technical issues surrounding long-term preservation of digital materials, compared to what is allocated to economic issues. An informal example illustrates the point: a Google search on 'digital preservation' yields over 64,000 results, while a search on 'costs of digital preservation' yields only about 400.[2] Richard Quandt (2003, 349) observes that 'the cost savings in producing electronic rather than paper journals tend to be overestimated, particularly because the costs of archiving are not adequately dealt with'.

But this is not to say the topic has been ignored entirely. A small but growing body of work has sought to articulate the scale and scope of digital preservation's costs – usually in the form of qualitative description, but occasionally in quantitative terms as well.[3] The brief excursion into the literature which follows, while not exhaustive, at least gives a sense of the knowledge that has accumulated to date on the costs of digital preservation.

Models to assess costs of digital preservation

Russell and Weinberger (2000) enumerate cost elements of digital preservation against the background of a digital collection manager's workflow, including selection, negotiation of intellectual property rights (specifically, the right to preserve and the right to provide access), determination of appropriate strategies for long-term preservation and access, validation of digital materials at the time of ingest, metadata creation, storage and repository administration. The authors' key insight is that digital preservation decisions and, by extension, digital preservation costs, are not compartmentalized within a distinct segment of digital collection management but, rather, are diffused throughout the workflow stages identified above, which in turn extend over much of the information lifecycle.

Sanett (2002, 2003) adopts a slightly narrower focus, confining herself to cost models specifically aimed at efforts to preserve authentic electronic records. Sanett identifies three components of long-term preservation costs: capital costs, which are upfront expenditures required to set up repository systems and processes (e.g. hardware and software development, interface design); direct operating costs, which are expenditures needed to sustain the repository's operations over a finite time period (e.g. selection, acquisition, storage, metadata creation, preservation activities); and indirect operating costs, which include the repository's overheads (e.g. support staff, facilities expense, administration). Sanett suggests a five-year cycle for evaluating costs, with operating costs calculated on an annual basis and adjusted to present value, and capital costs amortized over the entire period. A five-year cycle is suggested because it is likely to correspond with the useful life of initial hardware and software investments.

Chapman (2003) emphasizes the importance of understanding repository storage costs, in that they represent 'ongoing costs that apply to all materials designated to receive preservation services – however "preservation" is defined'. Chapman observes that managed storage forms the 'nucleus' of any preservation activity, and it is therefore essential that sources of sustained funding be found for this service. Repository storage costs are subject to a number of factors, including, but not limited to, the scope of the obligations and guarantees associated with a particular repository service, the pricing model, and the quantity and format of deposited materials. Chapman suggests that this multiplicity of factors must be taken into account when developing price schedules and payment mechanisms for managed storage services. He predicts that 'the majority of content owners will be consumers of centralized repository services, not developers and managers of local repositories or digital asset management programs'. In this event, it is vital that affordable storage costs and pricing models prevail if these centralized repositories are to attract content for deposit.

The Task Force report cited earlier includes a comparative assessment of the long-term costs of maintaining print and digital materials, respectively. This study is unusual in regard to the quantitative detail it provides; however, considering that the data underpinning the analysis is now about a decade old, it is probably best not to pay too much attention to the specific numbers reported in the study. But there may be some enduring qualitative lessons. Based on the estimates in the study, the author concludes that while the storage and access costs for digital materials will initially exceed that of their print equivalents, the digital and print cost trajectories will converge over time, eventually crossing so that, over the long term, maintaining digital materials becomes less expensive than maintaining print materials. This suggests that decision-makers must take care to adopt a longer view when evaluating the pros and cons of investing in digital repository capacity, and not to be excessively daunted by the significant initial costs such an investment would require.

Finally, a recent paper by Donald Waters (2002) focuses not on the structure of digital preservation costs, but on the prospects for meeting them in a sustainable way. Waters suggests that digital preservation exhibits attributes of a public good – goods such as national defence, public parks and environmental improvement – for which there are no practical means to exclude those who do not contribute towards the cost of provision. If one institution takes steps to preserve a particular set of digital materials, these materials are effectively preserved for all institutions, in the sense of being maintained as part of our collective cultural memory. Given this, it follows that the incentives are significantly reduced for any institution to be the one to take on the effort and expense of preserving the materials. It is far better, from a purely economic perspective, to wait for another institution to assume responsibility for this task; the benefits from preservation can then be enjoyed by all. A collective attitude of 'wait for someone else to do it' will result in a suboptimal level of preservation activity, with a corresponding diminution of our ability to maintain the scholarly and cultural record in its entirety. While some may question whether economic motives will be the controlling factor in preservation decision-making, the present age of static or shrinking budgets, coupled with enhanced opportunities for resource sharing occasioned by the rapid growth in network interconnectivity, implies that the so-called 'free-rider problem' must be taken seriously. Lavoie (2003) explores this and other economic issues impacting the incentives to preserve digital materials.

Categories of costs of digital preservation

Broadly speaking, the costs of digital preservation can be divided into two categories: *fixed costs*, which include the upfront expenditures needed to set up repository capacity, implement workflows such as ingest procedures and preservation processes, and assemble the necessary 'human capital' to administer the system; and *operating costs*, which include the ongoing costs of sustaining the repository and its constituent processes at a level sufficient to ensure that long-term preservation objectives are met. As more and more institutions invest in the infrastructure necessary to store and manage their digital assets, practical experience is accumulating, along with empirical data, in terms of the fixed costs of digital collection management generally, and digital preservation specifically. Yet most of these initiatives are still in their infancy, and have yet to produce a record of the complete cost trajectory underlying stewardship of digital materials through successive shifts in prevailing hardware and software environments.

As a consequence, the long-term operating costs of digital preservation remain, for the most part, uncharted waters, and it is the uncertainty over the future scale and scope of these costs that is most worrisome to institutions planning or currently maintaining a digital preservation programme. Why are these future costs so uncertain? A number of factors are of particular importance.

Factors causing uncertainty about future costs

One source of uncertainty is rooted in the current lack of consensus on best practice for carrying out digital preservation. Discussion of possible digital preservation techniques typically divides into two camps – format migration and emulation – although received wisdom now takes the view that rather than being substitutes, these techniques are likely to be used in combination depending on the nature of the archived material. But these strategies are, for the most part, untested, in terms of application to large-scale digital collections of diverse cultural heritage materials, maintained for current and future user communities with expectations that vary both within the community and across time.[4] It is difficult to anticipate the costs of an activity when the activity itself is not well defined.

Another factor contributing to uncertainty is time. Many – indeed, probably most – cultural heritage institutions have an open-ended commitment to preservation, in the sense that they expect to preserve content indefinitely. In contrast, preservation objectives are often much narrower for organizations in other domains: a commercial enterprise such as a bank may have to preserve digital records only for a relatively short, legally prescribed period. But a library, museum or archive must attach a much more distant horizon to its preservation responsibilities, extending to the next generation and beyond.

Preserving digital content not only for tomorrow, but for ten years, 20 years or even centuries from now drastically increases the variance attached to any forecast of long-term costs. The *raison d'etre* for digital preservation is the constantly evolving technological environment that threatens to 'orphan' digital materials when the technology needed to access them becomes obsolete or otherwise unavailable. But it is difficult to predict, *a priori*, the future obsolescence of current software and hardware, and, consequently, difficult to predict the timing, frequency, complexity and, ultimately, the cost of intervention. The more distant the time horizon to which digital preservation extends, the greater the uncertainty surrounding the effort and expense of maintaining digital materials in forms compatible with contemporary technology.

Finally, digital preservation costs are uncertain because the goals of digital preservation are themselves uncertain. For analogue artefacts, such as historical paper documents, paintings or even buildings, the goal of preservation is usually to maintain the object in its original form, or as close an approximation to the original form that is practical or possible. In contrast, the mutability of digital content, combined with the need to preserve its accessibility to users of both current and future technology, implies that the form in which a digital object is created may differ significantly from the form in which it is preserved.

Galloway (2003, 549) defines digital preservation as 'the activity of carrying digital objects from one software generation to another, undertaken for purposes beyond the original reasons for creating the objects'. This definition hints at one of the key challenges of digital preservation: determining which objectives should be the focus of digital preservation efforts. For example, is it sufficient to preserve only the 'intellectual content' of a digital object, or is it necessary to preserve all aspects of its original look, feel and functionality as well? Preserving just the intellectual content is likely to be cheaper than preserving a version that replicates, in form and functionality, the digital object in its original form. Deciding which strategy is appropriate will likely hinge on the future uses to which the archived digital object will be put, but how accurately can these uses be predicted in advance? It is here where uncertainty arises yet again, touching on the second part of Galloway's definition: 'for purposes beyond the original reasons for creating the objects'. Cultural heritage institutions must do their best to match preservation objectives with user expectations, but these expectations are likely to shift and evolve over time, making the cost of fulfilling them difficult to forecast.

Certainties about costs

So is there anything we can conclude about the costs of digital preservation? Several points seem to remain fairly constant in a sea of fluctuating uncertainty over preservation techniques, evolving technology cycles and shifting objectives. First, regardless of the specific manner in which digital preservation is carried out, it is likely to require a substantial, *ongoing* resource commitment. This includes not only the expensive upfront investment in the technological infrastructure constituting a long-term preservation repository for digital materials, but also the regular injections of funds needed to sustain the repository over the long term. In short, it will not be enough to fund digital preservation activities through one-time grants and other short-term funding sources, on which many current initiatives now depend. The commitment to long-term digital preservation will need to be made concrete through the allocation of ongoing, budgeted funds.

There is every indication that digital preservation will be more or less an ongoing activity, designed as a pre-emptive measure aimed at averting damage or obsolescence, rather than a reactive process applied at discrete intervals after damage or obsolescence has already set in. If this is the case, we can expect that digital preservation will extend throughout the digital information lifecycle, rather than being confined to the later stages; consequently, the costs of digital preservation will be incurred throughout the entire lifecycle as well, and the mechanisms by which digital preservation programmes are funded need to reflect this exigency.

The diffusion of digital preservation issues throughout the information lifecycle suggests a second point about costs: digital preservation and, by extension, digital preservation costs, will become increasingly inseparable from other aspects of digital collection management. For example, selecting a presentation format, a decision normally associated with the creative or publishing process, can have profound implications for future preservation. Is the chosen format a proprietary one, with only a small user community? Or is it a widely used, relatively stable format whose specifications are openly available?

The need to manage information with an eye toward its long-term preservation is of course not unique to the digital world – for example, publishers deliberately choose to print books on acid-free paper to extend their longevity – but this need is almost certainly amplified in the context of digital materials, where preservation's profile is much more visible throughout the information lifecycle. Format selection, metadata creation, fixity checking and so on are all activities that speak to the long-term 'preservability' of digital materials. As such, the costs needed to conduct these activities fall, at least indirectly, within the scope of the costs of digital preservation. This 'blending' of routine collection management with long-term preservation is not yet as apparent as it will be in the future: the relative newness of digital preservation issues implies preservationists must take digital information under their stewardship 'as is', with little input into the processes by which it was created and managed prior to archival retention. But it is very likely that in the future, the requirements for long-term preservation will filter down into the earlier stages of the information lifecycle. As this happens, it will become increasingly difficult to demarcate cleanly preservation as a distinct activity and, consequently, more difficult to separate the costs of long-term preservation from other costs associated with managing digital materials.

And, lastly, there are intangible costs to reckon as well: in particular, the costs of changing the mindset of *all* stakeholders in digital materials – creators, publishers, librarians, users and so on – to think of preservation as an immediate, ongoing issue for which everyone bears responsibility, and which is inextricably linked to sound digital collection management throughout the information lifecycle.

Cost and choice of preservation strategy

As mentioned in the previous section, the long-term cost of digital preservation will be determined at the point of intersection between numerous factors, variables and contingencies, embodying varying degrees of impact and predictability. It is difficult to generalize over a broad range of digital archiving contexts to say which of these factors should be considered of particular importance, but it seems reasonable to suppose that the choice of preservation strategy will figure heavily in the long-term costs associated with any given effort to preserve digital materials.

The range of digital preservation strategies currently being developed, tested or utilized by practitioners and researchers has been discussed in Chapter 1. In this section, the cost implications of five digital preservation strategies – media refreshment/migration, format migration, normalization, emulation and technology preservation – are examined and compared. The objective is not to recommend one strategy over another as being 'less costly' or more 'cost efficient', but simply to highlight some of the ways each strategy impacts the cost of long-term digital asset management, and to briefly consider similarities and differences across strategies in this regard.

Before taking up this task, it is useful to consider the five digital preservation strategies in the context of a simple framework representing what might be termed 'preservation intensity' – in other words, sets (or levels) of preservation objectives arranged in order of increasing complexity and scope. The framework can be expressed as follows:

- Bit preservation. Preserving digital materials so as to ensure that their bitstreams are recoverable from storage media using contemporary technology.
- Preservation of intellectual content. Preserving digital materials so as to ensure that their intellectual content can be rendered – e.g. displayed or interacted with in a prescribed way – using contemporary technology.
- Preservation of original form and functionality. Preserving digital materials so as to ensure that they can be rendered as close approximations of their original form – exhibiting the original look, feel and functionality – using contemporary technology.

The above framework describes increasingly ambitious preservation objectives, beginning with simple assurance that the digital object, viewed as a collection of bits, will survive over the long term. The next level demands more, requiring not only that the object survives, but also that future users are able to access, interpret and, ultimately, integrate into research and learning experiences the object's intellectual content, using technologies likely to be substantially different from those available today. To meet this objective, the digital materials may be translated into new forms compatible with these future technologies. Finally, preservation objectives may require that the digital object be maintained in a form as close to the original as possible, so that future users may experience the object in the same way as current users – but, again, using technologies that differ from those of today. In these circumstances, the underlying technology may change, but the form of the object presented to the user must not.

Digital preservation strategies are available to meet each of these broad preservation objectives. Bit preservation can be achieved through media refreshment/migration; preservation of intellectual content through format migration or normalization strategies; and preservation of original form and functionality through emulation or technology preservation. But, even without selecting a specific digital preservation strategy, implications begin to emerge concerning long-term costs merely from framing high-level preservation objectives. In general, the more of the object's original form, functionality and context a repository wishes to perpetuate for future users (or, put another way, the smaller the degree of tolerable information loss), the more complex and sophisticated – and hence more expensive – the preservation strategy needed to meet these objectives.

It is useful to explore this principle in the context of the digital preservation strategies mentioned above: media refreshment/migration, format migration, normalization, emulation and technology preservation. A leading reference in this regard is Tony Hendley's (1998) study, on behalf of the UK's Joint Information Systems Committee (JISC), looking at costs associated with a number of digital preservation strategies. Although the study can no longer be considered recent, it is still almost unique in its effort to examine long-term digital preservation costs in light of multiple perspectives, including information lifecycle stage, digital resource type and digital preservation strategy.

Media refreshment/migration

Media refreshment involves rewriting bits stored on digital media – e.g. magnetic tape, hard disk, CD-ROM – to a new instance of the same media. The purpose of this strategy is to counteract 'bit rot', the relatively rapid degradation of digital storage media, which can result in stored bitstreams becoming corrupted or otherwise unrecoverable.

Media migration involves transferring archived objects to new storage technologies (and new forms of digital media) as older technologies become obsolete.

Hendley subsumes media refreshment under the more general category of validation, which consists of a bundle of practices and procedures designed to maintain the integrity of archived digital materials. He notes that validatory procedures such as media refreshment are generally repeated at regular intervals, and therefore the costs of such procedures will be incurred repeatedly as well. The regularity of media refreshment is further reinforced by the availability of benchmark estimates of the useful life of most digital storage media.

Media migration is more complicated than media refreshment, because the useful life of a particular storage technology is difficult to predict. It is also more expensive, in that migrating from one storage technology to another likely involves changing a key infrastructure component of the digital archiving system itself, with all of the second-order challenges (and costs) of integrating the new storage technology with the legacy components of the archiving system.

Format migration

In contrast to media refreshment/migration, format migration involves changes to the archived bitstreams themselves. In particular, format migration involves an alteration in the way the 'ones and zeros' of a digital object are encoded, usually in order to make the object's bitstreams accessible and interpretable by contemporary software/hardware environments.

The costs of format migration hinge on a number of factors, including the frequency of occurrence, the availability of standardized tools for carrying out the migration, and the tolerance of information loss sustained as a byproduct of the migration process. Clearly, the more frequent the need to migrate archived objects to new formats, the greater the cost. Unfortunately, this factor is largely outside the repository's control, and lies instead in the hands of the pace of innovation and user expectations.

Standardized tools limit the costs of migration, and repositories can control this factor, to the extent that they can choose formats for which such tools exist; however, the flexibility of choice in this regard may again be limited by the expectations of users. Similar reasoning applies to the degree of tolerable information loss, which can be inversely related to the costs of migration, but also governed by the expectations of the user community.

Hendley notes that applications supporting multi-generational backward compatibility can lower the overall costs of format migration, at least in the short or medium term. But the costs of migrating across formats are likely to be higher; Hendley suggests that '[t]he simpler the digital resource the easier it is to interchange the resource between application programs without any significant loss of data and hence the lower the costs involved. The more complex the digital resource the more difficult it is to interchange the resource between two application programs without any significant loss of data.'

Normalization

Normalization involves the translation of digital objects from a potentially wide range of formats into a single, common format for long-term preservation. Normalization is a special case of migration, in which migration occurs at the time the object is ingested into the repository, and all objects are translated into the same format.[5] Of course, additional migrations may be necessary over time in order to ensure that the format used for normalization remains compatible with contemporary technology.

Normalization can potentially be cheaper than other forms of migration, because it minimizes the number of formats that the repository needs to manage over the long term. Moreover, if the format chosen for normalization is non-proprietary and stable, the repository can reduce or even eliminate the need for future migrations as technology continues to evolve.

But the costs of normalization can vary widely. Again, Hendley observes that the complexity of the object being normalized will be determinative in establishing the cost of this strategy: '[t]he simpler the digital resource, the easier and hence the cheaper it is to select a standard format and convert the digital resource'. Another cost to be taken into consideration is the potential information loss associated with normalization. Normalization can impact structure, appearance and functionality in widely differing ways, depending on the original format of the converted object. How much information loss is tolerable, and to what extent the repository is willing to take measures to avoid it, will strongly influence the overall cost of a normalization strategy.

Emulation

Emulation involves creating computer programs that are compatible with contemporary technology, yet mimic the hardware components of older, obsolete technologies. Emulation permits archived digital objects to be rendered in their original software environment, which in turn permits the original look, feel and functionality of the object to be preserved.

Many experts consider that of all digital preservation strategies, emulation harbours the highest potential costs. First, a library of emulators must be developed and maintained – of course, the greater the number of formats supported by the repository, the larger the library of emulators needed.[6] Second, the software environment for the archived digital objects, i.e. the operating system and application program, need to be preserved as digital objects in their own right, with all of the associated costs of doing so. And, finally, the emulators themselves represent digital objects subject to the vagaries of an ever-changing technological environment: as current technologies are eventually displaced and become obsolete, new emulators must be written that are compatible with whatever new environment emerges.

In his study, Hendley predicts that implementing emulation as a digital preservation strategy will require the emergence of third-party services specializing in the development of emulator programs. In these circumstances, a significant proportion of overall cost would take the form of fees charged by such services. It is likely these fees will become quite substantial if the work involves a significant degree of customization across repositories. Hendley concludes that emulation 'should be seen as a short to medium term strategy or a specialist strategy where the need to maintain the look and feel of the original digital resource is of great importance to the collection's user base'.

Of course, the circumstances Hendley suggests may warrant emulation – where preservation of the object in its precise original form is required – provide much of the explanation why the costs of emulation can potentially be so high. Emulation supports the most ambitious preservation objectives and, therefore, will likely entail the highest costs.

Technology preservation

Technology preservation is similar in spirit to emulation except that, instead of emulating obsolete hardware environments, the hardware environment itself is preserved along with the associated software environment and the archived object that is the focus of preservation.

There is a fairly strong consensus that technology preservation is probably impractical as a digital preservation strategy, largely because the number of hardware components requiring preservation would soon grow to unmanageable levels, while the cost of maintaining preserved hardware in working order would become increasingly expensive as the hardware aged. Moreover, hardware, as a physical object, requires physical space for storage, which would significantly increase the costs of preservation. On top of this, there would be additional costs involved in preserving the software intended to run on the preserved hardware, as well as the digital objects the preserved hardware and software are intended to support.

In short, technology preservation requires the preservation of every component of the original computing environment, along with archived content itself. While in some circumstances this may be desirable – e.g. a museum exhibit designed to offer visitors an authentic computing experience from earlier times – the costs are likely to be too high to warrant serious consideration of technology preservation as a general strategy for maintaining access to digital objects over long periods of time. Indeed, Hendley describes technology preservation as 'a relatively desperate measure in cases where valuable digital resources cannot be converted into hardware and/or software independent formats and migrated forward'.

General considerations about costs of preservation strategies

In considering the cost implications of these five digital preservation strategies, a number of general themes become apparent. Digital preservation costs tend to be directly related to the complexity of the preservation process, which can be interpreted to mean that costs will tend to rise as preservation objectives become more ambitious. When the goal is simply to ensure that a particular bitstream endures over the long term, preservation may involve nothing more than copying bitstreams from one media instance to another media instance of the same type – a straightforward process with little need for expensive customization or human intervention. But, as a repository's preservation commitments expand in scope – to include, for example, the guarantee that archived objects will be renderable using contemporary technology – the techniques needed to support this commitment will tend to be more complex and, as a result, more expensive to carry out. Indeed, complex strategies such as format migration or emulation are often built on top of less complex strategies, such as media refreshment/migration, implying that the costs of the latter represent only a subset of the costs of the former.

Simple and complex digital preservation strategies can also be distinguished on the basis of predictability of cost. Digital preservation strategies with limited objectives, such as media refreshment, are often implemented on a regular schedule, based on widely accepted estimates of media degradation rates, or 'bit rot'. In this sense, simple digital preservation strategies often have the virtue of limited costs that can be projected with reasonable accuracy far into the future. More complex strategies, such as format migration, are less predictable, depending largely on the pace and direction of technological change as well as user expectations. Such factors are difficult to anticipate *a priori*, and therefore the costs of preserving digital materials subject to these factors tend to be uncertain as well.

The cost implications associated with the relative simplicity or complexity of a digital preservation strategy can be linked to the *scope* of the overarching technical environment a repository chooses to preserve along with the archived object. Scope can be interpreted in both a 'vertical' and a 'horizontal' sense. The vertical interpretation comprises the layers of technology that sit between the user and digital content: storage technologies, network and computing resources, operating systems, application programs and so on. Relatively simple preservation strategies concern themselves with a small portion of this 'vertically stacked' environment – media refreshment/migration, for example, is limited to the storage layer. In contrast, technology preservation aims to preserve the *entire* technical environment. As the portion of the environment brought under the repository's custodianship increases, the costs of digital preservation will increase as well.

The horizontal interpretation addresses the variety, or *range* of environments – or portions of environments – the repository chooses to preserve. As the range expands, the repository's preservation costs are likely to expand as well. For example, a preservation strategy of format migration where a repository agrees to maintain a diversity of digital formats in renderable form will, all other things being equal, tend to be more expensive than a strategy of normalization, where the repository agrees to support a limited number of formats, or even only one.

Finally, all of the above considerations – degree of complexity of the chosen digital preservation strategy, predictability of costs, the portion of the technical environment the repository chooses to preserve, as well as the range of environments supported by the repository – are, in a sense, policy decisions that at least on the surface are resolved at the discretion of the repository. But as practitioners will be quick to point out, these decisions are usually guided and constrained, often to a considerable degree, by external influences beyond the repository's control, including, but not limited to, the pace and direction of innovation, the expectations of the user community, and the availability of funds to support the repository's operations. Ultimately, then, repository policies and, by extension, preservation costs, will likely emerge as a byproduct of negotiation and compromise between principal stakeholders and decision-makers, as well as the impact of continuing advances in digital technologies.

The 'other' cost: valuing digital preservation

It is customary to think of the costs of digital preservation in terms of the time, effort and resources needed to meet long-term preservation objectives. But this is only part of the story. The introduction to this chapter quotes a passage from the 1996 Task Force report: 'Failure to look for trusted means and methods of digital preservation will exact a stiff, long-term cultural penalty' (Task Force, 1996, 4). The 'stiff, long-term penalty' may be construed as a cost associated with digital preservation: in particular, the cost of *not* undertaking digital preservation.

Basic economic theory introduces the concept of *opportunity cost*: in brief, the idea that allocating scarce resources to one activity involves a cost measured in the loss of benefits that would have been realized had the resources been allocated to their 'next best' use. So it is with digital preservation. As any library administrator working with a static or shrinking budget can attest, finding funds for digital preservation programmes will likely come at the expense of less funding for other activities. But the reverse is equally valid: if we choose not to allocate funds to digital preservation, we will forgo benefits and, as the Task Force report argues, the scale of these lost benefits can be considerable. As Bickner (1983, 11) points out, 'costs are benefits lost'.

Allocation of scarce resources across competing activities is usually made through some form of cost/benefit analysis, where the gains from conducting each activity are weighed against the costs. Computing net benefits in this fashion helps to establish priorities and make choices. But, in many circumstances, cost/benefit analysis is difficult to carry out, because the benefits associated with a particular activity are resistant to quantification – particularly as a monetary, capitalized sum. Absent a common unit of measurement (i.e. dollars, pounds, euros and so on), and meaningful comparison of costs and benefits becomes impossible.

This problem is especially pervasive in the domain of preservation, digital or otherwise. How does one 'value' the long-term preservation of scholarly materials and cultural artefacts? In answering this question, one must usually resort to platitudes, such as 'the scholarly literature is of incalculable value' or 'this is a priceless artefact': evocative statements to be sure, but of little practical use in real-world decision-making. Hard as it is to reckon the costs of digital preservation, calculating the benefits is even more so.

And yet the ability to articulate quantitatively the benefits of digital preservation, even if only to an order of magnitude, is a vital tool for cultural heritage institutions, both in terms of justifying the significant cost of setting up and maintaining a digital preservation repository, and selecting digital materials worthy of long-term preservation.[7] The digital preservation research agenda which emerged from a recent National Science Foundation/Library of Congress workshop echoes this point, observing: 'Business planning and economic modeling are hampered by the lack of metrics for almost all aspects of digital preservation. Evaluation of digital archiving is impossible without concrete measures of costs, benefits, and values of digital objects' (Hedstrom, 2003a).

Methods for valuing benefits from services

There is growing interest on the part of cultural heritage institutions in methods for valuing the benefits generated from services rendered to their respective communities. The importance of creating demonstrable value is not new. John Cotton Dana, whose eminent career encompassed both libraries and museums, once observed: 'All public institutions . . . should give returns for their cost; and those returns should be in good degree positive, definite, visible, and measurable . . . Common sense demands that a publicly-supported institution do something for its supporters and that some part at least of what it does be capable of clear description and downright valuation' (OCLC, 2004, 30). But, in the current climate of stretched budgets and limited access to new funds, the need to marshal solid evidence speaking to the benefits of expensive new activities, such as digital preservation programmes, has never been greater.[8]

Three recent studies in the UK illustrate this view. The British Library commissioned a £150,000 study, completed in December 2003, aimed at demonstrating, in monetary terms, the economic value of the Library's services. The report estimates that for every £1 of public money invested in the Library, £4.40 of value was created, a return of nearly 350%. In addition, the report concludes that should the British Library cease to exist, the UK would lose nearly £300 million in economic value each year (British Library, 2003). More generally, the study aimed to disclose 'the benefit [the Library] provides relative to the public funding it receives, and the consequences were it to cease to exist. This was to increase accountability to government and the taxpayer, to validate its activities, to support its case for continued investment, to help it understand its impact more clearly and therefore to inform its thinking about products and services' (*Library & Information Update*, 2004, 16). One source suggests that the study may have been at least partly responsible for the British Library securing a subsequent increase in its grant-in-aid (*Library & Information Update*, 2004).

In March 2004, the National Museum Directors' Conference[9] (NMDC) released a report (Travers and Glaister, 2004) 'intended to take stock of the UK's national museums and galleries . . . and to assess their place within the wider social and economic framework of society'. A key emphasis was a quantitative assessment of the overall economic impact of NMDC institutions. According to the report, NMDC institutions took in, from a variety of sources, a total of £715 million in 2003–4. In addition to this total, which can be loosely interpreted as the 'cost' of funding the institutions' activities and services, the report estimates that £245 million was spent on activities ancillary to a museum visit – e.g. restaurants, hotels and so on – by domestic visitors, and a further £320 million by overseas visitors, for a total of over £1.2 billion. Assuming a multiplier of 1.5, the report concludes that the overall impact of NMDC institutions on the UK economy – i.e. the summation of first-order and higher-order effects – is approximately £2 billion, or 0.2% of gross domestic product.

Finally, in January 2004, the British Academy[10] sponsored a review (British Academy, 2004) aimed at 'demonstrat[ing] the value of the study of the arts, humanities, and social sciences in relation to the nation's wealth'. The report describes contributions in five distinct areas, including cultural and intellectual enrichment, new knowledge, public policy, education and economic prosperity. In regard to the last-named, the report notes, among other things, that the arts, humanities and social sciences play a key role in the generation of intellectual property, which the report argues is a key impetus to the UK's fastest growing economic sectors. The report also describes the importance of the arts, humanities and social sciences in equipping workers with the skills necessary to thrive in the 'knowledge-driven economy', citing in particular how knowledge of foreign languages and cultures might work to promote international trade.

These reports, although differing in their emphasis on quantitative methods, point up a keen interest in exploring new ways to demonstrate the value of their activities and services. But, as noted above, the output of cultural heritage institutions is, for the most part, resistant to quantification in monetary terms. How can these institutions provide evidence that they do indeed generate an appreciable 'return on investment', in ways that are 'definite, visible, and measurable', as John Cotton Dana requires?

Non-market valuation techniques

This question intersects with some work in economics that has been addressing similar issues for some time. This work, known as non-market valuation, has focused on developing techniques for estimating the value or benefit of goods and services conferred on society without the intermediation of markets. Questions such as 'What is the value of a public park?' or 'What is the benefit of saving the bald eagle from extinction?' fall within the scope of this analysis, the common theme being the need to value goods and services that are provided through mechanisms (i.e. decision-making processes) other than the usual price-based voluntary market transaction.[11]

There are a number of non-market valuation techniques, such as contingent valuation, travel cost models and hedonic pricing. The most widely used technique is probably contingent valuation, which employs survey methods to assess respondents' willingness to pay for a particular good or service, or, conversely, how much they would be willing to accept as compensation in the event they do *not* receive the good or service. These individual values are then used to estimate an overall non-market valuation. The British Library study described above uses contingent valuation as the basis for its analysis.

Assessing the benefits, or value, of preserving culturally

significant digital resources is a problem not very far distant from the ones addressed in the British Library, National Museum Directors' Conference and British Academy studies, as well as a host of valuation studies found in the economics literature, such as the benefits of conserving the bayou ecosystem around Houston, Texas, or the magnitude of the environmental damage sustained as a consequence of the *Exxon Valdez* oil spill in 1989 (Mathis, Fawcett and Konda, 2003). Indeed, a common application of non-market valuation techniques in the economics literature is determining the value of preserving a natural or environmental resource. Conceptually, then, a common theme emerges: estimating the value of preserving a societal asset, whether intellectual, cultural or natural, or in analogue, digital or physical form.

In the face of a likely need for a greatly expanded funding commitment to preservation, cultural heritage institutions must present persuasive evidence to funding sources that this expanded commitment is indeed justified. To do so, they must present evidence that the cost of preserving digital materials is exceeded by the benefits. In short, they must conduct some form of cost/benefit analysis of potential digital preservation activities. Non-market valuation techniques hold a great deal of promise in regard to quantifying the 'other costs' of digital preservation, providing cultural heritage institutions with the tools to conduct meaningful cost/benefit analysis, leading to a wise allocation of scarce preservation resources.

Conclusion

One theme encountered repeatedly in the digital preservation literature is that the toughest challenges in developing practical, sustainable strategies for the long-term stewardship of digital materials are not technical in nature, but instead have to do with the social, organizational and economic aspects of the problem. Which digital materials should be selected for preservation? Who is responsible for preserving these materials? How can we leverage scarce preservation resources in order to meet ambitious preservation objectives? And, of course, the one question which, in a sense, overarches all of the others: *How much will it cost?*[12]

Unfortunately, the answer to the question too often is *it depends*, but that should not preclude us from seeking generalizations and shared knowledge, at whatever level of specificity possible, across a wide range of digital preservation contexts. Even high-level cost frameworks can be useful guide posts to organizations entering the still largely uncharted realm of long-term digital preservation.

As government agencies, businesses and cultural heritage institutions find themselves custodians of more and more digital materials, they will continue to learn more about the long-term costs of digital preservation, through the accumulation of experience, the testing of models, the rejection of some approaches and the refinement of others. This underscores the need for case studies detailing the costs of digital preservation repositories. These case studies should include not just the costs of setting up the repository, but also its operational costs, with an emphasis on the costs of actions taken to preserve the archived digital content. Synthesizing cost data from case studies accumulated from a wide range of digital preservation experiences – whether these experiences involve the creation and maintenance of a library of emulators, or the migration of archived content over a disruptive technology cycle – is a necessary first step towards developing reliable benchmarks for the cost of long-term digital preservation.

Resolving the question of how much it will cost would also be aided by an answer to the related question of who will pay. The nature of digital materials and, by extension, the digital preservation process itself, has led to a blurring of preservation responsibilities across the wide range of stakeholders associated with the digital information lifecycle. The traditional demarcation of preservation responsibilities – cultivated over many years with analogue materials and confined largely to cultural heritage institutions such as libraries, archives and museums – will likely prove unsustainable when applied to the digital world.

The fact that the imperative to take action to preserve digital materials occurs fairly early in the information lifecycle – and reappears over and over again as the lifecycle unfolds – implies that digital preservation cannot be postponed until materials pass into the custody of cultural heritage institutions. Consequently, there is a potential that preservation responsibilities will not reside with a single library or archive, but instead will be diffused across many organizations and institutions. This in turn creates a need for 'cradle-to-grave' stewardship, involving well defined preservation roles and responsibilities for the diverse array of stakeholders associated with a particular class of digital materials – e.g. creators, publishers, aggregators and, ultimately, cultural heritage institutions. The cost ramifications of a digital preservation process distributed over multiple institutions and lifecycle stages are yet to be determined. It is likely, however, that the overall cost of cradle-to-grave digital preservation will vary inversely with the degree of co-ordination and co-operation prevailing across the relevant stakeholders.

Finally, any answer to the question of how much it will cost must be obtained in light of the larger context of digital collection management and its implications for library operations, workflows and user behaviour. Digital preservation is not so much a discrete activity as it is a set of 'careful digital asset management practices diffused throughout the information lifecycle' (Lavoie and Dempsey, 2004). As such, the *costs* of digital preservation are not necessarily separable from the overall costs of digital collection management. This suggests that estimating preservation costs cannot be done independently of other aspects of managing digital materials – everything from format selection at the time of creation, to choice of storage media and access policies, will influence the nature and scope of the actions required to make certain digital materials endure.

In this sense, digital preservation costs, to a large extent, fall out from an accumulation of other factors associated with acquiring, managing and providing access to digital materials, rather than being an additional expense layered on top of, and separable from, other collection management costs. Certainly there are some costs that arise directly from preservation decision-making, such as choice of digital preservation strategy (e.g. migration or emulation). But, even here, the choice may be driven by influences outside the control of the preservation manager – for example, user expectations that archived materials be maintained in their original form, rather than migrated to new formats – compared to a more isolated decision based solely on which strategy is cheapest and/or most efficient to implement.

In short, the issue of how much digital preservation will cost is perhaps only notional; in practice, we are really talking about the cost of long-term digital collection management, with the cost of preservation *per se* constituting only one highly interconnected component of overall cost.

Notes

1   This section is in part adapted from Lavoie (2003), pp. 5–10.
2   Search conducted on 12 October 2004. For completeness, a search was also made for 'digital preservation costs'. This yielded only about 60 results.
3   For an up-to-date bibliography on the costs of digital preservation, see the PADI website maintained by the National Library of Australia, www.nla.gov.au/padi/topics/5.html.
4   This is not to say that digital preservation techniques are not practised – for example, media refreshment is not uncommon, and Galloway (2003) points out that long-term retention of digital materials has been practised in some domains for several decades.
5   Or, more specifically, all objects in a particular class: for example, translating all textual documents into ASCII.
6   Assuming that a wide range of digital formats will necessitate a wide range of emulated hardware environments. If a single emulated environment supports a large number of formats, then the emulator library may be quite small compared to the number of formats represented in the repository.
7   This is not to say that quantitative analysis is the only tool for these purposes.
8   Not everyone subscribes to this view. The 'letter of the month' to a recent issue of CILIP's *Library & Information Update* is illustrative: 'What a sad indictment of our society that we need to convince governments – local or central – that public libraries are a good cause. Why do we have to defend their existence, let alone compete with commercial enterprises? Do politicians really need to be told that libraries are an essential underpinning to any structure of learning and culture in a civilized society?' The letter-writer goes on to lament the resources expended on government-required performance-monitoring and statistics gathering,

and suggests that the library profession should promote 'qualitative measures of service' (LIU, 2004, 18).

9 The members of the National Museum Directors' Conference include the national museums in England, Scotland, Wales and Northern Ireland, the three national libraries and the National Archives. The purpose of the Conference is, among other things, to 'represent the interests of national museums to government and other stakeholders; to play a key role in the development of the work of its members and their contribution to society and the economy' (from the NMDC website, see http://nationalmuseums.org.uk/).

10 The British Academy is 'an independent and self-governing fellowship of scholars, elected for distinction and achievement in one or more branches of the academic disciplines that make up the humanities and social sciences . . . The Academy aims to represent the interests of scholarship nationally and internationally; to give recognition to excellence; to promote and support advanced research; to further international collaboration and exchange; to promote public understanding of research and scholarship; to publish the results of research' (from the British Academy website; see www.britac.ac.uk/).

11 Note that some of these questions can be turned on their head and viewed as a cost question (e.g. 'what is the cost of *not* saving the bald eagle from extinction?'), in much the same way we are considering the question 'what is the cost of not preserving culturally significant digital materials?' This is simply a reaffirmation of the quote cited earlier, 'costs are benefits lost'.

12 In her survey of digital preservation, Lazinger (2001) titles one of the chapters with this very question.

7

It's money that matters in long-term preservation

Stephen Chapman

Introduction

Obsolescence is inevitable. Some objects are built to last longer than others, but all eventually become unusable. Preservation actions may be taken proactively to buy as much time as possible between interventions, or reactively to restore usability to compromised artefacts or content. Because these activities are generally perceived to be problematic and expensive, research agendas for digital preservation underscore the need to 'reduce the amount of human intervention in digital archiving processes' (Hedstrom, 2003b). Automation will be fundamental to archive electronic resources on a large scale, but it is highly unlikely that technology is going to make preservation cheap.

Preservation stakeholders – the 'designated communities' in OAIS parlance – serve cultural heritage materials well by acknowledging that preservation is not free. Even if digital object ingest, normalization, validation, monitoring, repair, transformation and other preservation actions become fully automated, and even if storage costs continue to decline, digital preservation is going to cost *something*.

How much will it cost? And who will pay whom? What terms and conditions will govern transactions for preservation services? For fee-based services, what happens to content for which organizations cannot pay the 'entry fee' for archiving, or when they stop paying the ongoing maintenance fees?

Policy guides and other documentation from emerging preservation[1] digital repositories provide preliminary answers to these and other questions about preservation costs. Professionally managed preservation repositories represent digital preservation as a business, where long-term use of stored objects will result from *quid pro quo* transactions between object owners (or stewards) and preservation professionals. Object owners appraise content, create or transform their objects to repository-compliant (or recommended) formats, produce metadata (lots of it) and pay fees; in exchange, repository managers provide an organizational commitment to digital preservation, make multiple copies, and monitor data, systems and obsolescence.

Repository terms and conditions may appear to be complex and onerous, and therefore needlessly expensive, but they have been conceived to make preservation affordable in the long term. Digital objects are inherently fragile, in part due to the rapid pace of manufactured hardware and software obsolescence. Strategies such as emulation, migration and universal virtual computing are being implemented to ensure that content remains usable.

Repository service providers are aware, however, that designated communities will likely abandon any option that proves too expensive to develop and sustain. In the business of preservation, both the service providers and the consumers of preservation services have a stake in controlling costs. Repository policies, service agreements and recommended practices for deposit ('ingest') reflect some of the assumptions and caveats that systems architects and analysts are making about long-term costs of data and content management. It remains to be seen whether consumers will literally buy in to these assumptions (by purchasing repository services), or whether they will withhold content from repositories as a means to negotiate for responsibilities they can fulfil and prices they can afford.

The bottom line

Digital repositories are relatively new. To date, no data are available to document proven methods and costs to sustain use of digital objects for time frames longer than a decade or so. To budget for medium- or long-term preservation, one must rely upon cost models. However, Maggie Jones notes that efforts to project costs are further hampered by difficulties in segregating and isolating the activities specific to preservation from those associated with producing, acquiring, identifying, disseminating and rendering digital objects (ERPANET, 2004a, 9). It is going to be difficult to track and compare archiving costs, and to develop business models and revenue streams for archiving, until communities agree to *what* should be counted, and accounted for, as preservation activity.

In the meantime, content owners interested in archiving can consider and critique preservation costs by studying the price lists (or pricing policies) for digital repository services. These lists and policies take some effort to parse, because repositories are likely to charge fees in several categories, at various increments. Current pricing categories include:

- one-time contributions for infrastructure ('development fee') (Portico, 2005)
- annual subscriptions or 'support fees' (OCLC, 2005; Portico, 2005)
- storage, priced annually (e.g. per Gb per year) (Harvard University Library, 2001; OCLC, 2005)
- ingest, per-batch (OCLC, 2005)
- transformations or other interventions, as needed (Harvard University Library, 2001).

These fee-for-service pricing categories convey that digital archiving requires capital for their start-up, ongoing and intermittent repository activities. Although pricing units, such as Gb, are frequently associated with content, perhaps the staffing costs (e.g. number of FTE per genre of formats) will prove to be most relevant to the development of business models to capitalize and sustain repository services.

Given the relatively small number of operational preservation repositories and the opaqueness of repository pricing, it is too soon to derive rule-of-thumb costs for digital archiving by comparing or normalizing fees for similar content stored in various archival repositories. One could, however, gain insight into the expenses of digital archiving by calculating the costs to archive one candidate collection at one repository. For example, if the Harvard University Library wished to deposit to the OCLC digital archive the master files of 2000 of the digitized books in its Open Collection Program's *Women Working* collection (ocp.hul.harvard.edu/ww), at current prices, what is the appropriate annual cost to cite for accounting purposes: $20,436 for the collection, or, by subtracting the subscription fee, only $7,936? See Table 7.1.

Table 7.1 Computed annual cost to manage a collection in the OCLC digital archive

Collection	Storage fee	Collection size	Storage total	Subscription fee	Grand total
2000 digitized books (average size = 127 Mb, 189 pp)	$32 per Gb	248 Gb	$7,936	$12,500	$20,436
Same collection, but added to existing account with over 1000 Gb of data	$15 per Gb	248 Gb	$3720	$12,500	$16,220

This relatively simple scenario (one type of digital material comprising one collection) demonstrates that preservation costs are relative. Previous papers (Ashley, 1999; Chapman, 2003; Shenton, 2005) cite and interpret the many factors that influence preservation costs. When evaluating repository services, one should assume that the units of pricing will be a meaningful variable in the equation of overall costs to archive a candidate collection.

The OCLC annual subscription fee certainly stands out in the *Women Working* books-at-OCLC scenario, but note that, in this case, size also matters. Cost data in Table 7.1 for one year can be extrapolated to project multi-year costs, but in several ways. How does one *fairly* interpret these annual costs to make long-term projections?

The total annual storage fee – either $3720 at the discounted rate or $7936 if this one collection (totalling less than 1001 Gb) were Harvard's only collection in the OCLC Digital Archive – applies to the collection of 2000 digitized books, when each averages 127 Mb. When also accounting for the annual subscription fee, which of the following 'bottom line' annual prices is appropriate (for OCLC and/or Harvard) to use in lifecycle planning for these works?

- $1.86 per vol. per year – excluding subscription, and provided that Harvard deposits another 753 Gb to the archive within the year
- $3.97 per vol. per year – excluding subscription, only collection in archive
- $8.11 per vol. per year – including full subscription, 1001+ Gb threshold exceeded within the year
- $10.22 per vol. per year – including full subscription, only collection in archive.

These cost differences are not insignificant, particularly if one of the calculations were to be used as a baseline in comparing pricing for comparable services from another digital repository, or as a baseline to estimate whether an institution could replicate the repository infrastructure internally at a comparable or lower cost.

The *Women Working* collection books are in fact stored and managed by the Harvard University Library Digital Repository Service (DRS). Consistent with Maggie Jones's observation that archiving costs are difficult to segregate from other services, Harvard librarians are hard pressed to calculate the per-volume, per-year DRS figure that could be fairly compared to the OCLC cost. Stewards of these 2000 *Women Working* volumes would be mistaken to account only for the $5.00 per Gb per year DRS fee for managed storage (Harvard University Library, 2001). In addition to this (calculated) fee of $0.62 per volume per year, Harvard librarians also pay an annual library systems assessment fee to support a range of common good services, including portions of DRS operating costs (hul.harvard.edu/ois/about/assessment.html).

Pricing models and fees are designed to generate revenue. Whether intentional or not, these models might also allocate equity –

or affect perceptions of whether preservation services are equitable. Annual pricing per Gb, for example, privileges relatively small objects such as datasets and structured text (e.g. XML), but potentially creates a fiscal barrier to manage comparable numbers of sound recordings, videos or other large objects. Repositories that strive to become safe harbours to shelter as much 'eligible' content as possible face significant challenges in designing simple pricing models for digital preservation.

In time, pricing categories for digital archiving may be as numerous and complex as those for public transportation. Riders of Boston's MBTA buses and subways, for example, do not pay the same fees to use the same services. Many riders pay the standard fare per ride. However, many pay discounted monthly rates because their employers subsidize a portion of the total cost. Others purchase discounted passes without subsidies. Young children ride for free, and seniors at discounted rates. Various taxes underwrite operational costs for Boston's transit authority. The MBTA pricing model generates operational revenue while providing incentives to maximize (or at least increase) passenger journeys.

Is diversity of pricing a good thing for stakeholders in digital archiving? This is a question best left to economists, but it is interesting to consider whether straight fee-for-service pricing models, without common-good subsidies, can ever fully recover operational costs.

Repository service providers – particularly those based within cultural heritage institutions – and the communities they serve are partners in the preservation enterprise, which benefits from economies of scale. If the mandate is to preserve as much of the collected electronic content as possible for use and inquiry by future generations, then service providers and the communities they serve should form partnerships to develop barrier-free pricing models.

The business relationship

Potential consumers of digital repository services quickly discover they must contribute more than money to the preservation enterprise. Repository policies point out that the 'promise' of preservation is conditional upon actions and decisions that the designated community will make periodically.

Levels of preservation service

Discussions of preservation strategies and costs were simpler – still complex, but simpler – when the content to be preserved could be described in concrete (physical) terms. Librarians have invested in strategies to preserve *books* because they have wanted to keep *books*; we keep books with the expectation that they will continue to be used.

Digital content, on the other hand, is inherently mutable and therefore abstract. Lavoie and Dempsey (2004) offer persuasive arguments that the parties who purchase archiving services need to make their desired preservation outcomes for any deposited content explicitly known. Alternatively, they point out that providers of digital repository services can 'articulate clearly what outcomes can be expected from the preservation process', affording the stakeholders an opportunity to adjust their expectations to what the repository can provide, or to negotiate with a change in service to bring the repository services in line with their needs.

Use agreements and submission agreements, such as the template *Library Agreement for Use of the FCLA Digital Archive* (Florida Center for Library Automation, 2005) incorporate mechanisms for one or both parties to specify or request 'levels' of preservation service. Service levels, as classified by LeFurgy (2002), might express low, medium and high confidence of persistence. In this context, levels function as caveats to the overarching promise 'to preserve'. As expressed in the FCLA Use Agreement, service levels distinguish the preservation outcomes applicable to deposited content: 'bit' preservation for persistent storage; 'full' preservation 'to ensure that information content of the files will remain usable into the indefinite future'. Other agreements may provide finer-grained definitions of preservation outcomes, as Lavoie and Dempsey recommend, both to document some of the significant properties of content (e.g. text indexing and searching) that must be preserved, as well as to specify the minimum or maximum intervals that content is to be retained.

In theory, service levels should act as levers upon the cost of repository service over time. Fee-based services for interventions such as format migration (of many files) would not apply to objects designated for bit preservation. By the same token, if a client wished to elevate the service level for an object or collection, could repository staff (or documentation) advise them how much the annual costs would increase?

Ross and Hedstrom (2005, 321) shed light on the challenges of applying multiple definitions of preservation by implicitly noting that levels of service should be accountable not only in terms of cost, but also in terms of loss. They observe: 'It will not always be possible or economical to preserve all of the features and functionality of original digital entities, but we lack metrics for measuring what is *acceptable loss*.' Research and development of tools in this arena will be fundamental to facilitate negotiations between repository service providers and designated communities in assigning service levels to various classes of material within their collections.

Use agreements may also state conditions of withdrawal of content from the repository, arguably the preservation outcome of greatest consequence. The FCLA Use Agreement (Florida Center for Library Automation, 2005, 2) includes a meaningful pay-to-play clause: 'Library agrees to satisfy Library's financial obligations within the terms and conditions of payment established by FCLA, or to withdraw its contributions from the FDA.'

Units of preservation service

Achieving common understandings of preservation obligations and outcomes requires common vocabularies. Repository analysts, programmers, and other technicians will perform routine activities on deposited content to manage it over time. As illustrated in Table 7.2, repository activities map to different units of content, all of which need to be precisely and consistently defined in documentation and other communications so that the designated community – particularly those paying for services – understand the impact of their decisions and the repository's policies upon their stored content over time.

Table 7.2 Repository activities associated with primary unit(s) of content

Activity	Collection	File	Format	Digital object	Object class	Version	Copy
Submission agreement	X				X		
Ingest				X			
Normalization			X				
Validation			X				
Storage		X				X	X
Backup		X				X	X
Integrity checking		X				X	X
Obsolescence monitoring			X		X		
Preservation planning					X		
Transformation (e.g. migration)					X		
Dissemination	X			X		X	
Deletion		X		X			X

Collections are presumed to be the main unit of deposit and preservation management. Digital collections are always comprised of files, which in turn encapsulate byte-streams. Files must be associated with each other to function as digital objects – the likely unit of retrieval from any descriptive metadata records. Finally, 'object classes' designate objects with shared significant properties – such as version (unique), outcome (do not delete) and format (colour still image) – that are critical to preservation planning. Efficiently managed repositories will apply interventions, such as migration algorithms, to the largest population of data (i.e. object class) that would be appropriately transformed.

Multiple units of preservation and multiple preservation services convey that digital storage is not synonymous with digital preservation. This statement bears repeating in any discussion of preservation costs. Many good storage solutions and services are marketed to cultural heritage institutions. These systems may do a good job of managing files or objects, but are not likely to have any internal 'knowledge' of formats, object classes or collections – all integral to cost-effective execution of full preservation services that sustain use in addition to preserving artefacts.

Accountability and affordability underpin repositories' complex classification scheme for units of preservation service. If repositories are to be entrusted to keep data usable in light of rapid changes in technology – over which cultural heritage institutions have little to no control – how, for example, are they to monitor obsolescence? Analysts and preservation experts (Abrams and Seaman, 2003) view formats as the components most susceptible to break as technologies change. Thus, monitoring relatively few formats and the files associated with them is more economical than monitoring many (all) files and attempting to render them periodically to ensure they remain usable.

Rationale for technical metadata

Repositories request technical metadata to facilitate automation and thereby save costs throughout the archiving lifecycle. Consistent with good practice in other digital library activities such as cataloguing and description, preservation metadata standards bring order to electronic information so that *both* machines and people can perform the necessary actions upon the correct set of data in the optimal way at any designated time.

Although potential repository users may baulk at the amount of complex metadata that many preservation repositories require as conditions of use (i.e. preconditions of deposit and ingest), they will accept these requirements if they, like the repository service providers, believe that future cost savings through automation will compensate for the high initial costs associated with ingest. Brown (2005) used a complex formula that computed an average ingest cost £18.76 per file in a case study of government records managed by the UK National Archives. Given enough time, metadata production and ingest costs as high as these could conceivably be recovered by downstream cost savings.

Of course, if the designated community of repository users does not specify a preservation outcome that benefits from downstream automation – perhaps they intend to preserve objects for a relatively brief period of time – they will be reluctant to provide metadata even if the repository provides them with tools and training.

Rationale for supported formats

Like preservation metadata, file format recommendations may be viewed in an economic as well as a technical context. In presenting the sustainability factors for preserving digital information at the Library of Congress, Arms and Fleischhauer (2004) note that format choices 'influence the likely feasibility and cost of preserving the information content in the face of future change in the technological environment in which users and archiving institutions operate'. Formats are likely to prove significant in the costs associated with migration to new formats, emulation of current software on future computers or a hybrid approach.

By minimizing the number of formats stored in a repository, and maximizing the number of files and objects associated with these formats, repositories minimize the costs to validate, monitor and transform files. As technology evolves – and with it, user expectations and demands – applications and algorithms will be needed to generate new delivery or master versions to sustain use of digital works. Repository systems and policies are being designed to seek efficiencies by employing few applications and algorithms to perform key operations on many files.

For files and objects intended to function as 'masters' in preservation repositories, maximizing the intervals between interventions is fundamental to risk as well as cost management. Any transformation to a byte-stream or its associated computing environment presents risk of error or loss.

It's going to take a village to preserve

The *quid pro quo* transactions between repository service providers and their clientele will not in and of themselves make preservation affordable in the long term. A relatively small collection of complex works – the accumulated work of a single faculty member, multimedia dissertations, websites – will produce a meaningful number of formats to monitor, files to manage and designated community expectations to document and to fulfil. These challenges will be replicated at preservation repositories worldwide.

For these reasons, 'local' repositories seek to form diverse and sometimes distant relationships to serve their constituents' needs professionally and cost effectively.

First and foremost, repository builders are looking to funders – not necessarily content owners or end users – to capitalize the costs of infrastructure development. Large-scale preservation repositories are expensive. Portico (2005) acknowledges that '[t]he Andrew W. Mellon Foundation, Ithaka, JSTOR and the Library of Congress – with a $3 million NDIIPP grant – are investing significantly in Portico's infrastructure development' so that it can become an operational non-profit repository with the mission 'to preserve scholarly literature published in electronic form'. Since 2003, the Koninklijke Bibliotheek (Koninklijke Bibliotheek, 2002) has been receiving more than €1.1 million annually 'for the operational costs of the E-Deposit . . . Continued work to make the system operational will require great effort from the KB in the years to come.'

Subsidies for these and other large-scale preservation repositories are fundamental to their evolution. Funding agencies are critical partners in establishing repository services, particularly in this transitional period to create new organizational models within and among libraries to accommodate electronic resources fully within a mission to acquire, describe, preserve and make information available for use.

Repository practitioners are also working to form alliances with each other, with digital library professionals and computer scientists, with academe, and with industry in at least two key areas, registries and centres for excellence, to make preservation affordable on a large scale.

Registries

Abrams and Seaman (2003) present a case for a global digital format registry to distribute the responsibilities of monitoring many formats among the experts whose organizations have the deepest vested interest in sustaining or transforming data files and objects in their domain. The expertise, documentation and tools from a relative few would benefit practitioners globally. The authors also underscore the necessity of 'generat[ing] a predictable yearly revenue stream' for repositories and their affiliated organizations, such as registries, in light of the fact that 'digital archives cannot afford service gaps'.

Proposals for format, metadata schema and software registries rely upon a marketing strategy that will convince a sufficiently large (or supportive) community to support these initiatives, regardless of whether they do so in support of the common good or simply to serve their parochial needs.

Centres for excellence

Like registries with ongoing governance and oversight, centres for excellence seek to leverage expertise and reduce redundancies. They implicitly promote affordability and scalability of repository services.

The Australian Partnership for Sustainable Repositories (Australian National University et al., 2003) seeks to draw upon an international 'expertise network' and, through a national services programme, 'to enhance cooperation between institutions so that costs can be minimized', to participate in standards development, and 'to maintain a technology watching brief'.

The UK's Digital Curation Centre (CANDO, 2003) has an even broader agenda, seeking 'to bring existing expertise together from different professions and disciplines', including the sciences and humanities, to inform research and innovation, and to 'establish a repository of tools and technical information to provide a focal point for digital curators'.

These centres have extraordinarily broad purviews and will be as challenging as repositories to sustain economically, yet the rationale is that spending money to support these multidisciplinary collectives – both formal and informal – will make repository services more affordable.

Conclusion

Lack of capital will hasten the obsolescence of digital works – whether they are managed within safe repositories or live in more threatening domains – because at some point people forget, they stop paying attention or they lack time, expertise, documentation, rights or tools.

In the emerging world of repository services, money can be used to delegate some measure of preservation responsibility, but it cannot be used *per se* to purchase longevity. By accepting the terms and conditions of participating with repositories, stakeholders may formally declare (and adjust as circumstances change) the desired preservation outcomes of their works, and, with good planning and policies within the repository, buy as much time as possible between interventions. When interventions must occur, they can be automated to the greatest extent possible.

Potential consumers of any repository service should carefully critique the units of pricing, actual costs per unit and the terms and conditions associated with that service. In calculating actual costs to use preservation repositories, designated communities might also consider what will be saved – in time, knowledge building, accountability and, of course, future costs.

Repository pricing and policies underscore that storage and preservation are not synonymous. The mandates of repository service are to identify, locate, retrieve and make digital entities available for use. Fulfilling these mandates challenges preservation stakeholders to communicate needs and outcomes clearly, to establish professional services, to create robust tools, and to distribute the work of monitoring obsolescence through registries, curation centres, technology watches and the like. Meeting these challenges — and none can reasonably be excluded — requires *significant* capital. It's money that matters in preservation. Can we make the case that these investments are sound, both today and for the long term?

Note

1   Used here, 'preservation' and 'preservation repositories' distinguish repositories with stated commitments to long-term preservation from institutional and other repositories that collect and store files and digital objects, but do not explicitly promise to sustain use – i.e. to deliver this content in forms that can be rendered by contemporaneous applications – over time.

8

Some European approaches to digital preservation

Peter McKinney

Introduction: a European approach?

After considering the title of this chapter for some time a question presented itself. Is there such a thing as 'a European approach'? How could this possibly be the case? Digital materials are consistent throughout the world. At least, they are consistent in their diversity: from New Zealand to Canada, to Brazil and Japan, these countries and their public and private organizations are creating a great mass of materials whose form can be recognized the world over. So can there be a 'European approach'? Yes. Despite the electronic medium passing through boundaries across the world globalizing practices, there are certain attitudes, positions and circumstances that have outlined what can indeed be termed a 'European approach'.

Of course, the examples given below do not necessarily reflect a uniform European approach, but there is more than a hint of a 'knowledge-space' that exists in Europe contained in them. This knowledge-space is the product of political boundaries and histories, knowledge, awareness and terminology, and is one of the major contributing factors to the shape of digital preservation work in Europe. Additionally, there is international recognition that the progress that Europe has made provides elements of an approach for others. Through the exploration of the European political climate and a discussion on some major shifts in terminology a uniqueness should appear, an indefinable 'something' that has come into being to allow us to say that there is a European approach to digital preservation which is distinctly recognizable.

For those not convinced of this view, there is a second angle to the chapter title. The title could also read: 'Some *other* European approaches'. What is apparent throughout all the literature on issues surrounding digital preservation is that there is a recycling of examples. Vitality is required to keep ideas fresh and momentum going, and the approaches discussed here should offer new perspectives to some of the issues that have been discussed in many fora. Outside the cultural heritage space there are companies and institutions dealing with the persistence of their digital assets as a matter of organizational and business need. Their experiences are instructive to the debates taking place in conferences, journals, newsletters and newsgroups. If nothing else, the examples below will expand horizons within digital preservation.

The European knowledge-space

'Collaboration' as a concept is ubiquitous in the digital preservation community. Almost all reports from conferences and meetings on various aspects of digital preservation end with a call for collaboration between stakeholders. This is an acknowledgement of the diversity, both physical and academic, of knowledge and that the problem is far larger than one group or individual can solve. It is also a sign of the relative newness of the field and the lack of integration into organizations; that is, those working in the field *must* seek out external help. The geographical and political map of Europe suggests that collaboration would flourish. Where Australia has one National Archive and one National Library, Europe has one of each in every country. Where the USA has the National Archives and Record Administration working on ingesting electronic records, Europe has the Archives de France, the Nationaal Archief in the Netherlands and the Schweizerisches Bundesarchiv (to name only a few) all working on issues.[1] The scope exists to divide and conquer the problem of digital obsolescence: problems can be addressed by different centres and different areas of expertise can focus on individual challenges.

However, it is not quite as neat and co-ordinated as this. There has not been a large degree of international collaboration. Indeed, there is confusion over what exactly the collaborative picture in Europe is. A recent survey of cultural heritage institutions found that digital preservation regulations existed in 46% of the countries that responded (Australia, Denmark, Finland, France, Germany, Greece, Italy, Latvia, Portugal, Slovenia, Sweden, Switzerland and the USA) (Lograno, Battistelli and Guercio, 2003). In contrast, Neil Beagrie found not one national digital preservation initiative across Europe and Oceania, but rather smaller initiatives attempting to tackle the problem (Beagrie, 2003, 12). These two reports seem to offer different insights into the European picture. On one level, there is a piecemeal and varied attempt at addressing the problem, yet, at a higher level, regulations are in place which seem to offer strong drivers to undertake action. What is the true picture?

Beagrie's synopsis is an accurate reflection of the international scene, and one that has perhaps not changed fundamentally since it was carried out. Guercio and her team at the University of Urbino found in 2004 a landscape fraught with confusion (Guercio, 2004). Varied institutions took part in a questionnaire undertaken for presentation at a conference on digital preservation hosted by the Italian Presidency of the European Commission (www.imss.fi.it/ memorie_digitali/). Participation was somewhat sporadic (Portugal being well represented and the UK and the Netherlands not represented) and due to time constraints the study was rushed. Despite these problems there is a great deal that can be teased from it. National regulations were reported in 46% of countries (Lograno, Battistelli and Guercio, 2003, 12), and these could include a multitude of regulations. Does the implementation of e-government provide blanket coverage that electronic records must be preserved? In the same way, have legal deposit rules been interpreted as requiring preservation of digital materials? It is unclear what interpretations have been made. Indeed, the report emphasizes this: 'in this context the meaning of regulations and dispositions is also uncertain, often leading to multiple interpretations' (Lograno, Battistelli and Guercio, 2003, 11). Beagrie's fragmentation of initiatives is perhaps a strong reflection of this confusion. Clear and concise legislation is only now coming in to national policies and, even where legislation includes digital materials, there is little consistency in the way digital materials have been treated. The need for high-level guidance has been identified by others and will be discussed below.

For the moment, it is still the case that the majority of practices in digital preservation are 'ad hoc and fragmentary' (Ross, Greenan and McKinney, 2004). Funding has come mostly from the European Commission or national funding bodies, and has been short term. Guercio has rightly pointed out that what has emerged is a 'picture of provisions, regulations, and plans as a multiple broken line, its continuity being undermined and its different segments being hard to integrate' (Guercio, 2004, 140). This is in contrast to other (geographical) areas, certainly in terms of national initiatives. In New Zealand and the USA large-scale funds have been made available to address particular national issues. The National Archives and Records Association in the USA has just awarded a contract worth over $308 million to build an Electronic Records Archive (National Archives and Records Administration, 2005). A similar strategy has been employed in New Zealand, where the National Library has received NZ$24 million, of which a portion will go towards the creation of a trusted digital repository (National Library of New Zealand, 2004). It seems that in Europe national institutions struggle to attract this degree of topic-specific investment. Work in Europe has begun to address the issue of sustainable funding but, as yet, it is in its infancy and, where urged by international bodies, is not being acted upon through practical implementation.

Awareness and knowledge

Awareness of the problems of digital obsolescence is relatively high within certain areas. While practitioners have been focusing limited resources on technical research, there has been a good deal of dissemination work to other practitioners and interested parties within the community. In Europe there have been (and are) a few conduits of information for the digital preservation community. These include NESTOR in Germany, the Digital Preservation

Coalition in the UK and the pan-European project ERPANET. The Electronic Resource Preservation and Access Network was funded by the European Commission in late 2001 to raise awareness of digital obsolescence and to disseminate knowledge and information on work that is being done to avert this problem.[2] Part of ERPANET's work involved interviews with a wide range of companies and other organizations throughout Europe, exploring their awareness of digital obsolescence and the practices put in place to solve it. Many interviewees in ERPANET's case studies demonstrated an awareness of the problem. This awareness included an understanding of some or all of the issues and a recognition that digital objects in their care would be at risk in a number of years' time. Sometimes there was even an awareness of possible solutions. However, awareness does not in many cases extend to knowledge (where knowledge is an under-standing through study and practice). Participants knew *of* preservation practices, but less of what they would entail. Awareness raising has usually taken place within the digital preservation community, drawing in those information professionals who are in the community and should be aware of the issues. Awareness outside this relatively small and easily convinced community is lacking. The community shares common goals and objectives. In fact, so much has now been written on digital preservation that the words are becoming redundant, familiar and dull (weak) to many. The words of the doomsayers have been heard many times now, but increasingly the prophecies do not actually mean that much to people. Unless it actually happens to them or their organization, it is likely that the message will be ignored or not understood, and until the work is being undertaken it is hard to fully comprehend the complexities. The BBC Domesday project has been cited widely to bring the problem to the attention of the public.[3] While the story is an excellent example of the issues at stake, it comes across as perhaps more of an embarrassment to the owners and creators, than as a transferable example to change attitudes and provoke activity.

In order to raise awareness among 'external' stakeholders, such as senior management and creators, freshness and direct interest are required, in addition to coherent and convincing business plans. Freshness comes only from novelty, and digital preservation has reached a stage where novelty can come only from practice, something by its very nature that is rare at the moment. It is also certainly true that members of the digital preservation community can talk to each other with very technical and specialized language, which means little to those external to this body of knowledge. The language, tropes and modes of communication are singular to the digital preservation community, and there has been little attempt so far to adapt these in order to communicate outside the community.

Preservation and curation

To be clear, Digital Preservation (with intentional capitals), within Europe at the very least, has come to symbolize a community, a need, a desire to stop a projected disaster of loss. The need is driven by an awareness that digital objects are at risk from the ravages of time to a far greater degree than traditional methods of conveying information. Because information has become the primary currency of many organizations and is represented more than ever in digital form, loss of this information is unthinkable. A community has grown around this need and, in Europe, initial community-building and knowledge-sharing have been successful. Are there any particular reasons why this is true in Europe in particular? It is not an exaggeration to suggest that most work exploring the issue of digital longevity is undertaken with either external grants or internal project funding (and indeed unfunded personal research). Common to all is the short-term nature of the funding: 18 months here, two years there. This is in direct contrast to the nature of the problem and the recognition that preservation is an ongoing process. While funding bodies see the need for research and work to be done, it is beyond their remit to offer sustained funding. This leaves the digital preservation community with several problems. With limited funding there are two options: try to do it all (potentially badly) in a short time-scale, or focus on small problems and hope the community will fill in the other gaps. This puts a lot of pressure on the formation of a community that must look at ways of disseminating information and ensuring there is no clustering of effort on the same problem and lack of work on other issues. Some projects have been funded only to look at this dissemination and community-building work, of which ERPANET is one of the best examples, but there has been no work to date at an international level to co-ordinate research and developments.

Without doubt, terminology is as yet relatively unstable and inconsistent across disciplinary boundaries. Within Europe 'curation' is beginning to become part of the lexicon. Curation as a term originated in the Joint Information Systems Committee (www.jisc.ac.uk)[4] and is beginning to be used more frequently in the community. The term was coined to 'distinguish the actions involved in caring for digital data beyond its original use, from digital preservation' (Macdonald and Lord, 2003, 5). Digital curation is an e-science term and relates directly to that community. There are some common misuses and misconceptions of what the term means, but the literature points to curation being an action that brings added value to a body of digital information (Lord et al., 2004; Lord and Macdonald, 2003). Scientific datasets can be enormous in size and are characterized by constant reuse and activities such as 'cleaning' and reinterpretation. These appear to be the defining activities of curation. Other activities mentioned in the literature (including appraisal, management, provision of context, retrieval and access) all relate to activities already understood to be within the broad remit of digital preservation. The term has injected some freshness and perhaps brought novelty and a rebranding of 'digital preservation'. It has also brought different sectors (e-science and cultural heritage) together to approach issues jointly. Within the UK, 'curation' has become a political term and been used by some funding bodies and projects to push forward the digital preservation agenda. Elsewhere, terms such as persistence, longevity and sustainability are being used to define exactly what is at stake.[5] It seems that the term 'digital preservation' is becoming something of an albatross. The term certainly lacks the ability to transfer its complex meaning and assumptions easily to decision-makers (and apparently some of the community).

The role of the European Commission

The European Commission has played a major role in creating the knowledge-space that exists in Europe. It has funded a number of projects exploring digital preservation issues and has managed to retain the longevity of digital heritage on the agendas of successive presidencies of the Union. Initiatives funded by the Commission have brought a certain coherence to the European picture. ERPANET, one of the very few projects to have focused solely on digital preservation, was used by the Commission to offer a picture of the state of practices and awareness throughout Europe. Through a number of workshops, seminars, interviews and meetings, ERPANET helped a large number of disparate stakeholders come together and share their expertise and knowledge. While ERPANET did not have a mandate to undertake a large amount of research itself, it has created a number of fora for other initiatives and projects to vocalize and to disseminate their research.

The background to the Commission's work has already been outlined in some reports (Hofman, 2004; Lunghi, 2004). Succinctly, in the 1990s there was a great drive towards digitization activities and making available electronically as much heritage and information as possible (this was also tied in with the e-Europe agenda).[6] It became increasingly obvious that digitization was being undertaken in a non-standard fashion and with little regard for the work of others. In response, the Lund Principles (European Content, 2001) offered recommendations for supporting co-ordination of digitization activities. With the creation of large amounts of digitized heritage and the e-government drive across Europe producing digital records and materials, recognition grew that accompanying action had to be taken to ensure that the objects (and investments) were not lost. The activities currently being undertaken at the European level revolve around the extension of the Lund Action Plan into a preservation-orientated sphere. The next step was the Council of the European Union's Resolution of 25 June 2002, created under the Spanish Presidency. In this document the Commission notes 'the need for long-term digital preservation work' and urges its member-states to undertake 'the development of policies for preserving digital culture and heritage' (European Union, 2002). This was a major milestone reiterating the concerns and thoughts of many experts in a political arena. Following relatively quickly on the heels of this resolution, an Experts' Workgroup on the Preservation of Digital Memory was created and drafted the Firenze Agenda (Experts' Workgroup, 2004). This outlines the requirements of work to be done in order to galvanize that which has already been undertaken in Europe and to push forward the community. The Agenda outlines three action areas:

1 Create awareness and co-operation mechanisms.
2 Exchange good practice and develop a common point of view.
3 Develop long-term policies and strategies.

While politics undoubtedly pervades much of this work, it is important to note that the Commission has responded to work that has been ongoing in the digital preservation community and is shaping a high-level response. At the moment though, the Commission is funding digital preservation work as part of other projects, rather than singularly.[7]

Some approaches

A large proportion of the literature produced in the area of digital preservation mentions some key cultural touchstones. Cedars, the Digital Preservation Coalition, NESTOR, the British Library, Scandinavian web-archiving projects and the Digital Preservation Testbed are all discussed with regularity. Rather than continue the repetition, it would perhaps be more instructive if different initiatives were discussed.[8] Most of the following examples featured in the various suites of ERPANET's case studies and come from areas that are distinct from the cultural heritage sector. Because they are, for the most part, examples of business responses to a need (that of maintaining their digital assets) they display different drivers to undertake work to ensure the longevity of digital assets. Outside the cultural heritage sector, rarely was the historical value of materials taken to be powerful enough to provide a case for longevity and unsurprisingly it was drivers such as legislative compliance and financial return that the most successful business cases were founded on.

ERPANET undertook a series of case studies to explore how companies and institutions deal with their digital assets.[9] The studies looked at three core areas: the institution's awareness of digital preservation issues (or, from a different angle, the value of its assets and the risk that the electronic format posed to this value); how the company managed its digital assets (were there policies in place for preservation, what systems was it using, did it have dedicated funding?); and future actions. The findings were varied, which perhaps is no surprise, reflecting the diversity of the types of organization ERPANET approached.[10] What perhaps is surprising was the overall divergence of awareness of the problems of digital persistence. Many companies that were approached decided not to undertake the study. They either did not understand the questions that were being asked or, where they did understand, realized they had not reached a point where they could discuss solutions. This contrasted sharply with some of the organizations that participated, which had thought long and hard about their digital assets and treated them with great care and skill.

Individual business needs

The European Investment Bank (EIB) is the financing institution of the European Union. The Bank is an excellent example of under-pinning records creation and management, in essence everyday work patterns, with strong preservation requirements. At the end of 2002 a massive IT programme was undertaken to replace ageing systems and reflect new thinking of its workflow. Although preservation was not part of the initial funding package put in place, forward-looking staff at the Bank ensured that practices which would benefit the preservation of the historical and vital records that they preserve were included in the overhaul. Staff at the Bank are now embarking on a plan to bring preservation to the attention of senior management and staff. Throughout the entire process of bringing in new records systems, a huge staff training programme was being run to ensure that staff understood why creation practices were changing and how this would benefit them.

The EIB recognized that it takes a fundamental shift in culture to embed new practices. It is a commonality of a number of projects that one of the principal obstacles to implementation of new practices is the time taken to understand and learn them. New ideas and practices that must be introduced to ensure successful preservation are met with obstacles. Particular types of technology have a large amount of personal effort invested in them. A new, unified way of reaching the same goal will be met with resistance. Certain requirements can help resolve this stalemate. If there are direct and immediately felt advantages for the user (or for senior management) then change can be easier to swallow. This is the fundamental problem that can be traced throughout every case study that ERPANET carried out; the impact of having (or not having) a sustainable digital preservation process is not immediately understood, or cannot displace more pressing concerns of the decision-makers. It is therefore perhaps of little surprise that senior management within the Bank have not explicitly funded digital preservation practices. The case studies all show that the persistence of digital objects, particularly beyond their legal and administrative lifetime, is not a concern that has immediate impact.

What does the example of the European Investment Bank tell us? That digital preservation can be reduced to the premise of good records management. Where regulations require only compliance for up to ten years, then a records management system that will keep data 'live' will for the most part be sufficient. The telecommunications sector, for example, has little need for long-term archiving. Records are rarely kept beyond ten years, and even this span is only for business records. Some information is retained for far shorter terms – three years for data such as invoices and six months for client-related data such as time and duration of calls. If we place this in the context of the life of many large companies' electronic record management systems, then there are fewer issues to contend with. Migration does not happen frequently; it occurs only when an upgrade or overhaul of the system is required.[11]

Interestingly in the case of telecommunications companies it is senior management that have led the drive for the clear management of records.[12] Their driver is most definitely the regulatory environment, as is the case with many organizations (all organizations have legislation to comply with, be it health records of employees, or regulations of professional bodies). Other studies in the suite show this as the most important driver – new legislation in the pharmaceutical sector states that records submitted to the US Federal Drug Agency in digital format must be kept in digital form for the required length of time.[13] At the moment, very few companies are making the jump to digital submission; they are waiting for suitable software and systems to be developed by companies to enable such management of the records.

The Schweizerisches Bundesarchiv has been archiving digital documents since 1980.[14] The ARELDA (Archiving of Electronic Data and Records) project at the Federal Archives is part of the Swiss e-government initiative and has as its ultimate aim the long-term preservation of digital records.[15] Around €11 million are earmarked for the initial planning and implementation of the systems that will enable the Archives to ingest and archive the materials as required by the regulations and requirements placed on them. Subsequent years will see around €3 million allocated for running the system. This money and the work of creating a digital system capable of maintaining the authenticity of records while migrating them over time has been undertaken mainly because of increasing pressures placed on the Archives. In addition to the Federal Archives Act of 1999 which clearly includes digital records within the requirement to archive federal administration records, the Archives have two areas of pressure. (Schweizerisches Bundesarchiv, 2001, 1). First, the proliferation of technology that can be used on desktop machines has given individual users without a strong background in IT the ability to create their own databases. Second, many of the databases used within administrative departments have reached a critical age. Older IT systems are now being updated and, rather than bear the cost of mass migration, older data are being transferred to the Archives. Additionally, the age of the data means that certain legal requirements are no longer relevant and, at the same time, some data are being deleted from the systems. The Archives, like all European government agencies, foresee having to manage a greater proportion of digital records as the government conducts a greater proportion of its business online.

Their approach is 'slowly and surely'. By 2008 the Archives will be able to preserve for the long term digital records as easily as they can with paper (Schweizerisches Bundesarchiv, 2001, 5). To get there, a step-by-step plan has been outlined which will see the services offered grow from ad hoc solutions implemented by the ARELDA Support Team in the early stages, through the outsourcing of systems creation and subsequent development and updating, to the additional functionality to allow audiovisual materials to be ingested.[16] In all, the process will take eight years to complete, but the systems will be able to guarantee the preservation of government records and their authenticity throughout the coming years no matter what technological changes there are.[17]

Recognizing collaborative value

The examples above reflect the scope of organizations that have to address issues of digital management and longevity, but they are individual responses driven either by business or judicial requirements. The studies ERPANET carried out did find examples of collaboration within other areas. In the meteorological sector, for example, there is a willingness to share information and work together and, while longevity issues are only now beginning to be addressed in a co-ordinated fashion, there seems to be a real sense of common purpose, reflecting the lack of boundaries of the phenomena the organizations investigate (ERPANET, 2004b, 2004c). Of course, in highly commercial sectors (such as the pharmaceutical sector), where there is a competitive advantage to be gained from any advances made, this is less likely to be the case.

The most synthesized and coherent sectoral work is in the broadcasting sector. Here the value of assets is understood, not only in relation to companies' own use of the materials, but also the financial gain from selling them (ERPANET, 2003a). This understanding of value is crucial to their preservation work. The European Commission has funded two major projects to explore the best way to deal with the vast quantities of audio, video and film material that is in real danger of being lost. Because a large amount of audiovisual materials are on increasingly rare and fragile media, the companies have the two-fold problem of the digitization of older, at risk materials, and the proper management of born-digital materials. The first funded project to look at this was PRESTO which found that 70% of the media was at risk throughout Europe; it reported on ways to reduce preservation costs by at least 50%.[18] The membership of PrestoSpace, the follow-up to the work done by PRESTO, comprises a number of national broadcasting companies, technology providers, industrial partners and universities. They have as their aim the provision of 'technical solutions and integrated systems for a complete digital preservation of all kinds of audio-visual collections' (www.prestospace.org/index.en.html). While lasting only for 40 months, the project will address the problem of short-term funding for this type of work. According to UNESCO, Europe has around 50 million hours of audiovisual holdings – an incomprehensible amount of history and heritage of Europe. PrestoSpace is hoping to create 'preservation factories' which will be self-sustaining (www.prestospace.org/project/objectives.en.html). This undertaking could only work with the backing of many different stakeholders, and is a display of what can be achieved with common agreement and understanding. Both projects, PRESTO and PrestoSpace, are iterations of work that goes on right across the broadcasting sector.[19] They are expressions of a desire to retain archives of our audiovisual heritage not only for financial gain, but also for the historical value of the material. Of real interest in these projects is the association of value with preservation. The value of the archival holdings is related directly to the cost of preservation, where 'one minute of sold or re-used archive material will pay for one hour of preservation' (Wright, 2001). Value, and the need to measure, understand and contextualize it, is the new focus for preservation work.

The new focus – value

The PrestoSpace project has identified the need to address 'economic factors' for sustainable actions to keep materials available for use into the future (www.prestospace.org/project/objectives.en.html). There is acknowledgement across the community that actions to keep assets usable are neither one off nor static; there is therefore a desperate need to attract long-term funding for continued work. Costing the processes of digital preservation is seen as the first step to sustained funding but it is a complex undertaking. Where is the point at which a process moves from day-to-day management to preservation practices? If it is held to be true that the process is in place since creation, then is the proper creation of materials also a cost? But this is a false dichotomy as the cost is one of ensuring that assets can be used when required and their value is not lessened by technological interference or obsolescence; it is a total creation and management cost. This means that there are no divisions between creation and archiving such as exist in the paper world. Of course, this is a distinctly holistic view of the digital asset that ignores traditional boundaries of departments and services in organizations and indeed the need to assign costs to different budget centres, but it is one that deliberately holds that the assets of an organization should be treated as such and not as personal/departmental property.

While costing work is at the moment being undertaken, the real challenge is the exploration of the value of digital materials. That is, materials that are valuable to an organization should be classed as assets, and kept into the long term and managed properly. Mapping the retention of assets into the strategic planning of the organization is fundamental.[20] This requires proper assessment of value through an exploration of the 'value-turn' of an object to an asset in order to understand the strength of its necessity to the organization (Currall, Johnson and McKinney, 2005). Once this is understood, it becomes far easier to convince others of the worth of retaining the asset. However, digital objects are intangible, and giving a value to intangibles is incredibly challenging. Senior management understand and act on bottom lines and, in most cases, these are in financial form. Intangibles do not lend themselves to be presented in this way. There are, however, a number of different methods to help in the valuation of intangibles.[21] Concisely, and somewhat simplistically, the methods attempt to put a financial figure on what cannot be readily quantified or to create ways of allowing senior management to view non-financial information with weighting equal to that of numerical information. The former have many flaws and detractors – no one method has gained acceptance and there are too many unknowns to be truly accurate (indeed, it would be only a slight exaggeration to suggest that the valuation can equal whatever is required). The latter look at 'balancing' different factors (Kaplan and Norton, 1992) to achieve greater efficiency and monitor the results of research investment. The espida project at the University of Glasgow is adapting the Kaplan and Norton methodology to explore the full value that digital materials can have (www.gla.ac.uk/espida). This involves not only a great deal of engagement work with all members of staff within an organization but also the use of terminology that senior management recognize and understand. This work aims to bring fruition to the term 'sustainable digital preservation'.

Conclusions

Digital preservation within Europe has taken a path that could be described as 'an approach'. The geographical and political shape of the continent has created various communities that have had to, and are still trying to, come together and create solutions to the obsolescence of digital materials.

There is a clear difference between the requirements of, say, a humanities, text-based computing world, and that of astronomical observations or pharmaceutical records. But one thing unites them: the question of value. It is neither practical nor desirable to keep everything. Indeed, this attitude is counter-productive when trying to make a case for sustained funding; no organization, whether private or public, will give money to an activity that does not have beneficial outcomes (be they financial or otherwise). The value of materials must be explored. When do they become assets, i.e. something that the organization can invest in and recoup the benefit of? A business case is far different from a cost model. A business case is made in order to justify allocation of money or resources, or to bring about organizational change. If the terms of value are worked out, then it becomes easier to make this case. What this really means is that digital preservation is not a unique action or actions, but something that must be embedded into practices and the everyday. The case must be made that the use of assets into the future is not 'a desirable', but rather 'a necessity'. This calls for a change of focus and belief from the digital preservation community. What do we want to preserve and, more importantly, why? Not everything can or should be preserved and the strategy of an organization should determine what objects are indeed assets and what are not. Until that change, digital preservation will remain a side issue of organizations.

To answer the initial question, yes, there is such a thing as a European approach to digital preservation. It is less unified than in North America and Australia yet, perhaps somewhat ironically, it has a strong sense of community. It is refreshing to see the community drawing in (and expanding out to) new areas such as e-science and medicine and continuing to make sure that what is of value today, remains of value in the future. There are new avenues to explore and, as more sectors join the community, new problems to be solved. But it is certain that the community is gaining enough knowledge and expertise to cope with these challenges, not the least of which is creating an organizational strategic platform from which digital assets can be created and sustained for the long term.

Notes

1   The Schweizerisches Bundesarchiv is interesting for two reasons. First, it has in place an impressive electronic records management system and, second, despite Switzerland being outside the European Union it has played a not insignificant role in the European digital preservation community.

2   ERPANET was funded under the FP Programme: IST-2001-32706.

3   The Digital Preservation Coalition (DPC) has used the BBC Domesday book effectively in its publicity campaign in the media. See, for example, BBC (2002) and Darlington, Finney and Pearce (2003).

4   The JISC 'supports further and higher education by providing strategic guidance, advice and opportunities to use Information and Communications Technology (ICT) to support teaching, learning, research and administration. JISC is funded by all the UK post-16 and higher education funding councils' (www.jisc.ac.uk).

5   See, for example, Hofman (2004). The NESTOR project also states that 'the emphasis is put on long-term *accessibility* of digital resources and not that much on pure *preservation* aspects' (www.langzeitarchivierung.de/index.php?newlang=eng).

6 The eEurope Action Plan outlined, among other things, the modernization of public services throughout Europe. See http://europa.eu.int/information_society/eeurope/2005/index_en.htm.

7 For example, as part of the DELOS II project. See Hofman (2004) for further information.

8 This is in no way a comment on the work mentioned, but rather an attempt to introduce different perspectives.

9 The information is taken from ERPANET (2003a, 2003b, 2003c, 2003d, 2004b, 2004c) and generalized from the other erpaStudies available at www.erpanet.org/studies/. These studies were carried out by the ERPANET team which comprised staff in the Nationaal Archief van Nederland, the Schweizerisches Bundesarchiv, the Università degli Studi di Urbino Carlo Bo and the Humanities Advanced Technology and Information Institute (HATII) based at the University of Glasgow.

10 These findings are discussed in Ross, Greenan and McKinney (2004) and various ERPANET presentations (see www.erpanet.org/ presentations.php#staff).

11 'Frequently' here would mean a timescale of less than every five years. It should also be noted that the EIB had some large problems when migrating its data to its new systems.

12 The ERPANET case study on the telecommunications sector managed to attract only two companies to take part, Swisscom and Orange. Many other companies cited a lack of resources and personnel. A major issue, and this holds true for the entire corpus of studies, was finding someone within an organization who could respond to the questionnaire.

13 The regulation is 21 CFR Part 11. For the FDA this is usually five years after the drug has been taken off the market; however, other countries such as Germany have far longer retention schedules (30 years after it has left the marketplace). See ERPANET (2004b, 10).

14 Its magnetic tape archive consists of around 1000 ½ inch tapes; it has 100,000 digital video documents in Digital Betacam, 120,000 digitized manuscript pages and 1000 audio documents on CD (Schweizerisches Bundesarchiv, 2001, 3–4).

15 See www.bar.admin.ch/bar/engine/ShowPage?pageName=ueberlieferung _elektronische_unterlagen.jsp for further information on electronic records in the Federal Archives.

16 This is detailed in Schweizerisches Bundesarchiv (2001, 56).

17 On the issue of migration and continued authenticity, see, as a starting point, ERPANET (2003d) and Heuscher (2003).

18 See http://presto.joanneum.ac.at/index.asp, and www.prestospace. org/project/index.en.html.

19 Collaborative work is also encouraged by various international organizations such as FIAT (International Federation of Television Archives), ASBU (Arab States Broadcasting Union) and ABA (North American Broadcasters' Association).

20 There is a lot of literature about aligning information strategies with the corporate strategy. See, in particular, Ryan (2005) and Hymans (2005).

21 An excellent starting point is Hunter, Webster and Wyatt (2005). The British Library (2004) has recently published results on the value of its collections and work to the British taxpayer using contingent valuation methods.

Digital preservation projects: some brief case studies

Jasmine Kelly and Elisa Mason

In this chapter, we present brief details of current digital preservation projects. These have been chosen to illustrate a wide range of different approaches to the preservation of divergent media, and to give a snapshot of worldwide activity in digital preservation. More details of all of these can be found on their websites. Projects are listed alphabetically.

ADAPT: An Approach to Digital Archiving and Preservation Technology

http://www.umiacs.umd.edu/research/adapt/index.html
The main aim is 'developing technologies for building a scalable and reliable infrastructure for the long-term access and preservation of digital assets'.
Lead partner: University of Maryland
Subject: Infrastructure development
Country: USA

UMIACS (University of Maryland Institute for Advanced Computer Studies) runs the ADAPT (Approach to Digital Archiving and Preservation Technology) project. Partners include the San Diego Supercomputer Center, George Mason University, the University of New Hampshire and Fujitsu Laboratories of America.

Recognizing the different access and maintenance requirements of scientific, business, cultural and governmental data storage and retrieval – ranging from near-continuous access, updating and analysis to restricted and sporadic archive availability – the ADAPT infrastructure is intended to provide a powerful, adaptable tool to manage and preserve digital objects. Its three-layer approach to data storage, manipulation, access and preservation is designed to enable maximum flexibility and adaptability to changing requirements and technologies.

Metadata for complex, often highly structured material needs to be detailed and must capture crucial features of the digital object, including behavioural information about lifecycle management and preservation – content, structure, context, preservation, presentation. ADAPT uses the Open Archival Information System (OAIS) reference framework, including overall terminology. Secure collaboration is central to ADAPT's development, with combinations of trusted entities and distributed archive infrastructures available.

Three pilot projects operated with external partners are currently running to test digital preservation methodologies. Concerned with the preservation of NARA (National Archives and Records Administration) electronic records and geospatial scientific collections, these projects have generated papers and slides available to download.

Archipol

www.archipol.nl/
'The aim of the project is to archive the web sites of political parties in the Netherlands.'
Lead partners: Documentatiecentrum Nederlandse politieke partijen (DNPP) and Universiteitsbibliotheek Groningen
Subject: Topic-specific web archiving
Country: Netherlands

Established in 2000 to archive the websites of political parties in the Netherlands, Archipol contains information in Dutch and English. The Archipol project was set up by the Documentation Centre for

Dutch Political Parties (Documentatiecentrum Nederlandse politieke partijen, DNPP), based at the University of Groningen and Groningen University Library. It is funded by the SURF Foundation, a higher education and research partnership organization for network services and information and communications technology (ICT) within the context of Innovation in Scientific Information Provision (Innovatie Wetenschappelijke Informatievoorziening, IWI), and the University of Groningen.

Archipol is intended to be a resource for journalists and researchers in many fields, and holds a chiefly Dutch-language archive of websites run by political parties in the Netherlands. All publicly accessible pages are archived, with the exception of certain interactive parts and hyperlinks to other websites. A single 'authentic' version of the site is downloaded annually.

In line with its purpose of developing a model for similar archiving schemes, information on the project and the archiving approach employed is available on the website. Links to other relevant articles and archive websites, and a search tool, are provided.

Archivierung Elektronischer Daten und Akten = Archiving of Electronic Data and Records (ARELDA)

www.bar.admin.ch/themen/00532/00536/index.html?lang=de
The key goal is 'to find long-term solutions for the archiving of digital records in the Swiss Federal Archives. This includes the accession, the long-term storage, preservation of data, description and access for the users of the Swiss Federal Archives.'
Lead partner: Swiss Federal Archives
Subject: Long-term preservation of digital records
Country: Switzerland

As part of its remit to preserve documents that contribute to the Swiss national heritage, the Swiss Federal Archives has set up ARELDA (Archiving of Electronic Data and Records). This e-government project supports and advises the records management team of the Federal Archives and departments of the federal government.

Concerned with preserving digital records, ARELDA takes an approach based on application-free archiving, thus aiming to circumvent the difficulties associated with long-term storage and retrieval of data that is stored, and increasingly created, in digital formats that change as software and hardware become more powerful. A key part of ARELDA's work is the development of long-term strategies to manage government information in digital form. Information is provided only in French, German and Italian.

ARROW: Australian Research Repositories Online to the World

http://arrow.edu.au/
The project 'will identify and test software or solutions to support best practice institutional digital repositories comprising e-prints, digital theses and electronic publishing'.
Lead partner: Monash University
Subject: Digital repository development
Country: Australia

The Australian Research Repositories Online to the World (ARROW) project is funded by the Australian Commonwealth Department of Education, Science and Training under the Research Information Infrastructure Framework for Australian Higher Education. The ARROW Consortium comprises the lead institution of Monash University, the National Library of Australia, the University of New South Wales and Swinburne University of Technology.

ARROW's chief objectives are to support best-practice policies in institutions' digital repositories of research output, and to improve metadata across the higher education and heritage sectors. ARROW aims to develop and test software and national 'resource discovery' services developed by the National Library of Australia by offering protocols and toolkits for institutions to manage access to, and preservation of, their research publications and information. Benefits of the scheme include the establishment of a secure open-standards-based infrastructure for capturing and recording research output of all kinds, metadata and identifier tools, improved access to, and enhanced visibility of, research, the creation of a publications history for academics that is globally indexable by search engines, and enhanced inter-institutional compatibility and collaboration.

ARROW makes available on its website news, project documentation, a glossary, and access to ARROW repositories hosted by partner institutions. Partners and members of ARROW may log into a restricted area.

Australian Partnership for Sustainable Repositories (APSR)

http://www.apsr.edu.au/

The objective is 'to establish a centre of excellence for the management of scholarly assets in digital collections'.

Lead partner: Australian National University
Subject: Centre of excellence
Country: Australia

The Australian Partnership for Sustainable Repositories (APSR) is one of the four projects funded by the Department of Education, Science and Training under the Systematic Infrastructure Initiative. Led by the Australian National University, other partners are the University of Sydney, the University of Queensland, the National Library of Australia, APAC (Australian Partnership for Advanced Computing) and the University of Melbourne.

Through its four project strands APSR's main objective is to set up a centre of excellence in the management of scholarly digital information. It aims to look in particular at the issues of access to and preservation of digital assets, to enhance national skills and expertise in this field, and to establish national services and international links. The partner institutions will provide models of digital information management to augment the growth of expertise and to encourage technical development. For example the Australian National University is producing a broad-spectrum repository, and the University of Sydney is investigating preservation of resources in a complex distributed environment.

Expertise is disseminated via publications on the website, such as working papers, reports, presentations and discussion papers, through public lectures, tutorials, discussion fora, conference participation and organization, and recommending reference works and online resources such as guidelines and standards. News and a blog are available, plus summaries and contact details for current projects. Visitors to the website may also read information on APSR jobs and contact staff while partners may enter a restricted area.

Business Plan Archive

www.businessplanarchive.org/
The archive 'collects and preserves business plans and related planning documents from the Birth of the Dot Com Era so that future generations will be able to learn from this remarkable episode in the history of technology and entrepreneurship'.
Lead partner: University of Maryland
Subject: Topic-specific digital archive
Country: USA

The Business Plan Archive is an online repository for business materials relating to the beginning of the 'dot com' era. Set up in 2002, the Archive's partners are the Library of Congress, the Center for History and New Media at George Mason University, and the University of Maryland Libraries. The Archive's contents will be deposited eventually in the Archives and Manuscripts Library at the University of Maryland. It is associated with the DotComArchive.

The archive is intended to be a resource for students and business entrepreneurs. Students in a number of universities use it as part of their course material. Website visitors who wish to access the archive must register, for reasons of commercial sensitivities. A higher level of access – 'approved researcher' – is available on the submission of a brief research proposal and then a copy of the deliverables specified in the proposal. Members can contribute material, including personal stories as well as business documentation; contributors can specify restrictions on access to their material.

The website highlights recent additions; provides project news and announcements, in a blog format; gives details of press coverage; allows visitors to register for e-mail updates; offers FAQs; and provides examples of what can be gained from the Archive. See also the DotComArchive.

Certification of Digital Archives

www.crl.edu/content.asp?l1=13&l2=58&l3=142
The purpose is 'to develop the processes and activities required to audit and certify digital archives'.
Lead partner: Center for Research Libraries
Subject: Certification
Country: USA

Certification of Digital Archives (CDL) is a project of the Center for Research Libraries (CRL), funded by the Andrew W. Mellon Foundation to further work required to audit and certify digital archives. Established in 2005 and running for 18 months, the project builds on the work of the RLG-NARA Digital Repository Certification Task Force to produce certification processes and metrics for digital archives.

As archiving digital content becomes of more pressing concern to institutions in the higher education and heritage sectors, and a variety of standards and systems is materializing, having robust assurance of the calibre of systems and processes on offer to these organizations is increasingly important. Ensuring secure access to and capable management of electronic resources over the long term as well as gaining value for money are key considerations for such bodies, especially when dealing with third parties, and the project aims to provide guidance in assessing such matters. CDL will produce specifications for auditing and certification, and create a business model for the certifying body.

Information about the project is provided on the website, including details of the repositories of digital content that are being tested against proposed criteria. These are the Koninklijke Bibliotheek (National Library of the Netherlands), which hosts the official digital archive for Elsevier Science Direct; Portico, which is creating a preservation repository of material from commercial and not-for-profit publishers for higher education institutions, libraries, publishers and government agencies; and the Inter-university Consortium for Political and Social Research (ICPSR), which maintains social science data; as well as the LOCKSS (LOts of Copies Keep Stuff Safe) distributed archive system.

CLASP: Classic Software Preservation Project

www.archive.org/details/clasp
Working to 'permanently archive classic, obsolete retail software from the late 1970s through the early 1990s'.
Lead partner: Internet Archive
Subject: Software preservation
Country: USA

The Classic Software Preservation Project (CLASP) was set up in 2004 by the non-profit Internet Archive to assist in the permanent archiving of retail software dating from the late 1970s to the early 1990s. Obsolete software of all types is stored in outdated and fragile formats, and the risk of losing the historical record of software development is therefore high.

CLASP is collecting original consumer software of the designated period in order to 'refresh' the data into current storage media. These media are then locked away until copyright obstacles are overcome, and the software may be made freely available. CLASP is permitted to conduct this work under a special exemption to the Digital Millennium Copyright Act but standard intellectual property rights are still held over these programs; the digital artefacts will be obsolete once the copyright expires.

CLASP has a public database of information about its archived software, which website visitors can search and sort by relevance, average rating and data added, media type, collection and creator. There are lists of recently reviewed items, most downloaded software, and 'top batting averages' of programs. There is an RSS feed and information about the Internet Archive. Users can register for free in order to access various collections in the Internet Archive and while logged-in can also write reviews of archived software.

CLOCKSS: Controlled LOCKSS

www.lockss.org/clockss/Home

The mission is to develop 'a distributed, validated, comprehensive archive that preserves and ensures continuing access to electronic scholarly content'.

Lead partner: Stanford University Libraries
Subject: Digital data archiving
Country: USA

Launched in 2006, the CLOCKSS pilot initiative is a collaborative circle of publishers, academic libraries and scholarly institutions that aims to produce a fail-safe archive for scholarly material using LOCKSS (LOts of Copies Keep Stuff Safe) technology. Edinburgh University, Indiana University, New York Public Library, Rice University, Stanford University and the University of Virginia are the academic members while the American Chemical Society, American Medical Association, American Physiological Society, Blackwell Publishing, Elsevier, Institute of Physics, Nature Publishing Group, Oxford University Press, SAGE Publications, Springer, Taylor & Francis and John Wiley & Sons are the other members.

The two-year pilot phase employs the community model of the LOCKSS system to create a 'large dark archive' of electronically published material made available by the publisher members, and to test a model of managing preservation and access in the long term, including 'orphaned or abandoned' content. The system is managed by the community and the outcome of the pilot stages will be disseminated among the wider community, with a view to creating a full-scale repository model for international use.

DACHS: Digital Archive for Chinese Studies

www.sino.uni-heidelberg.de/dachs/

The 'aim is archiving and making accessible Internet resources relevant for Chinese Studies'.

Lead partner: University of Heidelberg
Subject: Topic-specific web archiving
Country: Germany

The Digital Archive for Chinese Studies (DACHS) aims to collate internet resources for Chinese studies, particularly social and political thought available on websites in various Chinese languages. It is part of the European Centre for Digital Resources in Chinese Studies, at the Institute of Chinese Studies based at the University of Heidelberg. The University of Leiden in the Netherlands joined the scheme in 2003.

The Archive holds a varied collection of digital material, including political speeches, historical documents from non-Chinese collections, websites created in China or elsewhere, excerpts from discussion forums, journals, newsletters and films. With an emphasis on current affairs, the information is selected by scholars and non-academics within China and around the world, and is augmented by complete collections acquired by donation or purchase. Partly to comply with the diverse copyright situations of the material, access to the archive from outside the University of Heidelberg and the University of Leiden is limited to researchers with a password granted by the archive. The content includes 'snapshots' of web coverage of specific events and associated material as well as longer-term themes.

The metadata system used is the Open Archival Information System (OAIS). Harvesting metadata from the original sources or relying on full-text search engines are two scenarios currently envisaged.

The website provides detailed material on the initiative, including technical information, plus a newsletter and publications. The archive can be searched by index or most recent downloads but general access is closed. Website visitors can subscribe to the ChinaResourceNews e-mail newsletter, archives of which can be browsed by year or searched by word or author's e-mail address.

DAREnet: Worldwide access to Dutch academic research results

www.darenet.nl/en/page/language.view/home
Aims 'to demonstrate the network of the local collections of digital documentation held by all the Dutch universities and several related institutions, presenting them to the user in a consistent form'.
Subject: Digital repository development
Country: Netherlands

DAREnet (Digital Academic Repositories) is a network of research repositories of all universities and several other academic and research institutions in the Netherlands. It is a national initiative of all the Dutch universities, the National Library of the Netherlands (KB), the Royal Netherlands Academy of Arts and Sciences (KNAW), and the Netherlands Organization for Scientific Research (NOW), co-ordinated by the SURF Foundation, which is a partnership organization for network services and information and communications technology. Officially launched in 2004, DAREnet runs until the end of 2006 and is funded by the Ministry of Economic Affairs.

DAREnet acts as a national umbrella for repositories of research outputs from Dutch academia and research organizations, which retain responsibility for their own collections. Its Dutch- and English-language website allows free, unrestricted, full-text access to the repositories of all participating organizations, where copyright limitations permit. Visitors may search one or more repositories directly from DAREnet, but may only access restricted material via its host repository. The Cream of Science database showcases leading research and is browsable by surname, discipline and institute. News and project information is available, as well as material on individual repositories, and links directly to the collections.

As part of its remit to encourage the growth of the network of repositories, DAREnet makes grants to relevant projects, details of which are provided on the website. Individual repositories are also developing services to enhance their collections.

Data-PASS: Data Preservation Alliance for the Social Sciences

www.icpsr.umich.edu/DATAPASS/

The main goal is to 'identify, acquire and preserve important social science research collections that have not been archived'.

Lead partner: University of Michigan Inter-university Consortium for Political and Social Research

Subject: Topic-specific digital data archiving

Country: USA

The Data Preservation Alliance for the Social Sciences (Data-PASS) is a partnership run by the University of Michigan Inter-university Consortium for Political and Social Research (ICPSR), the Roper Center at the University of Connecticut, the Odum Institute at the University of North Carolina at Chapel Hill, the Harvard-MIT Data Center of the Institute for Quantitative Social Science at Harvard University, the Henry A. Murray Research Archive of the Institute for Quantitative Social Science at Harvard University, and the Electronic and Special Media Records Services Division of the National Archives and Records Administration (NARA). The project is supported by an award from the Library of Congress as part of the National Digital Preservation Program.

The goal of Data-PASS is to help preserve social science data in digital format over the long term in order to comprehend American society in all its aspects. The members of the Alliance consider information gathered from opinion polls, voting records, surveys and other social science investigations, and select and acquire content that is desirable and appropriate for preservation. A key aim of the project is to develop common standards for metadata, and to produce strategies that will enable scholars and policy-makers to analyse the selected data.

The website comprises a brief summary of the project's aims, a list of partners with hyperlinks, and contact details.

DCC: Digital Curation Centre

www.dcc.ac.uk/
It was 'established to help solve the extensive challenges of digital preservation and to provide research, advice and support services to UK institutions'.
Lead partner: University of Edinburgh
Subject: Centre of excellence
Country: UK

The UK Digital Curation Centre (DCC) is funded jointly by the Joint Information Systems Committee (JISC), an independent organization advising the further and higher education sectors on the use of information and communications technology (ICT), and the e-Science core programme created by UK academic research councils to improve collaboration and knowledge-sharing in scientific research. The DCC comprises the Database Research Group within the School of Informatics, the Arts and Humanities Research Council (AHRC) Research Centre for Studies in Intellectual Property and Technology Law and the EDINA national data centre, all based in the University of Edinburgh, the National e-Science Centre, the Humanities Advanced Technology and Information Institute (HATII), UKOLN and the Council for the Central Laboratory of the Research Councils (CCLRC).

The DCC intends to provide support and advice in the storage, preservation of and access to scientific and scholarly research. Using its Associate Network, the DCC aims to act as a national hub for the dissemination of good practice in, and research and development into, digital curation, and to offer services and tools to promote standards and best practice.

The website provides news on digital curation events and research, manuals, briefing papers, case studies, a glossary and user requirement interviews. A catalogue of appropriate tools, standards guidelines and other projects is available and members can participate in discussion forums. There is information on the Associates Network, membership of which is open to all UK higher and further education institutions. There is also an advisory team available to answer specific questions or offer guidance on particular situations and there is material on the UK pilot of Stanford's LOCKSS (Lots Of Copies Keep Stuff Safe) tool. Website visitors can add details of events they are organizing, read project papers and FAQs oriented towards different roles in the digital data lifecycle. They can also contact the team, establish RSS feeds and subscribe to the *International Journal of Digital Curation*.

DELOS Digital Preservation Cluster

www.dpc.delos.info/
The main 'focus [is] on those [tasks] designed to initiate collaborative interaction between institutions and individuals, focus and enable

digital preservation, and deliver tangible results by bringing together fragmented research results in different laboratories'.

Lead partner: Humanities Advanced Technology and Information Institute (HATII)

Subject: Theory and methodology for digital preservation research

Country: International

The DELOS Network of Excellence on Digital Libraries project is part of the European Union's Sixth Framework Programme. Led by the Humanities Advanced Technology and Information Institute (HATII) at the University of Glasgow, the DELOS network also includes UKOLN at the University of Bath, Technische Universität Wien in Austria, the Università degli Studi di Urbino Carlo Bo in Italy, the Nationaal Archief Nederlands, the Phonogrammarchiv, Österreich-ischen Akademie der Wissenshaften in Austria and the Universität zu Köln in Germany. Moving on from the work of an earlier project which ran from 2000 to 2003, DELOS aims to standardize and cultivate the development of next-generation digital library technology.

Launched in 2004, the DELOS programme intends to enhance the integration and collaboration of research conducted in the European digital library field, particularly that relating to preservation issues. Specific goals are the production of guidelines, frameworks, metrics and tools to manage the lifecycle of digital information, the construction of interoperable services suitable for multilingual use, the building of integrated content management appropriate for personal, global, specialist and popular uses and the establishment of an infrastructure in which research into all dimensions of digital libraries can be supported. Knowledge-sharing takes place among researchers, practitioners and interested experts in industry, with international collaboration furthered by an exchange programme. As part of its remit to disseminate knowledge, especially to promote co-operation between the library and research sectors and the industrial sector, and to foster international collaboration, DELOS has set up a Virtual Digital Library Competence Centre dedicated to defined communities of users, with access to tech-nologies, services and expert information. The Preservation Cluster (WP6), which focuses on preservation issues, is working to improve communication and collaboration among all participants in digital content preservation research and development and to ensure that research conducted in digital content preservation informs the evolution of digital library architecture and the work of other DELOS network clusters.

The DELOS website provides news and reports of the Research Exchange Programme and summer schools and offers publications from the Preservation Cluster in PDFs. Visitors can also contact leading partner HATII and members can log into a restricted area.

Digital Object Management (DOM)

www.bl.uk/about/policies/dom/homepage.html
The mission is 'to enable the United Kingdom to preserve and use its digital output forever'.
Lead partner: British Library
Subject: Long-term preservation solutions
Country: UK

As part of its legal deposit obligation, the British Library runs the Digital Object Management (DOM) programme to manage digital material of all formats and kinds of content.

DOM is intended to establish a technical method of securing the storage, preservation and access to such digital objects for ever, both to maintain the usefulness of digital-born material and data created as surrogates of analogue objects, and to protect the fragile originals. There are three scheduled software releases based on the core principle of distinguishing between physical and service requirements. The system uses a Microsoft .NET framework.

Visitors to the DOM part of the British Library website can read detailed information about the project, including conference papers and presentations, and access contact information.

Digital Preservation Coalition

www.dpconline.org/
It was 'established . . . to foster joint action to address the urgent

challenges of securing the preservation of digital resources in the UK and to work with others internationally to secure our global digital memory and knowledge base'.
Subject: Long-term preservation solutions
Country: UK

Founded in 2001, the Digital Preservation Coalition (DPC) was set up to encourage work on digital preservation in the UK and to collaborate internationally on issues of digital global memory.

The DPC aims to publicize research and good practice; to broaden the number of specialists in the UK; to advocate and raise awareness of the significance of preservation of digital content, especially global memory; to foster tools and standards for digital preservation; and to work closely with other organizations, including those in the commercial sector.

The website is a key part of the knowledge-dissemination agenda, containing detailed information on the organization's activities, events, meetings and reports, including relevant technology developments, and guidance papers, in addition to featuring a DPC member's projects and the quarterly digest *What's New in Digital Preservation*, which summarizes selected recent activity collated from Preserving Access to Digital Information (PADI) Gateway, the digital-preservation and padiforum-l mailing lists and other sources. There is also a searchable archive of the discussion list, a diary of events, material on relevant training, with discounts for DPC members, and membership information, including an application form, plus press releases and details of media coverage. Members have a protected space holding resources and material on invitation-only events and may have one of three types of paid membership.

DINI: Deutsche Initiative für Netzwerkinformation (German Initiative for Networked Information)

www.dini.de/
[In German only]
Subject: Certification
Country: Germany

The Deutsche Initiative für Netzwerkinformation (DINI, the German Initiative for Networked Information) was set up in 1999 to co-ordinate and assist in the evolving information infrastructure in universities and other research bodies. DINI is an initiative of four partner institutions – AMH (Arbeitsgemeinschaft der Medienzentren der deutschen Hochschulen), the Association of Media Centres of the German Universities; DBV (Deutscher Bibliotheksverband Sektion 4: Wissenschaftliche Universalbibliotheken), the German Library Association, section 4: Academic General Libraries; ZKI (Zentren für Kommunikation und Informationsverarbeitung in Lehre und Forschung e.V.), Centres for Communication and Information Processing in Teaching and Research – and professional organizations and others. The scheme is funded by membership fees, donations and public subsidies.

DINI's overall objective of boosting networked research is con-ducted by the specific tactics of improving the creation and availability of information, enhancing the efficiency of ICT systems in research and education organizations, promoting pedagogical soft-ware development and dissemination, advocating training and upgrading public access to scientific data.

On its German-language website, DINI provides manuals and guidelines, project papers and news of DINI conferences and work-shops, together with an archive of news items and papers and information regarding past conferences.

DORIA: Digital Object Management System

www.lib.helsinki.fi/english/libraries/DOMS_en.htm
'A project that aims to create a platform for preservation, cataloguing and distribution of digital collections.'
Lead partner: Helsinki University Library
Subject: Digital archiving system
Country: Finland

The Digital Object Management System (DORIA) is a project set up by Helsinki University Library to preserve and manage digital collections held by libraries in Finnish universities and polytechnics.

Helsinki University Library is also the National Library of Finland and therefore takes responsibility for the legal deposit of digital material.

The DORIA project incorporates maintenance, support and development in addition to software and hardware. Utilizing ENCompass software, the digital object management system permits users to search the digital collections of higher education institutions' libraries, either individually or severally. Material in the archive includes the Elektra database of scientific journals, samples from the collections of the National Library of Finland, dissertations, cultural and musical objects, and the writings of President Urho Kekkonen. The search pages are available in English and Swedish, as well as Finnish.

DotComArchive.org

www.dotcomarchive.org/
The archive 'focuses on the preservation of [largely born-] digital business records from the dot-com era'.
Lead partner: University of Maryland
Subject: Topic-specific web archiving
Country: USA

The DotComArchive is based at the Robert H. Smith School of Business at the University of Maryland. It was established to act as a repository for memories of those involved in the 'dot com era' of the late 1990s, which is highly significant in the histories of business and information communications technology (ICT).

The archive collects a multitude of data, including presentations, business plans and e-mails dating from that period, but its main focus is on the memories of volunteers offering experiences of all kinds from different internet companies through structured surveys, free narrative and interviews. See also Business Plan Archive above.

eDAVID: expertisecentrum DAVID (Digitale Archivering in Vlaamse Instellingen en Diensten)

www.expertisecentrumdavid.be/eng/index.php
This project was the first to address Flemish archiving issues.

Although it is now completed, the Flemish site continues to be updated with information on digital archiving by the Antwerp City Archives.
Lead partner: Fonds voor Wetenschappelijk Onderzoek, Stadsarchief Antwerpen
Subject: Topic-specific digital archiving
Country: Belgium

The Flemish initiative eDAVID (Digitale Archivering in Vlaamse Instellingen en Diensten) is the continuation of the DAVID project, which was formally completed in 2003. The four-year DAVID project was run by Antwerp City Archives and the Interdisciplinary Centre for Law and Information Technology (ICRI) at the University of Leuven.

The open standards DAVID project focused on digital archiving and was intended to make available public archives and improve co-operation between universities and archival institutions in Belgium, concentrating principally on digital-born archives with a Flemish component. Its main objective was to offer guidance on electronic archiving, in particular to create a manual. The manual was put online in January 2004 with the partner organizations undertaking to maintain its currency. The eDAVID scheme maintains the website and manual and continues to work on best practice and innovation.

Along with the manual, the eDAVID website provides detailed information about the DAVID project, including newsletters, guidelines and standards, reports, papers and presentations on electronic document management, including work on digital signatures, and examinations of how case studies have been put into practice in the Antwerp City Archives. Most of these publications are PDFs and are available in English as well as Flemish.

e-Depot

www.kb.nl/dnp/e-depot/e-depot-en.html
e-Depot is 'a digital information archiving system . . . primarily intended for archiving publications by Dutch publishers'.
Lead partner: Koninklijke Bibliotheek

Subject: Digital archiving system, emulation
Country: Netherlands

The Koninklijke Bibliotheek (KB, National Library of the Netherlands) e-Depot concept builds on earlier work conducted in the Netherlands-specific DNEP-IWI and NEDLIB (Networked European Deposit Libraries) projects. KB is the national deposit library of the Netherlands and e-Depot mainly archives online electronic publications from Dutch publishers and content stored in offline media for long-term preservation and access.

Operational from 2002, the e-Depot utilizes the NEDLIB process model for digital archiving, which distinguishes between archiving and other services necessary for digital libraries, such as search and authentication. e-Depot is a fully automated system, a development of the Deposit System for Electronic Publications (DSEP) and Open Archival Information System (OAIS), and is now fully embedded within the National Library.

The website makes available project information; of particular interest might be the six studies on aspects of the project and papers for a workshop entitled 'Digital Preservation, Technology and Policy' to mark the launch of e-Depot. Technical information is provided, along with future plans and contact details.

The ECHO DEPository Project, 2004–7

www.ndiipp.uiuc.edu/
Its 'activities include the development of new tools for selecting and capturing materials published on the Web, the evaluation of existing tools for storing and accessing digital objects, and research into the challenges of maintaining archived digital resources into the future'.
Lead partner: University of Illinois at Urbana-Champaign
Subject: Web archiving
Country: USA

The Exploring Collaborations to Harness Objects in a Digital Environment for Preservation (ECHO DEPository) Project is a digital preservation project designed to provide guidance and tools for digital preservation. ECHO DEPository Project is funded by the Library of Congress under the National Digital Information Infrastructure Preservation Program (NDIIPP) and is due to end in 2007. Based at the University of Illinois at Urbana-Champaign, this three-year project is run by a partnership including the Online Computer Library Center (OCLC), the National Center for Supercomputing Applications (NCSA), WILL TV and Radio, Tufts University, Michigan State University and state libraries from Arizona, Connecticut, Illinois, North Carolina and Wisconsin.

The project partners aim to conduct research into technologies, standards and practices in digital preservation, with the objective of producing aids to institutions that manage digital content. Evaluation of existing tools and standards is also a major goal of the project and so the website offers project information and downloadable resources.

ERPANET: Electronic Resource Preservation and Access Network

www.erpanet.org

The chief objective is to 'establish an expandable European Consortium, which will make viable and visible information, best practice and skills development in the area of digital preservation of cultural heritage and scientific objects'.

Lead partners: Humanities Advanced Technology and Information Institute (HATII), Nationaal Archief van Nederland, Istituto di Studi per la Tutela dei Beni Archivistici e Librari, Schweizerisches Bundesarchiv

Subject: Centre of excellence

Country: Europe

Set up in November 2001 with the intention of disseminating information, best practice and skills development in the expanding arena of the digital preservation of cultural heritage and scientific objects, the Electronic Resource Preservation and Access Network (ERPANET) is a European Commission-funded project.

With its Europe-wide outlook and multilingual scope, ERPANET aims to raise awareness among all types of users of digital preservation technologies, from software developers through institutions to individuals; to encourage research in digital preservation; and to support collaboration across all sectors with interests in this field, including government bodies, heritage institutions and commercial organizations in all industries. As a central part of its remit to champion the sharing of multi-disciplinary expertise, ERPANET publishes details of the workshops and training seminars it runs and provides advice, bibliographies, commentaries, searchable reviews and assessments of recent developments and software in addition to a professional directory and guidance in best practice. Detailed case studies and chatrooms are available in a members-only part of the site. User-generated content is a key part of the website, with visitors able to contribute ideas, feedback and advice; and users of the free open archives ePrints service, run in partnership with the Digital Curation Centre (DCC), may also upload papers.

espida: an Effective Strategic model for the Preservation and Disposal of Institutional Assets

www.gla.ac.uk/espida/
Its focus is on 'the creation of a model of the relationships, roles and responsibilities, costs, benefits and risks inherent in institutional digital preservation'.
Lead partner: University of Glasgow
Subject: Digital preservation models
Country: UK

The Effective Strategic model for the Preservation and Disposal of Institutional Assets (espida) is a plan to draw up a business-focused model for digital preservation at higher and further education institutions, which will be made available to the education sector. Based in the University of Glasgow, espida is funded by the Joint Information Systems Committee (JISC) and runs until December 2006.

The espida project aims to integrate digital preservation into institutions' strategic planning by producing a model for such institutions based on its experience of working closely with academic and managerial parts of the University of Glasgow. It continues work on digital content management conducted in the university, such as Daedalus and the Effective Records Management Project.

The website provides project information, including news and reports of workshops and events, conference papers and contact details.

GPO LOCKSS Pilot Project

www.access.gpo.gov/su_docs/fdlp/lockss/
A pilot scheme 'to make Federal Government e-journals available to select pilot libraries that are operating LOCKSS boxes'.
Lead partner: US Government Printing Office
Subject: Infrastructure development
Country: USA

The US Government Printing Office (GPO) runs the Federal Depository Library Program (FDLP), which provides public access to official federal government publications, both print and electronic. Print publications are available at various federal deposit libraries throughout the country, but digital material lacks an appropriate distribution framework that permits the preservation and management of such material.

The GPO established a pilot project to examine the viability of the LOCKSS (LOts of Copies Keeps Stuff Safe) software system, developed at Stanford University, in addressing these needs. LOCKSS is open-source software that permits an institution to safeguard its own, local copy of content. This year-long project involving 20 university libraries and ten e-journals was scheduled to end in March 2006.

International Internet Preservation Consortium (IIPC)

www.netpreserve.org/
The mission is 'to acquire, preserve and make accessible knowledge and information from the Internet for future generations everywhere, promoting global exchange and international relations'.

Lead partner: Bibliothèque nationale de France
Subject: Internet archiving
Country: International

The objective of the International Internet Preservation Consortium (IIPC) is to obtain, preserve and make available internet content generated around the world. The IIPC is spearheaded by the Bibliothèque national de France (National Library of France) and comprises: the Biblioteca Nazionale Centrale di Firenze (National Library of Italy, in Florence), the Kongelige Bibliotek (Royal Library, Denmark), Helsingin yliopiston kirjasto – Suomen Kansalliskirjasto (Helsinki University Library and the National Library of Finland), the US-based non-profit organization the Internet Archive, Kungliga biblioteket Sveriges nationalbibliotek (Royal Library, National Library of Sweden), Landsbokasafn Islands – Haskolabokasafn (National and University Library of Iceland), the Library and Archives of Canada, Nasjonalbiblioteket (National Library of Norway), the National Library of Australia, the British Library and the US Library of Congress.

Established in 2003, the consortium was initially agreed to last for three years and limited to charter institutions, but membership is now being opened to other national libraries. Specific IIPC goals are to facilitate the archiving of internet content sourced from around the world using preservation techniques that permit secure access into the future; to stimulate the emergence of standards and tools that foster the establishment of international archives; and to advocate archiving of the internet to national libraries as sources of cultural heritage and scholarly investigation. IIPC is structured into six working groups handling the specific topics of technical frameworks; ascertaining researchers' requirements; appraising access tools; defining metrics and an evaluation testbed; investigating accessing of the 'deep web'; and content management.

The website provides background material about the consortium, news and events, papers from conferences and workshops, details of member institutions, press releases and reports of events, and contact information. Visitors can also search the site, download software developed by the IIPC to assist in web archiving, and subscribe to a newsletter. See also Chapter 5 for more detail.

Internet Archive

www.archive.org/
'The Internet Archive is building a digital library of Internet sites and other cultural artifacts in digital form.'
Subject: Internet, born-digital archiving
Country: USA

Founded in 1996, the Internet Archive (IA) is a non-profit scheme to archive digital data for free, permanent access. Based in San Francisco, the archive collaborates with cultural and heritage organizations such as the Library of Congress and the Smithsonian Institution, and is working on tools to encourage the establishment of other such internet libraries in the USA and elsewhere. The Internet Archive accepts donations of money and stocks, and receives donations from Alexa Internet, the Kahle/Austin Foundation, the Alfred P. Sloan Foundation, the William and Flora Hewlett Foundation and the public.

The IA holds digital content in the form of websites, electronic books, live music recordings, moving images (including news and movies), software and texts. The Open Educational Resources Archive is designed for students, teachers and autodidacts of all levels and holds educational content such as coursework, study guides, exercises and lectures contributed by ArsDigita University, Hewlett Foundation, MIT, Monterey Institute and Naropa University.

The Wayback Machine is a search facility on the IA website that displays the world wide web as it looked on a specified date. Website visitors can become members and can then upload contributions and participate in fora in addition to downloading and viewing collections. Reuse of much of the material is free although copyright restrictions of the originating source may lead the IA, as it deems appropriate, to take steps to eliminate specific content or disallow access to certain content. The website also offers background information on the IA, including technical material, as well as user fora and discussion lists, contact details and directions to the IA's physical location.

IA has introduced a subscription service called Archive-It, which enables organizations to create, manage and search their own digital collection via a web-based interface without needing technical expertise.

InterPARES 2

www.interpares.org/

'In addition to dealing with issues of authenticity, it delves into the issues of reliability and accuracy from the perspective of the entire life-cycle of records, from creation to permanent preservation.'

Lead partner: University of British Columbia

Subject: Long-term preservation of authentic records

Country: Canada

The goal of the International Research on Permanent Authentic Records in Electronic Systems (InterPARES) is to augment expertise relating to the long-term preservation of digital records, with the eventual aim of producing exemplar policies, standards and strategies. The project has had two phases thus far.

The two-year-long InterPARES 1, launched in 1999, was based on the work of the Preservation of the Integrity of Electronic Records, which intended to produce standards for the creation and management of electronic records; it published DoD Standard 5015.2. Drawing on the expertise of specialists from around the world, InterPARES 1 concentrated on the problem of preserving the authenticity of administrative databases and document management systems once they were no longer needed routinely. It also examined long-term preservation of digital sound. The investigations and conclusions were published in book form but are also available to download from the website www.interpares.org/ip1/ip1_index.cfm.

Beginning in 2002, InterPARES 2 was due to end in 2006. Its main focus is the maintenance of the authenticity, accessibility and accuracy of digital records, particularly those produced as part of artistic, scientific and government activity. Another project fuelled by international collaboration, InterPARES 2 is based in the School of Library, Archival and Information Studies at the University of British Columbia in Canada. The majority of project funding comes from the Canadian Social Sciences and Humanities Research Council's Major Collaborative Research Initiatives (MCRI) programme, the National Historical Publications and Records Commission and the National Science Foundation of the United States.

kopal: Cooperative Development of a Long-term Digital Information Archive

http://kopal.langzeitarchivierung.de/

The principal goal is 'to develop a technological and organizational solution to ensure the long-term availability of electronic publications'.

Lead partner: Die Deutsche Bibliothek
Subject: Long-term preservation solutions
Country: Germany

kopal (Co-operative Development of a Long-term Digital Information Archive) is a German initiative to investigate solutions to the problems of obsolescence associated with electronic archiving. Funded by the Federal Ministry for Education and Research (BMBF) and based in Frankfurt am Main, the project was launched in mid-2004 and is scheduled to end in 2007. Project partners are Die Deutsche Bibliothek (German National Library), Göttingen State and University Library, Gesellschaft für wissenschaftliche Datenverarbeitung mbH Göttingen (GWDG) and IBM. The Koninklijke Bibliotheek (National Library of the Netherlands) is collaborating on a preservation plan.

Utilizing large deposits of all types of electronic media from partner institutions the National Library and the Göttingen State and University Library, kopal is piloting a technical solution that enables institutions to retain control of their data stored inside a specific institutional space within a larger, secure infrastructure while allowing their reuse by other, authorized organizations. Integration into extant library systems and adherence to international standards are important factors in kopal's design.

The core component, known as DIAS-Core, employs a 'universal object format' to permit multiple clients to access and manage data remotely within a flexible, scalable model. koLibRI software (kopal Library for Retrieval and Ingest) is a set of Java tools that can be used in whole or in part in other systems. The full set is due to be provided by the end of the project, although a beta release is available to be downloaded for evaluation, with feedback requested.

The website offers information in German and English, including news, project material, press information, technical details, a newsletter to which visitors can subscribe and search, an archive, a glossary and links to relevant organizations and projects.

Kulturarw³

www.kb.se/kw3/
Swedish web archive.
Lead partner: Swedish Royal Library
Subject: Domain-specific web archiving
Country: Sweden

Kulturarw³ is a scheme run by the Royal Library, the National Library of Sweden, to archive Swedish digital material for public access. Although the archiving project started in 1996, the archive opened in 2003. Kulturarw³ is part of the Nordic Web Archive.

Visitors to the library may look at the collection through on-site terminals, but access from outside is not permitted. The approach taken to collecting material is similar to that of the US-based Internet Archive Foundation, in which regular sweeps of the internet are made, to collect Swedish-language content, material produced and hosted in Sweden, information created by Swedish people abroad, and foreign-originated content relating to aspects of Swedish culture.

The website contains a historical record of the website of the Royal Library itself, which can be browsed online. It also provides information about the project, including statistical data, papers presented at international conferences, FAQs and contact details. Most pages are available in English, though some information is in Swedish only.

LIFE: Life Cycle Information for E-Literature

www.ucl.ac.uk/ls/lifeproject/
LIFE 'will examine the life cycles of key digital collections at UCL and the British Library and establish the individual stages in the cycle. These stages will then be costed to show the full financial commitment of collecting digital materials over the long term.'
Lead partners: University College London (UCL), British Library

Subject: Life cycle management
Country: UK

The LIFE (Life Cycle Information for E-Literature) project examines the lifecycle of digital material with a focus on archiving. University College London (UCL) Library Services and the British Library run the project, which is funded by the Joint Information Systems Committee (JISC). Launched in early 2005, the LIFE project ends in 2006.

LIFE applies the theory of lifecycle collection management to digital content in order to manage each stage in an item's existence in the most efficient manner. Creating and operating successful selection and management policies are aided by understanding fully the long-term costs and requirements of archiving electronic content. The project uses selected digital collections belonging to the partner institutions to examine these issues.

The website offers project background, news of activities and events, presentation papers, a bibliography, glossary and contact details.

Mandate: Managing Digital Assets in Tertiary Education

www.jwheatley.ac.uk/mandate/
The 'aim is to develop a toolkit to support the creation and implementation of digital asset management and preservation in the further education setting, and demonstrate its application'.
Lead partner: John Wheatley College
Subject: Digital preservation solutions
Country: UK

Mandate (Managing Digital Assets in Tertiary Education) is a UK project examining the management of unstructured electronic content with regard to the particular requirements of the further education (FE) sector. MANDATE is funded by the Joint Information Systems Committee (JISC) as part of its Supporting Digital Preservation and Asset Management in Institutions Programme, and is a partnership between the Centre for Digital Library Research and the John

Wheatley College in Glasgow, supported by the Scottish Library and Information Council.

By investigating the variety of creation and utilization processes and practices within the college, MANDATE aims to produce workflow models and templates specifically for wider application among further education institutions.

A draft toolkit derived from the John Wheatley College case study, scheduled to end in 2006, is available on the website. Aimed at managers and administrative and technical staff looking at digital asset management, the online toolkit offers detailed guidance on managing digital content in the FE environment with hyperlinks to relevant organizations and appraisals of existing systems and approaches. The MANDATE website also provides project and meeting papers, and contact information.

MetaArchive

www.metaarchive.org/

A process to 'develop a cooperative for the preservation of at-risk digital content with a particular content focus: the culture and history of the American South' and testing LOCKSS as the technology infrastructure.

Lead partner: Emory University
Subject: Topic-specific web archiving
Country: USA

MetaArchive is a three-year digital preservation project involving Emory University in Georgia, Georgia Tech, Virginia Tech, Florida State University, Auburn University in Alabama, the University of Louisville in Kentucky and the Library of Congress. Coming under the National Digital Information Infrastructure and Preservation Program (NDIIPP) and developing work conducted in the MetaScholar Initiative, MetaArchive was launched in 2004.

The primary concern of MetaArchive's work is the culture and history of the American South. The group selects prioritized content in this subject area held by members and is developing agreements and a distributed and secure technical infrastructure based on the

LOCKSS (LOts of Copies Keeps Stuff Safe) system.

The MetaArchive website is intended to act as a locus for sharing knowledge and therefore provides comprehensive project documentation, together with hyperlinks to relevant organizations, projects and tools, information on events and contact details.

National Archives

www.nationalarchives.gov.uk/preservation/digital.htm
The Digital Preservation department is 'playing an active role in storing and preserving digital material' for government departments and the public sector.
Subject: Electronic records management
Country: UK

The National Archives of England, Wales and the United Kingdom has a dedicated Digital Preservation Department, set up in 2001, to fulfil its legal obligation as a national deposit repository.

Electronic Records Online, a pilot repository of government documents, has been live since 2003, and users may browse for records of all types, such as government inquiries, royal commissions and parliamentary committees, and request copies. For the UK Government Web Archive, most government departmental websites are harvested weekly or at six-month intervals. The department conducts research into data formats and migration processes, with information on the trials in progress.

PRONOM is a searchable online registry of technical information to which website visitors can contribute, and also includes tools and services, such as DROID, an automatic file identification mechanism and PRONOM's Unique Identifier (PUID).

The UK National Archives website also provides guidance notes and technical papers, and offers lists of similar organizations and initiatives plus events and reports.

National Geospatial Digital Archive

http://ngda.org/index.php

The purpose is to establish a 'network for the archiving of geospatial images and data'.
Lead partners: University of California – Santa Barbara, Stanford University
Subject: Geospatial data archiving
Country: USA

Under the auspices of the National Digital Information Infrastructure and Preservation Program (NDIIPP) run by the US Library of Congress, the University of California – Santa Barbara, and Stanford University are collaborating on the National Geospatial Digital Archive (NGDA).

The NGDA project intends to establish a national network to archive geospatial information, including images, seek and archive potentially endangered geospatial data, and work on producing best-practice guidelines for presenting such data. It also aims to create policy agreements on inter-institutional procedures and collaborations as well as boosting long-term communication.

Visitors to the website can download project paperwork and documents on the work produced by the NGDA, and view contact details. The NGDA hosts meetings and workshops on achieving a federation of specialist archivists and also provides summaries and many presentations from these events on its website.

nestor

www.langzeitarchivierung.de/index.php?newlang=ger
'Network of Expertise in Long-Term Storage and Long-Term availability of Digital Resources in Germany.'
Lead partner: Die Deutsche Bibliothek
Subject: Centre of excellence
Country: Germany

The aim of nestor (Network of Expertise in Long-term Storage of Digital Resources) is to foster expertise in long-term management of digital information in Germany by creating an umbrella for such activities. Nestor concludes in mid-2006. Partners in the project are

the Deutsche Bibliothek, Niedersächsische Staats- und Universitäts-
bibliothek Göttingen, Computer- und Medienservice und Univer-
sitätsbibliothek der Humboldt-Universität zu Berlin, Bayerische
Staatsbibliothek in Munich, Generaldirektion der Staatlichen Archive
Bayerns, Institut für Museumskunde and the Bundesarchiv.

Nestor plans to produce an information resource for institutions
and individuals working in the field of digital management, and to
improve collaboration among libraries, museums and all
organizations using digital content. Nestor aims to disseminate best-
practice guidance and standards, and to enhance general awareness
of digital preservation in addition to laying the foundations for a
permanent organization to co-ordinate and represent digital
archiving in Germany.

This German- and English-language website holds detailed project
information, news of events and publications posted by members,
downloadable documents, papers from conferences and workshops,
questionnaires and statistics, and a newsletter plus archive. Visitors
can access the Subject Gateway, a searchable database of PADI and
nestor articles and case studies; propose additions to the database;
search for individuals by specialism, institution and place; participate
in surveys; and give feedback. Members may log in to post comments,
send news and personalize content. Some pages are in German only.

Netarchive.dk

http://netarchive.dk/index-en.php
The main aims are 'collecting and preserving the Danish portion of
the internet' as required under legal deposit law.
Lead partners: Statsbiblioteket, Det Kongelige Bibliotek
Subject: Domain-specific web archiving
Country: Denmark

Since July 2005 the State and University Library and the Royal Library
in Denmark have been required to archive Danish internet material.

The Netarkivet (Netarchive) collection is not open to the public.
Access is limited to research purposes with the prior permission of
the Danish Data Protection Agency.

The Netarkivet initiative website is in Danish and English, with some pages in Danish only. It offers news, links, FAQs, contact details and downloadable papers on subjects arising from the work conducted in the harvesting and archiving process. Under the GNU Public Licence website visitors may also freely download source code developed by Netarkivet.

New Zealand Trusted Digital Repository

www.natlib.govt.nz/bin/media/pr?item=1085885702
To establish 'a trusted digital repository . . . for the long-term preservation and maintenance of digital materials aimed at providing New Zealanders access to their digital heritage'.
Lead partner: National Library of New Zealand
Subject: Digital repository development
Country: New Zealand

As part of its 2003 Digital Strategy, the National Library of New Zealand created a digital repository in 2004 to collect and manage New Zealand online electronic material.

New Zealand websites are being harvested periodically along with particular websites such as government and event-related sites, for example those relating to the 2003 Americas Cup. In addition to selected material from the National Library's current collections of digital information, unpublished content created by New Zealanders, such as drafts of creative work, are included.

The National Library's website presents information in English and Maori, with summary information about the project available.

North Carolina Geospatial Data Archiving Project (NCGDAP)

www.lib.ncsu.edu/ncgdap/
The focus is 'on collection and preservation of digital geospatial data resources from state and local government agencies in North Carolina'.
Lead partner: North Carolina State University
Subject: Geospatial data archiving
Country: USA

One of the projects run under the US Library of Congress's National Digital Information Infrastructure and Preservation Program (NDIIPP), the North Carolina Geospatial Data Archiving Project is jointly managed by the North Carolina State University Libraries and the North Carolina Center for Geographic Information and Analysis (CGIA). Project partners are the Geographic Information Coordinating Council (GICC) and NC OneMap.

Launched in 2004, the project is concerned with gathering and preserving digital geospatial data created within government organizations in North Carolina. A key aim is the foundation of a digital repository technical framework for geospatial information using open-source software such as DSpace. Other goals are to improve current geospatial metadata using Metadata Encoding and Transmission Standards (METS), to examine automated data identification and capture techniques employing OpenGeoSpatial Consortium approaches, and to produce a pattern for archiving and time-series development.

The website offers information on research topics related to the project, such as file formats and spatial databases, project documents and presentations, links to relevant institutions, projects and themes, and contact details.

OCLC Digital Archive

www.oclc.org/digitalarchive/default.htm
A system that 'offers real-world solutions for the challenges of archiving and preservation in the virtual world'.
Lead partner: OCLC
Subject: Digital repositories
Country: USA

The international library organization OCLC provides a Digital Archive tool to manage digital collections.

Developed from the OAIS (Reference Model for an Open Archival Information System) ISO standards and METS (Metadata Encoding and Transmission Standard), OCLC Digital Archive is a third-party repository that allows users to create their own digital archives and is designed to be used with other OCLC tools. Users may harvest web content individually or archive whole electronic collections and specify the level of access to such resources. The digital collections are available in several ways, including FirstSearch, Connexion or website.

The website offers comprehensive information about the Digital Archive tool, including order methods and support documentation.

Our Digital Island

http://odi.statelibrary.tas.gov.au/
It 'provides access to Tasmanian Web sites that have been preserved for posterity by the State Library of Tasmania'.
Lead partner: State Library of Tasmania
Subject: Domain-specific web archiving
Country: Australia

The State Library of Tasmania in Australia provides public access to its archive of Tasmanian websites via Our Digital Island. Visitors can browse by subject or title and can suggest a site for archiving. Users click on a thumbnail image and then access the archived website, although all the original functionality may not be preserved.

PANDAS: PANDORA Digital Archiving System

http://pandora.nla.gov.au/pandas.html
PANDAS has been 'developed to provide an integrated, web-based, web archiving management system'.
Lead partner: National Library of Australia
Subject: Digital archiving system
Country: Australia

The National Library of Australia launched the PANDORA Digital Archiving System (PANDAS) in 2001, a web-based tool to manage the archiving of web content, particularly its PANDORA digital archive. Partner institutions are the Australian Institute of Aboriginal and Torres Strait Islander Studies, the Australian War Memorial, the

National Film and Sound Archive (ScreenSound Australia), the Northern Territory Library and Information Service; the State Library of New South Wales, the State Library of Queensland, the State Library of South Australia, the State Library of Victoria and the State Library of Western Australia.

Staff in the partner organizations use PANDAS to select, gather, create and manage specialist digital content that is then publicly available via the PANDORA website. PANDAS also supports management functions such as access restrictions and detailed management reports, using a unique, system-specific URL. End-users can employ a citation service which is designed to overcome any future structural alterations of the PANDAS website.

The website provides comprehensive technical information and project background. The National Library plans to make the PANDAS software freely available.

paradigm: Personal Archives Accessible in Digital Media

www.paradigm.ac.uk/

The chief aim is to 'explore the issues involved in preserving digital private papers through gaining practical experience in accessioning and ingesting digital private papers into digital repositories, and processing these in line with archival and digital preservation requirements'.

Lead partners: University of Oxford, University of Manchester
Subject: Personal archives
Country: UK

The two-year Personal Archives Accessible in Digital Media (paradigm) project was set up in January 2005 to investigate the preservation of digital personal papers. Coming under the Joint Information Systems Committee (JISC) programme Supporting Institutional Digital Preservation and Asset Management, paradigm employs the resources of the Bodleian Library and the John Rylands University Library in Manchester.

The Bodleian holds the Conservative Party Archives, while the Rylands Library has close relations with the Labour History Archives and Study Centre (LHASC). Covering the two chief political parties in the UK, the project takes advantage of these collections while working outside the formal management of these archives, which do not contain private papers. The project involves the active participation of a politician from each of these parties who is creating different types of electronic content that may be suitable for archiving purposes. A key goal of the paradigm project is to produce guidance on the harmonization of traditional archiving processes and digital content archiving, following the open-standard Open Archival Information System (OAIS) model. Other goals include the staged production of a best-practice workbook discussing issues relating to the archiving of digital private papers; the creation of policy templates for institutional use; and testing digital repository tools DSpace and Fedora. Another central objective is to examine the feasibility of utilizing the networked access potential of the Archives Hub, which holds information on archives held in British higher education institutions.

The paradigm website provides extensive project material, including the Workbook on Digital Private Papers and papers given by project staff, plus contact details and information on news and events.

PAT Project: Persistent Archives Testbed

www.sdsc.edu/PAT/

The goal is 'to conduct case studies that test the ability to implement the SDSC's Storage Resource Broker (SRB) data grid . . . technology using a variety of archival collections. This is an optimal opportunity to test a community model for electronic records management, with archival and technological functions practically and appropriately allocated in a distributed network.'

Lead partner: San Diego Supercomputer Center (SDSC)
Subject: Digital preservation solutions
Country: USA

The US project PAT (Persistent Archives Testbed) involves the San Diego Supercomputer Center (SDSC), the Michigan Department of History, Arts and Libraries, the Ohio Historical Society, Kentucky

Department for Libraries and Archives, Minnesota Historical Society and Stanford Linear Accelerator Archives (SLAC) and History Office. Other partners include National Archives and Records Administration (NARA), California State Archives, Kansas State Historical Society, University of Illinois Urbana-Champaign Archives, Yale Manuscripts and Archives, UCLA Center for Information as Evidence, National Archives of Korea, the *Los Angeles Times*, the Getty Research Institute, Georgia Tech, the University of Florida, the University of California and Ashford Computing.

Funded by the National Historical Publications and Records Commission, PAT was set up in 2004 to build on the capabilities of the SDSC's Storage Resource Broker (SRB). The SRB is a distributed network for managing electronic records of all kinds, which removes electronic content from its original infrastructure while retaining the context and structure required to safeguard its meaning and authenticity. Also known as the Archivist Grid, PAT's chief goals are to utilize the variety of electronic content of its partners to establish a Persistent Archives Testbed, test the automation of parts of the archival process – identification, deposition, description, preservation and availability – at individual sites and to produce case studies.

The PAT website holds comprehensive project information, contact details and a brief glossary.

PORTICO

www.portico.org/
'The mission of Portico is to preserve scholarly literature published in electronic form and to ensure that these materials remain accessible to future scholars, researchers, and students.'
Lead partner: Ithaka
Subject: Digital archiving solution
Country: USA

Established in 2005, Portico is a digital archiving service that continues the work begun in the Mellon Foundation's 2002 E-Journal Archiving Program, now Ithaka. Funded initially by the Andrew W. Mellon Foundation, Ithaka, Library of Congress and JSTOR, Portico now solicits contributions from journal publishers and libraries.

The main preservation approach Portico employs is the migration of electronic content from one file format to another to circumvent technological obsolescence. Portico's archival format derives from the open-standard Journal Archiving and Interchange DTD and uses source files supplied by publishers.

The website offers background material on the initiative, including news, conference papers presented by staff, and details of the advisory committee and participating publishing houses.

PRESERV: PReservation Eprint SERVices

http://preserv.eprints.org/
PRESERV is a 'project investigating and developing infrastructural digital preservation services for institutional repositories'.
Lead partner: Southampton University
Subject: Digital preservation services
Country: UK

The PRESERV project is funded by the Joint Information Systems Committee (JISC) as part of its Supporting Digital Preservation and Asset Management in Institutions Programme. It aims to examine and develop digital preservation services for archives, with a focus on the technical framework. Southampton University, the National Archives, the British Library and University of Oxford are partners in PRESERV, which runs from 2005 to 2007.

PRESERV utilizes the Open Archival Information System (OAIS) model for institutional archives and Eprints software, one of the leading institutional repository systems, with PRONOM software to handle file formats. The project aims to pilot an ingest service that is integrated into the Eprints deposit process and to develop a software-independent preservation archive based on OAI.

The PRESERV website provides project material including news, papers and presentations, and a bibliography of digital preservation resources.

Preserving Digital Public Television

www.ptvdigitalarchive.org/
The principal aim is to design a 'preservation repository that the [American] public television system can afford to maintain and use'.
Lead partner: Channel 13/WNET, New York (Educational Broadcasting Corporation)
Subject: Topic-specific web archiving
Country: USA

The project Preserving Digital Public Television comes under the National Digital Information Infrastructure Preservation Program (NDIIPP) of the Library of Congress. Its remit is to design a repository for television programmes produced, and increasingly transmitted, digitally. The EBC (Educational Broadcasting Corporation) Thirteen/WNET station, PBS (Public Broadcasting Service) and WGBH public television companies are partners in this endeavour, along with New York University.

The project intends to produce standards, processes and workflows to preserve digital television assets long term, both as whole programmes and the components that constitute programmes. These will be tested in a practical environment and the evaluations disseminated to the wider industry.

This project utilizes work already conducted by organizations such as the Association of Moving Image Archivists (AMIA) as well as project partners, such as WGBH's Universal Preservation Format, which is a 'wrapper' for software-independent content, and WGBH's Media Archives and Preservation Center, which holds programming from the 1960s onwards.

The project website provides exhaustive project information, including technical details, news of events, links to relevant resources and contact information.

PrestoSpace: Preservation towards Storage and Access: Standardised Practices for Audiovisual Contents in Europe

www.prestospace.org/
The 'objective is to provide technical solutions and integrated systems

for digital preservation of all types of audiovisual collections. The project intends to provide tangible results in the domain of preservation, restoration, storage and archive management, content description, delivery and access.'

Lead partner: Institut national de l'audiovisuel
Subject: Archiving audiovisual materials
Country: Europe

PrestoSpace falls under the European Commission's Sixth Framework Programme for Research Theme of Information Society Technologies. Lasting from 2004 to 2007, the PrestoSpace project is based at the Institut national de l'audiovisuel (Ina) in France and involves commercial and non-commercial broadcasting and production organizations, archive owners and academic and research institutions from around Europe. Seven core partners comprise the steering board, with some 30+ associate partners.

The project intends to follow an integrated 'preservation factory' approach, entailing a partly automated technical solution to the problems associated with migrating existing analogue audiovisual content into digital formats and preserving this content. The main goal of PrestoSpace is to produce amenities and services for archiving audiovisual content, with specific objectives in the areas of preservation, restoration, management, metadata, storage and access. A key driver is the growing pan-European need to create scalable integrated systems that are viable within legal and commercial constraints.

Comprehensive information on the project is available on the PrestoSpace website, including presentation papers, archived details of meetings, news and events, and training resources. Website visitors can register to receive the newsletter and participate in the online forum, and may complete a questionnaire on audiovisual holdings across Europe. The public and archivists may browse the 'Digitization and Storage Guide' subsite, which offers material and tools to assist digitization projects. Project members may log into a restricted area.

reUSE

www2.uibk.ac.at/reuse/

The scheme will 'focus on the publications of public sector institutions. Together with the printed material the digital originals will be collected, preserved and made available.'

Lead partner: University Library of Innsbruck
Subject: Digital archiving solution
Country: Austria

The two-year reUSE project is based at the University of Innsbruck, Austria, and is a European Commission-funded initiative, under its eContent programme, to create integrated print and digital collections contributed by public sector archives. reUSE is a collaboration among the National and University Library of Slovenia, the National Library of Estonia, the Media and Library Centre of Humboldt University, Berlin, the National Library of Austria, Austrian Literature Online (composed of the University Library of Innsbruck, the University Library of Graz and the University of Linz), the National Library of Germany and the University of Lubljana.

The volume of public sector publications in electronic formats is increasing but the archiving focus has remained on printed matter. Set up in 2004, the reUSE project is a multi-partner initiative to co-ordinate the collection and management of digital artefacts that will be accessible to users through existing library access mechanisms, such as electronic catalogues. Pilot projects were evaluated to enable publishers and institutions to use best the various approaches used by different partners to suit their circumstances. Standards of interoperability and usability across Europe are key to the project.

The English-language website provides project material, including reports and surveys, plus details of partner organizations that are demonstrators of reUSE technology and procedures, and contact information.

SHERPA DP: Creating a Persistent Preservation Environment for Institutional Repositories

http://ahds.ac.uk/about/projects/sherpa-dp/

The objective is to 'create a collaborative, shared preservation environment for the SHERPA project framed around the OAIS Reference Model'.
Lead partner: Arts and Humanities Data Service (AHDS)
Subject: Digital preservation solutions
Country: UK

A project established by the UK Arts and Humanities Data Service (AHDS), SHERPA DP is a two-year project funded by the Joint Information Systems Committee (JISC) and Consortium of University Research Libraries (CURL) under the FAIR programme, which investigated metadata and preservation. SHERPA DP aims to produce a collaborative preservation context for the SHERPA project, which is concerned with developing open-access digital collections in research universities to promote knowledge-sharing. The University of Nottingham is lead institution on SHERPA DP and other partners are the University of Edinburgh, the University of Glasgow, the White Rose Partnership of the universities of Leeds, Sheffield and York, and the London LEAP Consortium, comprising University College London, Birkbeck, Imperial, King's College London, the London School of Economics (LSE), the School of Oriental and African Studies (SOAS) and Royal Holloway.

Based on a disaggregated OAIS Reference Model, SHERPA DP – which examines central issues in disseminating research data, such as intellectual property rights – integrates the SHERPA system with AHDS's preservation repository in a manner that allows SHERPA repositories to concentrate on their collection work while AHDS provides a shared space specifically for preservation. The work undertaken into management, technical and metadata requirements and workflow processes is intended to produce a body of material for wider dissemination, a Digital Preservation User Guide. SHERPA DP is looking in particular at the application of open-source and grid technologies in long-term digital archiving, in addition to DSpace and EPrints software.

The project website offers detailed material on the initiative.

Sound Directions: Digital Preservation and Access for Global Audio Heritage

www.dlib.indiana.edu/projects/sounddirections/
An archiving project to 'create best practices and test emerging standards for digital preservation of archival audio'.
Lead partner: University of Indiana
Subject: Audio archives solution
Country: USA

Funded by the National Endowment for the Humanities, Sound Directions is an 18-month project run by the Indiana University Archives of Traditional Music (ATM) and the Archive of World Music (AWM) at Harvard University. Beginning in early 2005, Sound Directions is an initiative to develop digital archiving technologies and procedures for preservation of audio content.

The chief goal of producing compatible packages of audio preservation software and protocols derives from investigation of the lifecycle of digital audio material, including in many cases conversion from analogue to digital formats, based on pilot projects carried out individually by each university. Other major aims are to create best practice and evaluate emerging standards, to establish digital archiving plans at each university, and to preserve valuable field recordings of national interest that are currently at risk.

The website provides comprehensive project documentation, including a slideshow of photographs, and contact details.

Sun Center of Excellence for Trusted Digital Repositories

www.coe.hu-berlin.de/sun/software/sun/index_html
The goal is to develop 'a framework . . . to handle preservation mechanisms within a trusted digital archive, a user interface for accessing the trusted digital archives and methods to apply digital signatures and time stamps to the digital documents'.
Lead partner: University Library of Innsbruck
Subject: Digital repository development
Country: Austria

A partnership of the Austrian Literature Online Consortium (ALO), Humboldt University Berlin, XiCrypt GmbH in Austria, and Sun Microsystems, the Sun Center of Excellence for Trusted Digital Repositories aims to produce and implement a digital repository model that builds on the Open Archival Information System (OAIS) Reference Model and the RLG report on Trusted Repositories.

Set up in 2004, the Center of Excellence is constructing an architecture to manage preservation mechanisms in a digital archive, a user interface to access holdings, and ways of adding digital signatures and time stamps to electronic information, developing previous work undertaken by individual partners.

The website provides material on the work of the Center of Excellence, and contact details.

Sun Centre of Excellence for Digital Futures in Libraries

www.lianza.org.nz/news/newsroom/news1131595738.html

The aim is to 'develop an advanced information lifecycle management system, which will serve as an international model for digital repositories and preservation management'.

Lead partner: National Library of New Zealand
Subject: Lifecycle management
Country: New Zealand

In late 2005 the National Library of New Zealand was named as an international model for electronic heritage preservation by the Sun Microsystems Centre of Excellence for Digital Futures in Libraries programme.

The government of New Zealand has established a nationwide Digital Strategy, a key plank of which is the National Content Strategy. The National Library is running the National Digital Heritage Archive (NDHA) scheme, which is a major contributor to the latter. Recognizing the ambition and scope of the project, the award inaugurates a partnership between Sun and the National Library to work on the management of the lifecycle of digital artefacts. It is envisaged that the results of this work in technology and best practice will be applicable to other digital repositories around the world.

TAPE: Training for Audiovisual Preservation in Europe

www.tape-online.net/

The principal aim is 'to explore the requirements for continued access to audiovisual materials and the application of new technologies for opening up collections that provide living documentation of the world of the 20th century'.

Lead partner: European Commission on Preservation and Access
Subject: Audiovisual preservation
Country: Europe

Part of the European Union's Culture 2000 scheme, the TAPE (Training for Audiovisual Preservation in Europe) project aims to improve awareness and training across Europe. Primary partners are the European Commission on Preservation and Access (ECPA) based in Amsterdam in the Netherlands, the Finnish Jazz and Pop Archive (JAPA), the Head Office of the State Archives (NDAP) in Poland, Phonogrammarchiv (PHA) at the Austrian Academy of Sciences (OEAW) and the Reproduction, Binding and Restoration Centre for the State Archives of Italy (CFLR), with associate partners located around Europe.

Formally beginning in 2004, TAPE is a three-year project that concentrates on working with archives held outside the main national institutions and which have the majority of their collections in other materials. Its chief objective is to aid plans to preserve audiovisual electronic data by creating a training programme in audiovisual preservation for non-specialists. Assisting collaboration between technological research and cultural heritage institutions is also a core goal. TAPE plans to produce a survey of such collections, collate best practice and develop training approaches and materials, to be disseminated in courses and publications.

The TAPE website provides detailed project information, including news of events, meetings and papers, and contact information for partners. Website visitors can register for European or national training, sign up to receive the discussion list and browse through a database of literature.

Tufts and Yale: Fedora and the Preservation of University Records

http://dca.tufts.edu/features/nhprc/index.html

'To synthesize electronic records preservation research with digital library repository research in an effort to develop systems capable of preserving university electronic records at both institutions. This project will test the potential of Fedora (the Flexible Extensible Digital Object and Repository Architecture) to serve as the architecture for such an electronic records preservation system.'

Lead partners: Tufts University, Yale University

Subject: Electronic records preservation

Country: USA

The US National Historical Publications and Records Commission (NHPRC)'s Electronic Records Project is intended to test the capacity of Fedora (the Flexible Extensible Digital Object and Repository Architecture) to be used as architecture for a preservation system. The 18-month project is run by Digital Collections and Archive (DCA) at Tufts University along with Manuscripts and Archives (MSSA) of Yale University Library.

FEDORA is a well established method of managing digital libraries and this project, begun in July 2004, applies the principles of archiving to investigate the feasibility of using this tool simultaneously to manage a digital library and to meet the requirements of a digital repository.

The website offers project information, such as plans, presentations and reports, plus contact information.

Virtual Archives Laboratory (VAL)

www.archives.gov/era/research/virtual-archives-lab.html

The objective is 'to design and test a model for a Federated Persistent Archives that will examine and address requirements for large-scale, long-term preservation of electronic records'.

Lead partner: US National Archives

Subject: Digital preservation testbed

Country: USA

Part of the US National Archives and Records Administration (NARA), the Electronic Records Archive (ERA) hosts the Virtual Archives Laboratory (VAL).

Set up in 2004, VAL is an environment provided to test technologies for digital collections management and archival initiatives, thereby aiding collaborative research among ERA partnerships. Project partners such as the San Diego Supercomputer Center (SDSC), the University of Maryland Institute for Advanced Computer Studies (UMIACS), and the US Army Research Laboratory (ARL) experiment with prototypes in VAL. Projects tested in VAL include the Persistent Archives Project, which plans to develop software for a federated model for dispersed, large collections of electronic records.

The website provides a brief overview of VAL's mission and work.

Web Archiving Consortium

www.webarchive.org.uk/
A 'consortium of six leading UK institutions . . . working collaboratively on a project to develop a test-bed for selective archiving of UK websites'.
Lead partner: British Library
Subject: Domain-specific web archiving
Country: UK

The UK Web Archiving Consortium is a collaborative initiative to develop a pilot for archiving selected UK websites. The lead partner on this two-year project is the British Library; other partners are the National Archives, the National Library of Wales, the National Library of Scotland, the Joint Information Systems Committee (JISC) and the Wellcome Trust.

The project began in 2004 and utilizes PANDAS software, with each institution focusing on material in its specialist field. The planned archive is browsable and searchable through the website; it is similar to the PANDORA archive established by the National Library of Australia.

The website offers project information, such as background

material, reports, presentations and papers, in addition to providing access to the archive itself. Website visitors can also suggest sites for archiving consideration.

WebArchiv: Archive of the Czech Web

http://en.webarchiv.cz/
'The main aim of the WebArchiv project is to implement a comprehensive solution in the field of archiving of the national web, i.e. [Czech] online-born documents. That includes tools and methods for collecting, archiving and preserving web resources as well as providing long-term access to them.'
Lead partner: National Library of the Czech Republic
Subject: National web archiving
Country: Czech Republic

Launched in 2000, the WebArchiv was set up to archive Czech online materials. Led by the National Library of the Czech Republic as part of its national legal deposit obligations, the WebArchiv initiative has several partners, including the Moravian Library and the Institute of Computer Science at Masaryk University.

The WebArchiv is currently in the pilot stage, and is concerned with establishing tools and methodology for harvesting, archiving, preserving and managing long-term access to online content. Selective preservation and large-scale automated gathering of Czech-language web material are both being tested as selection approaches.

The website provides Czech-language project information, presentations and papers. Background information and criteria for selection and preservation are available in English, along with contact details.

Web Archiving Program

www.rlg.org/en/page.php?Page_ID=399&projGo.x=25&projGo.y=15
The objective is to 'help RLG members create archives of Web-based information, capturing this important source of information for the historical record and future research'.

Lead partner: RLG (Research Libraries Group)
Subject: web archiving
Country: USA

In 2006 RLG initiated a programme of activities designed to help its members around the world – national libraries, archives, museums, universities and historical societies – handle the issues associated with archiving web material.

The Web Archiving Program covers elements such as collaboration and knowledge-sharing, metadata, usability, intellectual property, practical procedures for archiving web content and assessment of specialist services and software. RLG plans to offer members the Internet Archive's Archive-It tool.

The website provides contact details and a summary of the project's scope.

The Web at Risk: A Distributed Approach to Preserving Our Nation's Political Cultural Heritage

www.cdlib.org/inside/projects/preservation/webatrisk/
The aim is to 'develop web archiving tools that will be used by libraries to capture, curate, and preserve collections of web-based government and political information'.
Lead partner: California Digital Library
Subject: Topic-specific web archiving
Country: USA

The Web at Risk: A Distributed Approach to Preserving Our Nation's Political Cultural Heritage project is a three-year initiative to develop web archiving tools focusing on online government and political content. Funded by the Library of Congress National Digital Information Infrastructure and Preservation Programme (NDIIPP), the Web at Risk scheme was set up in 2004 and was based at the California Digital Library (CDL). Advised by the National Library of France, the project partners include New York University, the University of North Texas, the Texas Center for Digital Knowledge, San Diego Supercomputer Center (SDSC), Stanford University, Sun

Microsystems Inc., Arizona State Library and Archive and other libraries in the University of California.

Building on earlier research undertaken by CDL, the project concentrated on developing tools to aid libraries in gathering, managing and archiving digital political material, particularly local activities, such as the 2003 California gubernatorial recall election. The software in development is open source, modular and intended to be extensible. This allows it to be used in conjunction with existing processes and archives to create seven separate digital collections. Another major aim of the project is to produce guidelines, case studies and best-practice advice for libraries working in this area.

The website provides project information and contact details.

Bibliography

All the references in the text are to be found here, as well as some key works on various aspects on digital preservation that are not explicitly referred to in the text. There are many useful bibliographies on digital preservation to be found online, compiled by some of the key organizations concerned with digital preservation. These include the Arts and Humanities Data Service, http://ahds.ac.uk/preservation/bibliography.htm, and the Preserv Project, at http://preserv.eprints.org/Preserv-bibliography.html.

Erpanet has a bibliography of digital preservation policies available at www.erpanet.org/assessments/ERPANETbibliography_Policies.pdf, and PADI (Preserving Access to Digital Information) has put online a large, annotated bibliography on long-term digital preservation at www.nla.gov.au/padi/topics/18.html. The Digital Preservation Coalition (DPC) also has a useful 'What's new in digital preservation' service which it runs jointly with PADI. This is to be found at www.dpconline.org/graphics/whatsnew/. All URLs were valid and in working order on 19 June 2006 unless dated otherwise.

5th International Web Archiving Workshop (IWAW05), www.iwaw.net/05/index.html.

AAF Association, http://aafassociation.org/index.html.

Abiteboul, S. et al. (2002) A First Experience in Archiving the French Web. In Agosti, M. and Thanos, C. (eds), *Research and Advanced Technology for Digital Libraries: 6th European Conference, ECDL 2002, Rome, Italy, September 16–18, 2002: proceedings,*

Lecture Notes in Computer Science, vol. 2458, Berlin, Springer.

Abrams, S. L. (2005) Establishing a Global Digital Format Registry, *Library Trends*, **54** (1), 125–43.

Abrams, S. and Seaman, D. (2003) Towards a Global Digital Format Registry. In *World Library and Information Congress: 69th IFLA General Conference and Council, Berlin, Germany, 1–9 August 2003*, The Hague, IFLA, www.ifla.org/IV/ifla69/papers/128e-Abrams_Seaman.pdf.

Adams, D. (1999) How to Stop Worrying and Learn to Love the Internet, *The Sunday Times*, (29 August), www.douglasadams.com/dna/19990901-00-a.html.

Antoniol, G. et al. (1999) Web Sites: files, programs or databases? In Tilley, S. (ed.), *Proceedings of WSE '99: 1st International Workshop on Web Site Evolution, October 5, 1999, Atlanta, GA*, Riverside, Web Site Evolution, www.websiteevolution.org/1999/WSE99.pdf.

Archive Server Deposit.ddb.de, http://deposit.ddb.de/index_e.htm.

Archive-it, www.archive-it.org/.

Arms, C. and Fleischhauer, C. (2004) Sustainability Factors. In *Sustainability of Digital Formats: planning for Library of Congress collections*, Washington DC, Library of Congress, www.digitalpreservation.gov/formats/sustain/sustain.shtml.

Arvidson, A. (2002) The Collection of Swedish Web Pages at the Royal Library: the web heritage of Sweden. In *68th IFLA Council and General Conference, August 18–24, 2002, Glasgow, Scotland*, The Hague, IFLA, www.ifla.org/IV/ifla68/papers/111-163e.pdf.

Arvidson, A., Persson, K. and Mannerheim, J. (2000) The Kulturarw³ Project: the Royal Swedish Web Archiw3e: an example of 'complete' collection of web pages. In *66th IFLA Council and General Conference, Jerusalem, Israel, 13–18 August 2000*, The Hague, IFLA, www.ifla.org/IV/ifla66/papers/154-157e.htm.

Aschenbrenner, A. and Kaiser, M. (2005) *White Paper on Digital Repositories*, Innsbruck, reUSE Project, www2.uibk.ac.at/reuse/docs/reuse-d11_whitepaper_10.pdf.

Ashley, K. (1999) Digital Archive Costs: facts and fallacies. In European Commission (ed.), *Proceedings of the DLM-Forum on Electronic Records, Brussels, 18–19 October 1999*, Luxembourg, Office for

Official Publications of the European Communities, 121–8,
http://europa.eu.int/ISPO/dlm/dlm99/dlm_proceed99_03.pdf.

Audio Engineering Society (2002) *Process History Metadata Draft*,
unpublished.

Australian National University et al. (2003) *Towards an Australian
Partnership for Sustainable Repositories: a national infrastructure
development proposal*, Canberra, Australian National University,
www.apsr.edu.au/documents/APSR.pdf.

Ayre, C. and Muir, A. (2004) *Right to Preserve? The Copyright and
Licensing for Digital Preservation Project final report*, Leicestershire,
Department of Information Science, Loughborough University,
www.lboro.ac.uk/departments/ls/disresearch/CLDP/Project_
reports.htm.

Badenoch, D. et al. (1994) The Value of Information. In Feeney, M.
and Grieves, M. (eds), *The Value and Impact of Information*,
London, Bowker Saur.

Bailey, S. and Thompson, D. (2006) UKWAC: building the UK's first
public Web archive, *D-Lib Magazine*, **12** (1),
http://dlib.org/dlib/january06/thompson/01thompson.html.

BAT: BnfArcTools, http://bibnum.bnf.fr/downloads/bat/.

BBC (2002) Digital Domesday Book Unlocked, *BBC News*, (2 December), http://news.bbc.co.uk/1/hi/technology/2534391.stm.

Beagrie, N. (2003) *National Digital Preservation Initiatives: an overview
of developments in Australia, France, the Netherlands, and the United
Kingdom and of related international activity*, Washington DC,
Council on Library and Information Resources and Library of
Congress.

Beagrie, N. and Jones, M. (2001) *Preservation Management of Digital
Materials: a handbook*, London, British Library,
www.dpconline.org/graphics/handbook/.

Bearman, D. (1999) Reality and Chimeras in the Preservation of
Electronic Records, *D-Lib Magazine*, **5** (4),
www.dlib.org/dlib/april99/bearman/04bearman.html.

Bearman, D. and Trant, J. (1998) Authenticity of Digital Resources:
towards a statement of requirements in the research process,
D-Lib Magazine, (June), 1–12,
www.dlib.org/dlib/june98/06bearman.html.

Bekaert, J., Hochstenbach, P. and Van de Sompel, H. (2003) Using MPEG-21 DIDL to Represent Complex Digital Objects in the Los Alamos National Laboratory Digital Library, *D-Lib Magazine*, **9** (11), www.dlib.org/dlib/november03/bekaert/11bekaert.html.

Benjamin, W. (1992) The Work of Art in an Age of Mechanical Illustration, *Illuminations*, Fontana.

Bergman, M. (2001) The Deep Web: surfacing hidden value, *Journal of Electronic Publishing*, (August), www.press.umich.edu/jep/07-01/bergman.html.

Berners-Lee, T. (1994) *Universal Resource Identifiers in WWW: a unifying syntax for the expression of names and addresses of objects on the network as used in the world-wide web*, RFC 1630, unpublished, www.w3.org/Addressing/rfc1630.txt.

Berners-Lee, T. et al. (1994) The World-Wide Web, *Communications of the ACM*, **37** (8), 76–82.

Bibliothèque nationale de France (n.d.) *Dépôt Légal Internet à la BnF*, Paris, Bibliothèque nationale de France, www.bnf.fr/pages/infopro/depotleg/dl-internet_intro.htm.

Bickner, R. (1983) Concepts of Economic Cost. In King, D., Roderer, N. and Olsen, H. (eds), *Key Papers in the Economics of Information*, White Plains, NY, Knowledge Industry Publications.

Bowman, L. M. (2001) Bush Camp Takes Charge of Whitehouse.gov in Transition, *CNET News.com*, (9 January), http://news.com.com/2009-1023-250743.html.

Boyko, A. (2004) *Test Bed Taxonomy for Crawler*, Washington DC, Metrics and Testbed Working Group, International Internet Preservation Consortium, www.netpreserve.org/publications/reports.php?id=002.

British Academy (2004) *'That Full Complement of Riches': the contributions of the arts, humanities, and social sciences to the nation's wealth*, London, British Academy, www.britac.ac.uk/reports/contribution/index.html.

British Library (2003) *£363 Million a Year Knowledge Dividend to UK Economy: UK national library reveals results of ground-breaking research*, London, British Library, (10 December), www.bl.uk/cgi-bin/press.cgi?story=1399.

British Library (2004) *Measuring Our Value: results of an independent economic impact study commissioned by the British Library to measure the Library's direct and indirect value to the UK economy*, London, British Library, www.bl.uk/pdf/measuring.pdf.

Brown, A. (2005) Cost Modelling: the TNA experience. In *Report for the DCC/DPC Workshop on Cost Models for Preserving Digital Assets*, York, Digital Preservation Coalition, www.dpconline.org/docs/events/050726brown.pdf.

Brügger, N. (2005) *Archiving Websites: general considerations and strategies*, Århus, Centre for Internet Research, http://cfi.imv.au.dk/pub/boeger/bruegger_archiving.pdf.

Burner, M. (1997) Crawling towards Eternity: building an archive of the world wide web, *New Architect*, (May), www.webtechniques.com/archives/1997/05/burner/.

CAMiLEON (2003a) *CAMiLEON Project*, University of Leeds and University of Michigan, www.si.umich.edu/CAMILEON/.

CAMiLEON (2003b) *BBC Domesday*, University of Leeds and University of Michigan, www.si.umich.edu/CAMILEON/domesday/domesday.html.

Campbell, L. (2002) Update on the National Digital Infrastructure Initiative. In *The State of Digital Preservation: an international perspective: conference proceedings*, Washington DC, Council on Library and Information Resources, 49–53, www.clir.org/pubs/reports/pub107/pub107.pdf.

CANDO (2003) *Hosting the National Digital Curation Centre: the CANDO proposal, November 2003*, unpublished, www.dcc.ac.uk/docs/cando_bid_minus_fullcosting-and-letters.pdf.

Caplan, P. and Guenther, R. (2005) Practical Preservation: the PREMIS experience, *Library Trends*, **54** (1), 111–24.

Cedars (2002) *Cedars Project*, University of Leeds, University of Oxford and University of Cambridge, www.leeds.ac.uk/cedars/.

Cedars Project Team and UKOLN (2000) *Metadata for Digital Preservation: the Cedars Project outline specification: draft for public consultation*, unpublished, www.leeds.ac.uk/cedars/MD-STR~5.pdf.

Chakrabarti, S. (2002) *Mining the Web: discovering knowledge from hypertext data*, San Francisco, Morgan Kaufmann Publishers.

Chapman, S. (2003) Counting the Costs of Digital Preservation: is repository storage affordable?, *Journal of Digital Information*, **4** (2), http://jodi.ecs.soton.ac.uk/Articles/v04/i02/Chapman/.

Chapman, S., Conway, P. and Kenney, A. R. (1999) Digital Imaging and Preservation Microfilm: the future of the hybrid approach for the preservation of brittle books, *RLG DigiNews*, **3** (1), www.thames.rlg.org/preserv/diginews/diginews3-1.html#feature1.

Charlesworth, A. (2003) *Legal Issues relating to the Archiving of Internet Resources in the UK, EU, USA and Australia*, London, JISC and Wellcome Trust, www.jisc.ac.uk/uploaded_documents/archiving_legal.pdf.

Christensen-Dalsgaard, B. (2004) Web Archive Activities in Denmark, *RLG DigiNews*, **8** (3), www.rlg.org/en/page.php?Page_ID=17661#article0.

Coleman, M. S. (2006) *Google, the Khmer Rouge and the Public Good: address to the Professional/Scholarly Publishing Division of the Association of American Publishers* (6 February), www.umich.edu/pres/speeches/060206google.html.

Commission of the European Communities (2003) *Communication from the Commission to the Council, the European Parliament, the Economic and Social Committee and the Committee of the Regions: eEurope 2002 final report*, COM(2003) 66 final, Brussels, Commission of the European Communities, http://europa.eu.int/eur-lex/en/com/cnc/2003/com2003_0066en01.pdf.

CompuServe (1990) *Graphics Interchange Format*, Columbus OH, CompuServe, www.w3.org/Graphics/GIF/spec-gif89a.txt.

Consultative Committee for Space Data Systems (2002) *Reference Model for an Open Archival Information System*, CCSDS 650.0-B-1, Blue Book 1, Washington DC, National Aeronautics and Space Administration, http://public.ccsds.org/publications/archive/650x0b1.pdf.

Consultative Committee for Space Data Systems (2004), *XML Formatted Data Unit (XFDU) Structure and Construction Rules*, White Book, Washington DC, National Aeronautics and Space Administration, www.ccsds.org/docu/dscgi/ds.py/GetRepr/File-1912/html.

Cope, J., Craswell, N. and Hawking, D. (2003) Automated Discovery of Search Interfaces on the Web. In Schewe, K.-D. and Zhou, X. (eds), *Proceedings of the Fourteenth Australasian Database Conference on Database Technologies 2003*, vol. 17, Conferences in Research and Practice in Information Technology Series, Darlinghurst, Australian Computer Society.

Craig-McFeely, J. and Deegan, M. (2005) Bringing the Digital Revolution to Medieval Musicology: the Digital Image Archive of Medieval Music (DIAMM), *RLG DigiNews*, **9** (3), www.rlg.org/en/page.php?Page_ID=20666#article1.

Cullen, C. T. (2000) Authentication of Digital Objects: lessons from a historian's research. In *Authenticity in a Digital Environment*, Washington DC, Council on Library and Information Resources, 1–7, www.clir.org/pubs/reports/pub92/pub92.pdf.

Currall, J., Johnson, C. and McKinney, P. (2005) *The Organ-grinder and the Monkey: making a business case for sustainable digital preservation: presentation at EU DLM Forum Conference, 5–7 October 2005, Budapest, Hungary.*

CyberCemetery, http://govinfo.library.unt.edu/.

Danish Ministry of Culture (2002) *Presidency Conclusions from the Workshop on Digital Preservation, Copenhagen, December 11, 2002*, Copenhagen, Danish Ministry of Culture, www.kum.dk/graphics/kum/billeder/Temaer/formandskab/Workshop/Workshop_on_digital_preservation_presentations_etc/Conclusions_Copenhagen.doc.

Darlington, J., Finney, A. and Pearce, A. (2003) Domesday Redux: the rescue of the BBC Domesday Project videodiscs, *Ariadne*, (July), www.ariadne.ac.uk/issue36/tna/.

Day, M. (1999) Issues and Approaches to Preservation Metadata. In *Joint RLG and NPO Preservation Conference: guidelines for digital imaging*, www.rlg.org/preserv/joint/day.html.

Day, M. (2003) *Collecting and Preserving the World Wide Web*, London, JISC and Wellcome Trust, www.jisc.ac.uk/uploaded_documents/archiving_feasibility.pdf.

Deegan, M. and Tanner, S. (2002) *Digital Futures: strategies for the information age*, London, Library Association.

Denmark. The Royal Library. Department of Legal Deposit (2005)

Legal Deposit, Copenhagen, The Royal Library,
www.kb.dk/kb/dept/nbo/da/pligtafl/index-en.htm.

Digital Archive for Chinese Studies (DACHS),
www.sino.uni-heidelberg.de/dachs/.

Digital Forensics Center (n.d.) *Digital Forensics Legal Summary*,
unpublished,
http://dfc.cs.uri.edu/resources/LegalSummary.html.

Disaster Relief for Museums (n.d.) *Indonesia*, Paris, International
Council of Museums
http://icom.museum/disaster_relief/indonesia.html.

DOI (2005) *The Digital Object Identifier System*, Oxford, International
DOI Foundation, www.doi.org/.

Dublin Core (2006) *Dublin Core Metadata Element Set, Version 1.1:
reference description*, Dublin Core Metadata Initiative,
http://dublincore.org/documents/dces/.

Duranti, L. (1994), The Concept of Appraisal and Archival Theory,
American Archivist, **57** (2), 328–44.

Edwards, E. (2004) Ephemeral to Enduring: the Internet Archive
and its role in preserving digital media, *Information Technology
and Libraries*, **23** (1), 3–8.

Electronic Collection: a virtual collection of monographs and
periodicals,
www.collectionscanada.ca/electroniccollection/003008-200-e.html.

EMC (2004) *EMC Centera*, Hopkinton MA, EMC Corporation,
www.emc.com/products/systems/centera.jsp.

ERPANET (2003a) *ErpaStudies: broadcasting*, Glasgow, ERPANET,
www.erpanet.org/studies/docs/erpaStudy_Broadcasting.pdf.

ERPANET (2003b) *ErpaStudies: Meteorological Service (UK)*, Glasgow,
ERPANET, www.erpanet.org/studies/docs/erpaStudy_meto.pdf.

ERPANET (2003c) *ErpaStudies: pharmaceuticals*, Glasgow, ERPANET,
www.erpanet.org/studies/docs/erpaStudy_Pharmaceutical.pdf.

ERPANET (2003d) *ErpaStudies: telecommunications*, Glasgow, ERPANET,
www.erpanet.org/studies/docs/erpaStudy_telecoms.pdf.

ERPANET (2003e), *Trusted Digital Repositories for Cultural Heritage:
ERPANET workshop report, Rome, 17–19 November 2003*, Glasgow,
ERPANET,
www.erpanet.org/events/2003/rome/RomeFinalReport.pdf.

ERPANET (2004a) *Business Models related to Digital Preservation,
Amsterdam, 20–22 September 2004*, Glasgow, ERPANET,
www.erpanet.org/events/2004/amsterdam/Amsterdam_Report.
pdf.

ERPANET (2004b) *ErpaStudies: Koninklijk Nederlands Meteorologisch
Instituut*, Glasgow, ERPANET,
www.erpanet.org/studies/docs/erpaStudy_KNMI.pdf.

ERPANET (2004c) *ErpaStudies Special Report: electronic records
management training at the European Investment Bank*, Glasgow,
ERPANET,
www.erpanet.org/studies/docs/erpaStudy_EIBTraining.pdf.

European Content in Global Networks Coordination Mechanisms
for Digitisation Programmes (2001), *The Lund Principles:
conclusions of experts meeting, Lund, Sweden, 4 April 2001*,
Luxembourg, CORDIS,
http://eprints.erpanet.org/49/01/lund_principles-en.pdf.

European Union (2002) Council Resolution of 25 June 2002 on
Preserving Tomorrow's Memory: preserving digital content for
future generations (2002/C 162/02), *Official Journal of the
European Union*, **45** (C162), 4–5,
http://europa.eu.int/eur-lex/pri/en/oj/dat/2002/c_162/
c_16220020706en00040005.pdf.

Eva: the acquisition and archiving of electronic network
publications, www.lib.helsinki.fi/eva/english.html.

Experts' Workgroup on the Preservation of Digital Memory (2004)
Firenze Agenda. In Tola, V. and Castellani, C. (eds), *The Future
of Digital Memory and Cultural Heritage: Florence, 16–17 October
2003, conference proceedings*, Roma, ICCU,
www.erpanet.org/events/workgroup/documents/firenze%20
agenda.pdf .

Feeney, M. (ed.) (1999) *The Digital Culture: maximising the nation's
investment. A synthesis of JISC/NPO studies on the preservation of
electronic materials*, London, National Preservation Office,
www.ukoln.ac.uk/services/elib/papers/other/jisc-npo-dig/.

Florida Center for Library Automation (2005) *Library Agreement for
Use of the FCLA Digital Archive (FDA)*, unpublished,

www.fcla.edu/digitalArchive/pdfs/FCLALibraryAgreement_FDA.
doc.

Foo Labs (2004) *Xpdf*, www.foolabs.com/xpdf/about.html.

Furrie, B. (2003) *What Is a MARC Record, and Why Is It Important?*,
Washington DC, Library of Congress,
www.loc.gov/marc/umb/um01to06.html.

Galloway, P. (2003) Preservation of Digital Objects, *Annual Review of
Information Science and Technology*, **38**, 549–90.

Gellman, R. and Gilbert, D. (1994) *BeebEm: BBC Micro and Master
128 Emulator*, www.mikebuk.dsl.pipex.com/beebem/.

Geser, G. and Mulrenin, A. (2002) *The DigiCULT Report:
technological landscapes for tomorrow's cultural economy – unlocking
the value of cultural heritage*, Luxembourg, European
Commission, www.digicult.info/downloads/html/6/6.html.

Giles, L. et al. (1998) Access to Information on the Web, *Science*,
280 (5371), 1815.

Gillies, J. and Cailliau, R. (2000) *How the Web was Born: the story of
the world wide web*, Oxford, Oxford University Press.

Gleick, J. (2000) *Faster: the acceleration of just about everything*,
London, Abacus.

Gould, S. J. (1980) *The Panda's Thumb: more reflections in natural
history*, New York, London, Norton.

Granger, S. (2000) Emulation as a Digital Preservation Strategy, *D-
Lib Magazine*, **6** (10),
www.dlib.org/dlib/october00/granger/10granger.html.

Guercio, M. (2004) Digital Memory Preservation: policies and
regulations in Europe. In Tola, V. and Castellani, C. (eds), *The
Future of Digital Memory and Cultural Heritage: Florence, 16–17
October 2003, conference proceedings, Roma, ICCU*.

Hakala, J. (2003) Archiving the Web: European experiences,
Tietolinja, **2**, www.lib.helsinki.fi/tietolinja/0203/webarchive.html.

Halgrimsson, T. (2005) *Special Presentation: The International Internet
Preservation Consortium (IIPC)*, Rio de Janeiro, Conference of
Directors of National Libraries,
http://consorcio.bn.br/cdnl/2005/HTML/
Presentation%20Thorsteinn%20Halgrimsson.htm.

Harvard University Library (2005) *Global Digital Format Registry*,

Cambridge MA, Harvard University,
http://hul.harvard.edu/gdfr/.

Harvard University Library, Office for Information Systems (2001) *DRS Policy Guide*, Cambridge MA, Harvard University Library, http://hul.harvard.edu/ois/systems/drs/policyguide.html.

Hedstrom, M. (1998) The Role of National Initiatives in Digital Preservation, *RLG DigiNews*, **2** (5), www.rlg.org/legacy/preserv/diginews/diginews2-5. html#feature2.

Hedstrom, M. (2002) The Digital Preservation Research Agenda. In *The State of Digital Preservation: an international perspective: conference proceedings*, Washington DC, Council on Library and Information Resources, 32–6, www.clir.org/pubs/reports/pub107/pub107.pdf.

Hedstrom, M. (2003a) *It's About Time: research challenges in digital archiving and long-term preservation: final report: workshop on research challenges in digital archiving and long-term preservation, April 12–13, 2002*, Washington DC, National Science Foundation and Library of Congress, www.digitalpreservation.gov/about/NSF.pdf.

Hedstrom, M. (2003b) Research Challenges in Digital Archiving and Long-term Preservation. In *Wave of the Future: NSF post digital library futures workshop, Chatham, Massachusetts, 15–17 June 2003*, Pittsburgh, School of Information Sciences, University of Pittsburgh, www.sis.pitt.edu/~dlwkshop/paper_hedstrom.html.

Hendley, T. (1998) *Comparison of Methods and Costs of Digital Preservation*, British Library Research and Innovation Report 106, London, British Library Research and Innovation Centre, www.ukoln.ac.uk/services/elib/papers/tavistock/hendley/hendley.html.

Hercules (2001) *Hercules 370/390 Emulator*, www.schaefernet.de/hercules/index.html.

Heritrix, http://crawler.archive.org/index.html.

Heuscher, S. (2003) *Today's Design of Tomorrow's Trust in Digital Archives: considerations from the ARELDA project: ERPANET Workshop on Trusted Digital Repositories for Cultural Heritage, Rome 17th–19th November 2003*, unpublished, www.erpanet.org/events/2003/rome/presentations/Heuscher.pdf.

Hofman, H. (2004) Enabling Persistent and Sustainable Digital Cultural Heritage in Europe: section 2: position paper. In *Coordinating Digitisation in Europe: progress report of the National Representatives Group: coordination mechanisms for digitisation policies and programmes 2004*, Rome, MINERVA, www.minervaeurope.org/publications/globalreport/globalrep2004.htm.

Holdsworth, D. (1992) The *LEEDS File Archive*, Leeds University, www.leeds.ac.uk/iss/systems/archive/.

Holdsworth, D. (1996) The Medium Is NOT the Message. In *Proceedings of the 5th NASA Goddard Mass Storage Systems and Technologies Conference*, NASA publication 3340, http://esdis-it.gsfc.nasa.gov/MSST/conf1996/A6_07Holdsworth.html.

Holdsworth, D. (2001) *C-ing Ahead for Digital Longevity*, University of Leeds, www.si.umich.edu/CAMILEON/reports/cingahd.html.

Holdsworth, D. (2002) *Architecture of CEDARS Demonstrator*, www.leeds.ac.uk/cedars/archive/architecture.html.

Holdsworth, D. and Sergeant, D. M. (2000) A Blueprint for Representation Information in the OAIS Model. In *Eighth NASA Goddard Conference on Mass Storage Systems and Technologies/17th IEEE Symposium on Mass Storage Systems*, http://romulus.gsfc.nasa.gov/msst/conf2000/PAPERS/D02PA.PDF.

Holdsworth, D. and Wheatley, P. (2000) *Emulation, Preservation and Abstraction*, Leeds, CAMiLEON Project, http://cedarsgw.leeds.ac.uk/CAMiLEON//dh/ep5.html.

Holdsworth, D. and Wheatley, P. (2001) Emulation, Preservation and Abstraction, *RLG DigiNews*, **5** (4), www.rlg.org/preserv/diginews/diginews5-4.html#feature2.

Holdsworth, D. and Wheatley, P. (2004) Long-term Stewardship of Globally Distributed Representation Information. In *12th NASA Goddard/21st IEEE Conference on Mass Storage Systems and Technologies*, NASA/CP-2004-212750, http://romulus.gsfc.nasa.gov/msst/conf2004/Papers/MSST2004-03-Holdsworth-a.pdf.

Hunter, L., Webster, E. and Wyatt, A. (2005) *Measuring Intangible Capital: a review of current practice*, Intellectual Property Research Institute of Australia Working Paper 16/04, Victoria, Intellectual Property Research Institute of Australia, www.ipria.org/publications/workingpapers/ IPRIA%20WP%2016.04.pdf.

Hymans, F. (2005) Tying in Information to Business Strategy, *Library & Information Update*, **4** (5), 18–20.

IMS Global Learning Consortium (2004) *Content Packaging Specification*, Burlington, IMS, www.imsglobal.org/content/packaging/.

International Council of Museums (ICOM) Disaster Relief for Museums Website, http://icom.museum/disaster_relief/.

International Federation of Library Associations and Institutions (2005) *In Banda Aceh, Sumatra all of the major libraries suffered extensive damage*, (March), www.ifla.org/V/press/tsunami-Indonesia1.htm.

International Internet Preservation Consortium, www.netpreserve.org/.

InterPARES Project (2001) *The Long-term Preservation of Authentic Electronic Records: findings of the InterPARES Project*, Vancouver, InterPARES Project, www.interpares.org/book/index.cfm.

InterPARES 2 Project, www.interpares.org/ip2.htm.

ISO/IEC 21000-2:2003 *Information Technology – Multimedia Framework (MPEG-21) – Part 2: Digital Item Declaration*, International Standards Organization.

JHOVE: JSTOR/Harvard Object Validation Environment, http://hul.harvard.edu/jhove/.

Kaplan R. S. and Norton D. P. (1992) The Balanced Scorecard: measures that drive performance, *Harvard Business Review*, (January–February), 71–9.

Kenney, A.R. (1996) *Digital to Microfilm Conversion: a demonstration project 1994–1996*, Ithaca NY, Cornell University Library, www.library.cornell.edu/preservation/publications/comfin.html.

Kenney, A.R. (2006) *Surveying the E-Journal Preservation Landscape*, ARL Bimonthly Report 245, Washington DC, Association of Research Libraries, www.arl.org/newsltr/245/preserv.html.

Kenney, A. R. and Stam, D. C. (2002) *The State of Preservation Programs in American College and Research Libraries: building a common understanding and action agenda*, Washington DC, Council on Library and Information Resources, www.clir.org/pubs/reports/pub111/pub111.pdf.

Knight, S. (2005) Preservation Metadata: National Library of New Zealand experience, *Library Trends*, **54** (1), 91–110.

Koerbin, P. (2005) *Report on the Crawl and Harvest of the Whole Australian Web Domain Undertaken during June and July 2005*, Canberra, National Library of Australia, http://pandora.nla.gov.au/documents/domain_harvest_report_public.pdf.

Koninklijke Bibliotheek (2002) Long-term Digital Archiving. In *Koninklijke Bibliotheek Strategic Plan 2002–2005*, The Hague, Koninklijke Bibliotheek, www.kb.nl/bst/beleid/bp/2002/2002-en.html.

Kuhn, T. S. (1970) *The Structure of Scientific Revolutions*, Chicago, University of Chicago Press.

Lage, J. P. et al. (2002) Collecting Hidden Web Pages for Data Extraction. In *Proceedings of the Fourth International Workshop on Web Information and Data Management*, New York, ACM Press.

Lagoze, C. and Payette, S. (2000) Metadata: principles, practices and challenges. In Kenney, A. R. and Rieger, O. Y. (eds) *Moving Theory into Practice: digital imaging for libraries and archives*, Mountain View, Research Libraries Group.

Lavoie, B. (2003) *The Incentives to Preserve Digital Materials: roles, scenarios, and economic decision-making*, Dublin, OCLC Online Computer Library Center, www.oclc.org/research/projects/digipres/incentives-dp.pdf.

Lavoie, B. F. (2004) Of Mice and Memory: economically sustainable preservation for the twenty-first century. In *Access in the Future Tense*, Washington DC, Council on Library and Information Resources, 45–54, www.clir.org/pubs/reports/pub126/pub126.pdf.

Lavoie, B. and Dempsey, L. (2004) Thirteen Ways of Looking at . . . Digital Preservation, *D-Lib Magazine*, **10** (7/8), www.dlib.org/dlib/july04/lavoie/07lavoie.html.

Lawrence, S. and Giles, C. L. (1999) Accessibility of Information on the Web, *Nature*, **400** (6740), 107–9.

Lazinger, S. (2001) *Digital Preservation and Metadata: history, theory, and practice*, Englewood CO, Libraries Unlimited.

Lecher, H. E. (2006) Academic Web Archiving: DACHS. In Masanès, J. (ed.), *Web Archiving*, Berlin, Springer (forthcoming).

LeFurgy, W. (2002) Levels of Service for Digital Repositories, *D-Lib Magazine*, **8** (5),
www.dlib.org/dlib/may02/lefurgy/05lefurgy.html.

LeFurgy, W.G. (2005) Building Preservation Partnerships: The Library of Congress National Digital Information Infrastructure and Preservation Program, *Library Trends*, **54** (1), 163–72.

Lessig, L. (1999) *Code and Other Laws of Cyberspace*, New York, Basic Books.

Lev, B. (2001) *Intangibles: measurement, management and reporting*, Washington DC, Brookings Institution Press.

Lev, B. et al. (2003) *Study on the Measurement of Intangible Assets and Associated Reporting Practices*, Brussels, European Communities Enterprise Directorate General,
http://europa.eu.int/comm/enterprise/services/business_related _services/policy_papers_brs/intangiblesstudy.pdf.

Library & Information Update (LIU) (2004) Demonstrating Value at the BL: update reports, *Library & Information Update*, **3** (10), 16–17.

Lievesley, D. and Jones, S. (1998) *An Investigation into the Digital Preservation Needs of Universities and Research Funders: the future of unpublished research materials*, British Library Research and Innovation Centre 109, London, British Library,
www.ukoln.ac.uk/services/papers/bl/blri109/datrep.html.

Lin, K.-I. and Chen, H. (2002) Automatic Information Discovery from the 'Invisible Web'. In *International Conference on Information Technology: Coding and Computing*, Washington DC, IEEE Computer Society.

Lograno, L., Battistelli, A. and Guercio, M. (2003) *Legislation, Rules and Policies for the Preservation of Digital Resources: a survey*, F. Marini (trans.), Florence, ICCU and ERPANET,
www.erpanet.org/events/workgroup/documents/Regulations_

Policy%20_Dossier_English%20version.pdf.

Lord, P. and Macdonald, A. (2003) *e-Science Curation Report: data curation for e-science in the UK: an audit to establish requirements for future curation and provision*, unpublished, www.jisc.ac.uk/uploaded_documents/e-ScienceReportFinal.pdf.

Lord, P. et al. (2004) From Data Deluge to Data Curation. In Cox, S. J. (ed.), *Proceedings of the UK e-Science All Hands Meeting 2004, Nottingham, UK, 31st August–3rd September*, Nottingham, EPSRC, www.allhands.org.uk/2004/proceedings/papers/150.pdf.

Lorie, R. A. (2001) A Project on Preservation of Digital Data, *RLG DigiNews*, **5** (3), www.rlg.org/legacy/preserv/diginews/diginews5-3.html#feature2.

Lunghi, M. (2004) Enabling Persistent and Sustainable Digital Cultural Heritage in Europe: section 1: the Netherlands questionnaire responses summary. In *Coordinating Digitisation in Europe: progress report of the National Representatives Group: coordination mechanisms for digitisation policies and programmes 2004*, Rome, MINERVA, www.minervaeurope.org/publications/globalreport/globalrep2004.htm.

Lupovici, C. (2005) Web Archives Long Term Access and Interoperability: the International Internet Preservation Consortium activity. In *World Library and Information Congress: 71st IFLA General Conference and Council, Oslo, Norway, 14–18 August 2005*, The Hague, IFLA, www.ifla.org/IV/ifla71/papers/194e-Lupovici.pdf.

Lyman, P. (2002) Archiving the World Wide Web. In *Building a National Strategy for Preservation: issues in digital media archiving*, Washington DC, Council on Library and Information Resources and Library of Congress, www.clir.org/pubs/reports/pub106/contents.html.

Lynch, C. (1999) Canonicalization: a fundamental tool to facilitate preservation and management of digital information, *D-Lib Magazine*, **5** (9), www.dlib.org/dlib/september99/09lynch.html.

Lynch, C. (2000) Authenticity and Integrity in the Digital Environment: an exploratory analysis of the central role of trust.

In *Authenticity in a Digital Environment*, Washington DC, Council on Library and Information Resources, 32–50, www.clir.org/pubs/reports/pub92/pub92.pdf.

Macdonald, A. and Lord, P. (2003) *Report of the Task Force Strategy Discussion Day*, Digital Data Curation Task Force, www.jisc.ac.uk/uploaded_documents/CurationTaskForceFinal1.pdf.

MacKenzie, G. (2000) Searching for Solutions: electronic records problems worldwide, *Managing Information*, (July/August), 59–65.

Magraeth, M. (2001) Museum of Modern Art, private communication.

Making of America II, http://sunsite.berkeley.edu/MOA2/.

Masanès, J. (2002a) Archiving the Deep Web. In *2nd ECDL Workshop on Web Archiving, September 19, 2002, Rome, Italy*, unpublished, http://bibnum.bnf.fr/ecdl/2002/BnF/BnF.html.

Masanès, J. (2002b) Préserver les Contenus du Web. In *4èmes Journées Internationales d'Etudes de l'Arsag*, unpublished, http://bibnum.bnf.fr/conservation/migration_web.pdf.

Masanès, J. (2004) *International Internet Preservation Consortium Press Release*, unpublished, www.netpreserve.org/press/pr20040505.php.

Masanès, J. (2005a) IIPC Web Archiving Metadata Set. In *5th International Web Archiving Workshop, September 22–23, 2005, Vienna, Austria*, unpublished, www.iwaw.net/05/masanes2.pdf.

Masanès, J. (2005b) Web Archiving Methods and Approaches: a comparative study, *Library Trends*, **54** (1), 72–90.

Masanès, J. (2006) Collecting the Hidden Web. In Masanès, J. (ed.), *Web Archiving*, Berlin, Springer (forthcoming).

Mathis, M., Fawcett, A. and Konda, L. (2003) *Valuing Nature: a survey of the non-market valuation literature*, Houston, Houston Advanced Research Center, http://files.harc.edu/Projects/Nature/LiteratureSurvey.pdf.

Mellor, P., Wheatley, P. and Sergeant, D. (2002) Migration on Request, a Practical Technique for Preservation. In Agosti, M. and Thanos, C. (eds), *Research and Advanced Technology for Digital Libraries: 6th European Conference, ECDL 2002, Rome, Italy*,

September 16–18, 2002: proceedings, Lecture Notes in Computer Science, vol. 2458, Berlin, Springer.

METS: Metadata Encoding and Transmission Standard, www.loc.gov/standards/mets/.

Milinovic, M. and Topolscak, N. (2005), Architecture of DAMP: a system for harvesting and archiving Web publications, *Widwisawn*, **3** (3), http://widwisawn.cdlr.strath.ac.uk/Issues/Vol3/issue3_3_1.html.

MINERVA Web Preservation Project, http://lcweb2.loc.gov/cocoon/minerva/html/minerva-home.html.

Mohr, G. et al. (2004) Introduction to Heritrix, an Open Source Archival Quality Web Crawler. In Masanès, J. and Rauber, A. (eds), *4th International Web Archiving Workshop, September 16, 2004, Bath, UK* (forthcoming).

Moore, R. et al. (2004) Data Grid Management Systems. In *12th NASA Goddard/21st IEEE Conference on Mass Storage Systems and Technologies*, NASA/CP-2004-212750, http://romulus.gsfc.nasa.gov/msst/conf2004/Papers/ MSST2004-01-Moore-a.pdf.

Moore, R. W. and Marciano, R. (2005) Prototype Preservation Environments, *Library Trends*, **54** (1), 144–62.

MPEG-21, Information Technology, Multimedia Framework (2003) Part 2: Digital Item Declaration, *ISO/IEC 21000–2:2003*, March.

NASA/IEEE (2004) *12th NASA Goddard/21st IEEE Conference on Mass Storage Systems and Technologies*, NASA/CP-2004-212750, www.storageconference.org/2004/.

National Archives (2004) *PRONOM*, www.nationalarchives.gov.uk/pronom/.

National Archives and Records Administration, 2004 Presidential Term Web Harvest, www.webharvest.gov/collections/peth04/.

National Archives and Records Administration (2004) *National Archives Names Companies to Design Archives of the Future*, (2 August), www.archives.gov/press/press-releases/2004/nr04-73.html.

National Archives and Records Administration (2005) *National Archives Names Lockheed Martin to Build Archives of the Future*, (8 September), www.archives.gov/press/press-releases/2005/nr05-112.html.

National Library of Australia (2002) *Digital Preservation Policy*, Canberra, National Library of Australia, www.nla.gov.au/policy/digpres.html.

National Library of Australia (2004) *Themes Emerging from Archiving Web Resources: issues for cultural heritage organisations*, Canberra, National Library of Australia, www.nla.gov.au/webarchiving/ConferenceReport.rtf.

National Library of Australia (2005) *Online Australian Publications: selection guidelines for archiving and preservation by the National Library of Australia*, Canberra, National Library of Australia, http://pandora.nla.gov.au/selectionguidelines.html.

National Library of New Zealand (2004) *National Library to Capture New Zealand's Digital Heritage*, (30 May), www.natlib.govt.nz/bin/media/pr?item=1085885702.

Negroponte, N. (1995) *Being Digital*, London, Coronet.

netarchive.dk, http://netarchive.dk/index-en.php.

NISO (2004) *Technical Metadata Standard for Still Images,* Bethesda MD, NISO, www.niso.org/committees/committee_au.html.

NSF-DELOS Working Group on Digital Archiving and Preservation (2003) *Invest to Save: report and recommendations of the NSF/DELOS Working Group on Digital Archiving and Preservation*, Washington DC, National Science Foundation and Brussels, European Union, http://delos-noe.iei.pi.cnr.it/ activities/internationalforum/Joint-WGs/digitalarchiving/ Digitalarchiving.pdf.

NutchWAX, http://archive-access.sourceforge.net/projects/nutch/.

OCLC, Online Computer Library Center (2004) *The 2003 OCLC Environmental Scan: pattern recognition*, Dublin, OCLC, www.oclc.org/reports/2003escan.htm.

OCLC, Online Computer Library Center (2005) *OCLC Digital Archive Preservation Policy and Supporting Documentation*, Dublin, www.oclc.org/support/documentation/digitalarchive/ preservationpolicy.pdf.

OCLC/RLG Working Group on Preservation Metadata (2002) *Preservation Metadata and the OAIS Information Model: a metadata framework to support the preservation of digital objects*, Dublin, OCLC, www.oclc.org/research/projects/pmwg/pm_framework.pdf.

Oltmans, E. and Kol, N. (2005) A Comparison between Migration and Emulation in Terms of Costs, *RLG DigiNews*, **9** (2), www.rlg.org/en/page.php?Page_ID=20571#article0.

PADI (n.d.) *Web Archiving*, Canberra, National Library of Australia, www.nla.gov.au/padi/topics/92.html.

PANDORA, http://pandora.nla.gov.au/index.html.

Pant, G., Srinivasan, P. and Menczer, F. (2003) Crawling the Web. In Levene, M. and Poulovassilis, A. (eds), *Web Dynamics*, Berlin, Springer.

Paradigma, www.nb.no/paradigma/eng_index.html.

Pearce, A. (n.d.) *Domesday 1986,* LongLife Data, http://domesday1986.com/.

Phillips, M. (2003) Collecting Australian Online Publications, *Australian Academic & Research Libraries*, **34** (3), http://alia.org.au/publishing/aarl/34.3/phillips.html.

Phillips, M. E. (2005a) Archiving Web Resources International Conference: issues for cultural heritage organizations, *RLG DigiNews*, **9** (1), www.rlg.org/en/page.php?Page_ID=20522#article2.

Phillips, M. E. (2005b) Selective Archiving of Web Resources: a study of acquisition costs at the National Library of Australia, *RLG DigiNews*, **9** (3), www.rlg.org/en/page.php?Page_ID=20666#article0.

Phillips, M. E. (2005c) What Should We Preserve?: the question for heritage libraries in a digital world, *Library Trends*, **54** (1), 57–71.

Pope, M. (1975) *The Story of Decipherment*, London, Thames & Hudson.

Portico (2005) *Sustaining the Archive,* www.portico.org/about/sustain.html.

PREMIS: PREservation Metadata Implementation Strategies, www.oclc.org/research/projects/pmwg/.

PREMIS Working Group (2005) *Data Dictionary for Preservation Metadata: final report of the PREMIS Working Group*, Dublin, OCLC Online Computer Library Center and Mountain View, RLG, www.oclc.org/research/projects/pmwg/premis-final.pdf.

Price, G. (2003) A New Demo: keyword search the Wayback

Machine with Recall, *ResourceShelf Blog*, (4 September),
www.resourceshelf.com/2003/09/04/no-kidding-keyword-search-
the-wayback-machine/.

Price, G. (2004) Recall Update, *SearchEngineWatch Blog*, (13
October), http://blog.searchenginewatch.com/blog/041013-
123930.

PRONOM: the technical registry,
www.nationalarchives.gov.uk/pronom/.

Quandt, R. (2003) Scholarly Materials: paper or digital?, *Library
Trends*, **51** (3), 349–75,
www.findarticles.com/p/articles/mi_m1387/is_3_51/ai_1022708
82.

Raghavan, S. and Garcia-Molina, H. (2001) Crawling the Hidden
Web. In Apers, P. et al. (eds), *Proceedings of the 27th International
Conference on Very Large Data Bases, September 11–14, 2001, Roma,
Italy*, San Francisco, Morgan Kaufmann Publishers,
www.vldb.org/conf/2001/P129.pdf.

Reich, V. and Rosenthal, D. S. H. (2001) LOCKSS: a permanent web
publishing and access system, *D-Lib Magazine*, **7** (6),
www.dlib.org/dlib/june01/reich/06reich.html.

Research Libraries Group, Automatic Exposure: technical metadata,
www.rlg.org/en/page.php?Page_ID=2681.

Research Libraries Group and OCLC (2002) *Trusted Digital
Repositories: attributes and responsibilities*, Mountain View,
www.rlg.org/legacy/longterm/repositories.pdf.

Roche, X. (2006) Copying Web Sites. In Masanès, J. (ed.), *Web
Archiving*, Berlin, Springer (forthcoming).

Ross, S. (2000) *Changing Trains at Wigan: digital preservation and the
future of scholarship*, London, National Preservation Office,
British Library, www.bl.uk/services/npo/pdf/wigan.pdf.

Ross, S. (2003) *Digital Library Development Review: final report*,
Wellington, National Library of New Zealand,
www.natlib.govt.nz/files/ross_report.pdf.

Ross, S. (2004a) Il Ruolo di ERPANET per l'Acceso a Lungo
Termine del Patrimonio Culturale. In Tola, V. and Castellani, C.
(eds), *Futuro delle Memorie Digitali e Patrimonio Culturale: atti del
Convegno internationale, Firenze 16–17 October 2003*, Roma,

Istituto centrale per il catalogo unico delle biblioteche italiane e per le informazioni bibliografiche.

Ross, S. (2004b) The Role of ERPANET in Supporting Digital Curation and Preservation in Europe, *D-Lib Magazine*, **10** (7/8), www.dlib.org/dlib/july04/ross/07ross.html.

Ross, S. and Gow, A. (1999) *Digital Archaeology: rescuing neglected and damaged data resources*, London: South Bank University, Library Information Technology Centre, www.ukoln.ac.uk/services/elib/papers/supporting/pdf/p2.pdf.

Ross, S., Greenan, M. and McKinney, P. (2004) Digital Preservation Strategies: the initial outcomes of the ERPANET case studies. In *Preservation of Electronic Records: new knowledge and decision-making*, Ottawa, Canadian Conservation Institute, 99–111.

Ross, S. and Hedstrom, M. (2005) Preservation Research and Sustainable Digital Libraries, *International Journal on Digital Libraries*, **5** (4), 317–24.

Rothenberg, J. (2000a) Preserving Authentic Digital Information. In *Authenticity in a Digital Environment*, Washington DC, Council on Library and Information Resources, 51–68, www.clir.org/pubs/reports/pub92/pub92.pdf.

Rothenberg, J. (2000b) *Using Emulation to Preserve Digital Documents*, The Hague, Koninklijke Bibliotheek, www.koninklijkebibliotheek.nl/pr/publ/usingemulation.pdf.

Royal Library, Sweden (2005) Kulturarw[3]: long time preservation of electronic documents, Stockholm, The Royal Library, www.kb.se/kw3/ENG/.

Rusbridge, C. (2006) Excuse Me: some digital preservation fallacies, *Ariadne*, (January), www.ariadne.ac.uk/issue46/rusbridge/.

Rusbridge, C. et al. (2005) The Digital Curation Centre: a vision for digital curation. In *Proceedings from Local to Global: data interoperability: challenges and technologies, Sardinia, Italy*, http://eprints.erpanet.org/archive/00000082/01/DCC_Vision.pdf.

Russell, K. (1999) *Digital Preservation: ensuring access to digital materials into the future*, Leeds, Cedars Project, www.leeds.ac.uk/cedars/Chapter.htm.

Russell, K. and Weinberger, E. (2000) *Cost Elements of Digital*

Preservation, unpublished,
www.leeds.ac.uk/cedars/documents/CIW01r.html.

Ryan, F. (2005), Surviving and Thriving in a Harsh World, *Library & Information Update*, **4** (5), 26–9.

Saltzer, J., Reed, D. and Clark, D. (1984) End-to-end Arguments in System Design, *ACM Transactions on Computer Systems*, **2** (4), 277–88.

Sanett, S. (2002) Toward Developing a Framework of Cost Elements for Preserving Authentic Electronic Records into Perpetuity, *College and Research Libraries*, **63** (5), 388–404, www.ala.org/ala/acrl/acrlpubs/crljournal/backissues2002b/ september02/sanett.pdf.

Sanett, S. (2003) The Cost to Preserve Authentic Electronic Records in Perpetuity: comparing costs across cost models and cost frameworks, *RLG DigiNews*, **7** (4), www.rlg.org/legacy/preserv/diginews/diginews7-4. html#feature2.

Schneider, S. and Foot, K. (2005) Web Sphere Analysis: an approach to studying online action. In Hine, C. (ed), *Virtual Methods: issues in social science research on the internet*, Oxford, Berg Publishers.

Schneider, S. et al. (2003) Building Thematic Web Collections: challenges and experiences from the September 11 web archive and the Election 2002 web archive. In Masanès, J., Rauber, A. and Cobena, G. (eds), *3rd Workshop on Web Archives, Trondheim, Norway, August 21st, 2003: proceedings*, unpublished, http://bibnum.bnf.fr/ecdl/2003/index.html.

Schweizerisches Bundesarchiv (2001) *Archiving of Electronic Digital Data and Records in the Swiss Federal Archives (ARELDA)*, Bern, Schweizerisches Bundesarchiv.

SCORM, www.adlnet.org/scorm/index.cfm.

Shenton, H. (2005) Real Time, Deep Time, Life Time: spanning digital and traditional collections life cycles. In *Archiving 2005: final program and proceedings of the IS&T archiving conference held on 26–29 April 2005 in Washington, DC*, Springfield IL, Society for Imaging Science and Technology.

Simpson, D. (2004) *National Assessment Survey for the Digital Preservation Coalition*, unpublished, www.dpconline.org/docs/reports/dpcsurvey.pdf.

Singh, S. (1999) *The Code Book: the science of secrecy from ancient Egypt to quantum cryptography*, London, Fourth Estate.

Smith, C. (2005) Building an Internet Archive System for the British Broadcasting Corporation, *Library Trends*, **54** (1), 16–32.

Smith, M. (2005) Exploring Variety in Digital Collections and the Implications for Digital Preservation, *Library Trends*, **54** (1), 6–15.

Stack, M. (n.d.) *Full Text Search of Web Archive Collections*, San Francisco, Internet Archive, http://archive-access.sourceforge.net/projects/nutch/iwaw/iwaw-wacsearch.pdf.

Steenbakkers, J. F. (2005) Digital Archiving in the Twenty-first Century: practice at the National Library of the Netherlands, *Library Trends*, **54** (1), 33–56.

Sun Microsystems (2006) *Open Office*, www.openoffice.org/.

Tanner, S. (2004) Reproduction Charging Models and Rights Policy for Digital Images in American Art Museums (a Mellon Foundation study), http://kdcs.kcl.ac.uk/USart/.

Task Force on Archiving of Digital Information (1996) *Preserving Digital Information: report of the Task Force on Archiving of Digital Information*, Washington DC, Commission on Preservation and Access and Mountain View, Research Libraries Group, www.rlg.org/legacy/ftpd/pub/archtf/final-report.pdf.

Taylor, D. J. (2001) Curse of the Teenage Cybergeeks: review of Michael Lewis, The Future Just Happened, *Sunday Times Culture*, (15 July), 34–5.

Travers, T. and Glaister, S. (2004) *Valuing Museums: impact and innovation among national museums*, London, National Museum Directors' Conference, http://nationalmuseums.org.uk/images/publications/valuing_museums.pdf.

Typed Object Model, http://tom.library.upenn.edu/.

UNESCO (2003) *Charter on the Preservation of the Digital Heritage*, Paris, United Nations Educational, Scientific and Cultural Organization.

van Nuys, C. et al. (2004) The Paradigma Project and its Quest for

Metadata Solutions and User Services. In *World Library and Information Congress: 70th IFLA General Conference and Council, 22–27 August 2004, Buenos Aires, Argentina,* The Hague, IFLA, www.ifla.org/IV/ifla70/papers/009e-Nuys.pdf.

Voerman, G. et al. (2002) Archiving the Web: political party web sites in the Netherlands, *European Political Science,* **2** (1), www.essex.ac.uk/ECPR/publications/eps/onlineissues/ autumn2002/information.htm.

W3C (2006) *W3C: World Wide Web Consortium,* www.w3.org/.

Waller, M. and Sharpe, R. (2006) *Mind the Gap: assessing digital preservation needs in the UK. A report prepared for the DPC,* Digital Preservation Coalition, www.dpconline.org/docs/reports/ uknamindthegap.pdf.

Waters, D. J. (ed) (1997) Digital Archiving: the report of the CPA/RLG Task Force. In *Preservation and Digitization: principles, practices and policies,* London, National Preservation Office.

Waters, D. (2002) Good Archives Make Good Scholars: reflections on recent steps toward the archiving of digital information. In *The State of Digital Preservation: an international perspective,* Washington DC, Council on Library and Information Resources, www.clir.org/pubs/abstract/pub107abst.html.

The Web at Risk: a distributed approach to preserving our nation's political cultural heritage, www.cdlib.org/inside/projects/preservation/webatrisk/.

Web Capture, www.loc.gov/webcapture/index.html.

Web InfoMall, www.infomall.cn/index-eng.htm.

WebArchiv, www.webarchiv.cz/.

WERA, http://archive-access.sourceforge.net/projects/wera/ index.html.

Wettengel, M. (1998) German Unification and Electronic Records. In Higgs, E. (ed.), *History and Electronic Artefacts,* Oxford, Clarendon Press.

Wheatley, P. (2001a) Migration: a CAMiLEON discussion paper, *Ariadne,* (September) www.ariadne.ac.uk/issue29/camileon/.

Wheatley, P. R. (2001b) *Representation Networks: a case study,* www.leeds.ac.uk/reprend/repnet/casestudy.html.

Wheatley, P. R. et al. (2003) *Representation and Rendering Project,*

University of Leeds, www.leeds.ac.uk/reprend/.

Wiggins, B. (2005) IFLA Survey on Inclusion of Electronic Resources in National Bibliographies. In *World Library and Information Congress: 71th IFLA General Conference and Council, 'Libraries – a voyage of discovery', August 14th–18th 2005, Oslo, Norway*, The Hague, IFLA, www.ifla.org/IV/ifla71/papers/177e-Wiggins.pdf.

Wright, R. (2001) *Broadcast Archives: preserving the future*, unpublished, http://presto.joanneum.ac.at/Public/ICHIM%20PRESTO%2028_05_01.pdf.

Index

Managing Electronic Records
Julie McLeod and Catherine Hare

'My own institution is in the early stages of considering these issues and I shall certainly be making use of many of the ideas and lists in this book, which truly offers something for everyone...'   ARIADNE

Bringing together for the first time the views, experience and expertise of international experts in the records management field in the public and the private sectors, this book covers the theory and practice of managing electronic records as business and information assets.

It focuses on the strategies, systems and procedures necessary to ensure that electronic records are appropriately created, captured, organized and retained over time to meet business and legal requirements. In addition to chapters covering principles, research and developments, there are case studies relating to practice and lessons learned. The chapters are written by a fully international line-up of contributors. They cover:

- the wild frontier ten years on
- the use of standards and models
- metadata matters
- digital preservation
- research in electronic records management
- technologies for preservation
- legal issues
- ethics and electronic recordmaking
- competencies - the asset that counts most
- records management - case studies in the private sector
- electronic recordkeeping in the public sector
- playing the long game.

This book explores issues and offers solutions, not only for records professionals but also for information, IT and business administration specialists, who, as key stakeholders in managing electronic information, may have taken on crucial roles in managing electronic records in their organization. It will also be a key textbook for records management courses.

2005; 336 pp; hardback; ISBN 978-1-85604-550-6; £39.95

Digitizing Collections
Strategic issues for the information manager
Lorna M. Hughes

'This book is a valuable contribution to the series on this complex topic and it manages to deliver a great deal of practical information.'

INFORMATION WORLD REVIEW

This book presents information managers with all the strategic and practical issues to consider when making the decision to digitize their collections. It runs through the digitization process step by step, outlines the different techniques available to deal with a wide range of library resources, and explores the opportunities offered by a collaborative approach to digitization. Fully case- and evidence-based, the text is supported by examples of digitization projects carried out in various types of libraries around the world, and by an extensive list of sources of further information. Divided into two main sections, 'Strategic Decision Making' and 'Digitizing Collections', the chapters include:

* Why digitize? The costs and benefits of digitization
* Selecting materials for digitization
* Intellectual property, copyright and other legal issues
* The institutional framework
* The importance of collaboration
* Project planning and funding
* Managing a digitization project
* Digitization of rare and fragile materials
* Digitization of audio and moving image collections
* Digitization of text and images.

This key international text offers information managers the benefit of a fully strategic approach to digitization and substantial experience drawn from leading digitization projects. It is also essential reading for managers in heritage institutions such as museums, galleries and local archives, and for students of information science.

Digital Futures series – series editors Marilyn Deegan and Simon Tanner

2004; 344 pp; hardback; ISBN 978-1-85604-466-0; £39.95

Essential Classification
Vanda Broughton

This much-needed text leads the novice classifier step by step through the basics of subject cataloguing, with an emphasis on practical document analysis and classification. It deals with fundamental questions of the purpose of classification in different situations, and the needs and expectations of end users. The novice is introduced to the ways in which document content can be assessed, and how this can best be expressed for translation into the language of specific indexing and classification systems.

The characteristics of the major general schemes of classification are discussed, together with their suitability for different classification needs. Key areas covered are:

- the need for classification
- first principles of classification
- varieties of classification: systems and structures
- the classification schemes: internal structure
- types of classification scheme
- order in the classification scheme
- content analysis: document description and practical constraints
- controlled indexing languages
- word-based approaches to retrieval
- Library of Congress Subject Headings
- applying a classification scheme
- Library of Congress Classification
- Dewey Decimal Classification
- Universal Decimal Classification
- faceted classification
- managing classification.

'What a pleasure to look through this extensive well researched and practical resource on almost every aspect of classification written by an internationally recognized expert in classification research, with over 30 years of experience.'
    LIBRARY MANAGEMENT

This guide is essential reading for library school students, novice cataloguers and all information workers who need to classify but have not formally been taught how. It also offers practical guidance to computer scientists, internet and intranet managers, and all others concerned with the design and maintenance of subject tools.

2004; 336 pp; paperback; ISBN 978-1-85604-514-8; £29.95